Greek Lit in Translation

D0147893

# GREEK LYRIC

# GREEK LYRIC

# An Anthology in Translation

Translated,
with Introduction and Notes, by
Andrew M. Miller

Hackett Publishing Company, Inc.
Indianapolis/Cambridge

Copyright © 1996 by Hackett Publishing Company, Inc.

All rights reserved
Printed in the United States of America

19 18 17 16 15          4 5 6 7 8

For further information, please address
  Hackett Publishing Company, Inc.
  P.O. Box 44937
  Indianapolis, Indiana 46244-0937

  www.hackettpublishing.com

Cover and text design by Dan Kirklin

**Library of Congress Cataloging-in-Publication Data**
Greek lyric: an anthology in translation/translated, with
  introduction and notes, by Andrew M. Miller.
        p.   cm.
    Includes bibliographical references (p.   ).
    ISBN 0-87220-292-5 (cloth)   ISBN 0-87220-291-7 (pbk.)
    1. Greek poetry—Translations into English.   I. Miller, Andrew
  M., 1947–
  PA3622.M53   1996
  884'.0108—dc20                          95-45733
                                           CIP

ISBN-13: 978-0-87220-292-4 (cl.)
ISBN-13: 978-0-87220-291-7 (pbk.)

The paper used in this publication meets the minimum
requirements of American National Standard for Information
Sciences—Permanence of Paper for Printed Library Materials,
ANSI Z39.48–1984.
∞

# CONTENTS

To Bell

κοινὰ τὰ τῶν φίλων

# PREFACE

This anthology of translations is drawn from the little that remains of the lyric poetry produced in the Greek world during the seventh, sixth, and fifth centuries B.C. Following ample precedent, it includes not only monody and choral lyric but also short poems and fragments in the elegiac and iambic meters, even though the latter do not fit the etymological definition of lyric as "poetry composed to be sung to the lyre." In the case of fragments, the general criterion for inclusion has been intrinsic and/or extrinsic value; in other words, I have chosen pieces which either are in sufficiently complete shape to make some sort of literary analysis possible, or, failing that, at least offer something of interest from a historical, literary-historical, or cultural perspective. In the case of the complete (or near-complete) poems of Pindar and Bacchylides, where choice was rendered difficult by the relative abundance of material, I have aimed at variety of scale and treatment. The poems selected range from short and straightforward examples of the victory ode as a genre (Pindar's *Olympians* 12 and 14, Odes 2 and 4 of Bacchylides) to "major" odes for princes (*Olympians* 1 and 2, *Pythians* 1 and 3, Bacchylides, Odes 3 and 5); they include as well Pindar's earliest and latest datable poems (*Pythians* 10 and 8) and four odes written for members of a single family (*Nemean* 5, *Isthmians* 5 and 6, and Bacchylides, Ode 13).

In the process of translation itself, I have proceeded on the assumption that many of the aesthetic qualities and stylistic effects of the texts I was dealing with (e.g., meter and rhythm, sound-texture, lexical nuance and interaction, the flexibility of word order made possible by grammatical inflection) are indivisible from the Greek language itself and hence can be recreated in English only rarely and faintly and by happy accident. The goal upon which I have concentrated my efforts is that of preserving as faithfully as possible what I believe *can* be preserved, namely the poems' conceptual content and important elements of their formal organization, without too grossly misrepresenting their stylistic level or their emotional and ethical tone. To this end I have attempted to render the "plain prose sense" of the original as straightforwardly as is compatible with (a) English idiom and (b) at least minimal standards of stylistic appropriateness and rhythmical flow. In practice, it should be noted, the degree of literalness yielded by this principle varies from poet to poet; for example, I have allowed myself to be freer and more overtly "poetic" in my handling of Pindar, with his self-consciously "grand" style and bold playing-off of syntax against word order, than I have in the case of the quasi-formulaic elegiacs of Tyrtaeus or Theognis. Although I have made no attempt either to reproduce the metrical patterns of the original texts or to devise different fixed patterns by way of equivalent, I have tried where I could (and often it was not possible) to preserve the general disposition of semantic content within the different units of discourse demarcated by those metrical patterns, whether lines, couplets, strophes, or triads.

In my handling of textual lacunae, which are unfortunately all too common in the case of poems and fragments preserved on papyrus, I have adopted two different approaches. In many cases where only one or two words in a line are missing and conjectural supplements have won general acceptance from scholars, I have simply incorporated the supplements without indicating the fact through the use of square brackets or any other typographical convention that might prove distracting to readers. (Pieces in which such silent suppletions are particularly numerous include Alcaeus 3, 4, and 11, Sappho 3 and 5, and Simonides 13.) In the case of longer gaps, or when the proposed supplements are more than usually uncertain or controversial, I have used triple dots (or in the case of whole lines, square brackets) to indicate that text is missing. In elegiac passages missing lines or couplets are marked by a single row of spaced dots.

In the rendering of Greek names I have been, quite frankly, inconsistent. Unless one adopts a policy of universal Latinization, some degree of inconsistency seems inevitable; even the most committed transliterationists stop short of Pindaros and Platon, Homeros and Aristoteles. The particular compromise I have adopted is to use the traditional (i.e., Latinate or Anglicized) spelling for (a) all authors, (b) a number of common geographical names (e.g., Aegean, Athens, Corinth, Delphi, Sicily, Thessaly), and (c) certain collective names (e.g., Ethiopians, Cyclopes, Centaurs, Phoenicians). Otherwise, and for all proper names of mythological and historical figures, I have used transliterated forms (with *ch* representing χ and *y* representing υ), although even within this last-mentioned category I have permitted a handful of exceptions (e.g., Helen, Priam, Achilles, Ajax, Oedipus, Croesus) to conform to my own invariable spoken usage.

The basic texts that I have worked from (without feeling bound to follow them in every particular) are as follows: for Pindar and Bacchylides, B. Snell and H. Maehler, *Pindari Carmina cum Fragmentis*, 2 vols. (Leipzig 1987, 1989) and *Bacchylidis Carmina cum Fragmentis* (Leipzig 1970); for Sappho and Alcaeus, E. M. Voigt, *Sappho et Alcaeus: Fragmenta* (Amsterdam 1971); for Alcman, Stesichorus, and Ibycus, M. Davies, *Poetarum Melicorum Graecorum Fragmenta* (Oxford 1991); for the rest of the lyric poets proper, D. L. Page, *Poetae Melici Graeci* (Oxford 1962); for the elegiac and iambic poets, M. L. West, *Iambi et Elegi Graeci ante Alexandrum Cantati*, 2 vols. (Oxford 1989, 1992); for Xenophanes' hexametric pieces, H. Diels and W. Kranz, *Die Fragmente der Vorsokratiker*, Vol. 1 (Dublin/Zurich 1966); for Simonides' epigrams, D. L. Page, *Epigrammata Graeca* (Oxford 1975). In numbering lines I have followed the conventions adopted by the various editors, which means that in the case of Pindar's victory odes (though not of Bacchylides, nor of Pindar's fragments) an indented line is reckoned as an extension of the preceding line instead of being counted separately. Other works that I have consulted with profit include D. A. Campbell, *Greek Lyric*, Vols. 1–4 (Cambridge, Mass., and London 1982, 1988, 1991, 1992) and *Greek Lyric Poetry: A Selection of Early Greek Lyric, Elegiac and Iambic Poetry* (London, Melbourne, Toronto 1967); J. M. Edmonds, *Greek Elegy and Iambus*, 2 vols. (Cambridge, Mass., and London 1931); D. E. Gerber, *Euterpe* (Amsterdam 1970); D. L. Page, *Alcman, The Partheneion* (Oxford 1951) and *Sappho and Alcaeus: An Introduction to the Study of Ancient Lesbian Lyric* (Oxford 1955); H. Maehler, *Die Lieder des Bakchylides, Erster Teil: Die Siegeslieder*, 2 vols. (Leiden 1982); W. J. Slater, *Lexicon to Pindar* (Berlin 1969). During the several years that I spent on the project three anthologies covering much the same material appeared in print: Barbara Fowler, *Archaic Greek Poetry: An Anthology* (Madison 1992), David Mulroy, *Early Greek Lyric Poetry* (Ann Arbor 1992), and M. L. West, *Greek Lyric Poetry* (Oxford 1993); these I did not look at until after I had completed my translations. I greatly profited from the many excellent suggestions for improvement offered by William Race and Emmet Robbins; in those instances where I persisted in ignoring their advice, I did so with trepidation. I would also like to extend my thanks to Paul Coppock for getting me started on the project, and to my students in

numerous classics-in-translation courses at the University of Pitts-
burgh for suffering through earlier drafts and helping me to see
where changes should be made.

# GENERAL
# INTRODUCTION

Lyric poetry is, along with epic and drama, one of the three major poetic "kinds" bequeathed to western civilization by the ancient Greeks. The historical period during which it flourished as the dominant mode of poetic expression in the Greek world extended roughly from the first half of the seventh century B.C. (the time of Archilochus and Tyrtaeus) through the first half of the fifth century, when choral lyric reached its culmination in the work of Bacchylides and Pindar. This Lyric Age of Greece, as it has been dubbed by some modern historians, was an era of far-reaching developments in the political, social, and intellectual life of the Greek city-states. The Greek world itself had already begun to expand through the founding of new cities, most notably in Sicily and southern Italy and on the Black Sea. A number of cities experienced protracted political struggles among aristocratic factions or between aristocrats and the lower social orders, and not infrequently the result was that a single enterprising individual fought or maneuvered his way to the top and established himself as tyrant (*tyrannos*). This term, which is apparently Lydian in origin, properly denoted the extralegal methods by which power was obtained rather than the manner in which it was exercised, and in fact the Greek tyrants were often fairly enlightened in their policies; they also served, in several notable instances (e.g., Polykrates of Samos and Hipparchos of Athens in the sixth century and Hieron of Syracuse in the fifth), as patrons to poets and other artists. In the case of Athens, moreover, the period of tyranny proved to be simply one phase in a gradual process of expanding political enfranchisement which culminated, during the fifth century, in the establishment of full *demokratia* or "rule by the people" ("the people" being defined as free adult males). On the other side of the Aegean Sea, meanwhile, Ionian Greeks like Thales, Anaximander, and Anaximenes were engaging in speculation about the nature and origin of the cosmos and so laying the foundation for later advances in philosophy and science.

It was during these two and a half centuries that the nineteen poets included in this volume[1] lived and wrote. As a group they exhibit considerable diversity. All but two of the nineteen, it is true, were male, but in view of the generally unfavorable conditions under which women lived in ancient Greece, it is perhaps more surprising that there should have been *any* female poets than that the number should have been so small.[2] Geographically, the poets represent most of the major regions of the Greek world, including not only the Greek mainland itself (the Boiotians Pindar and Corinna, the Athenian Solon, the Megarian Theognis, the Spartans Tyrtaeus and Alcman) and the islands of the Aegean (Archilochus, Semonides, Bacchylides, and Simonides from the Cyclades, Alcaeus and Sappho from Lesbos), but also the Ionian coast of Asia Minor (Anacreon, Callinus, Hipponax, Mimnermus, Xenophanes) and Sicily and southern Italy (Stesichorus and Ibycus). Thematically, their poems deal with the full gamut of human experience: erotic love (both hetero- and homosexual), politics, war, sports, drinking, money, youth, old age, death, the heroic past, the gods. Moreover, the poems were composed for performance on a wide range of occasions, from drinking-parties (*symposia*) and other private gatherings to civic or religious festivals embracing the community as a whole, and for a wide variety of purposes: to entertain friends, to attack enemies, to instruct the young, to raise the morale of soldiers, to articulate and defend public policies, to celebrate victorious athletes, to eulogize the dead. Finally, in composing their poems the poets made use of a wide variety of metrical forms, all of them involving the alternation of long and short syllables in various combinations and patterns (traditional English verse, by contrast, is based upon syllabic stress, not syllabic length). Although in the process of translation no attempt has been made to reproduce this aspect of the original Greek texts, it deserves a few words here because it was largely in terms of metrical form (with which mode of performance was associated) that the various poetic traditions within which Greek poets worked were defined and distinguished.

The category most copiously represented in this volume is *lyric*

---

1.  With the possible exception of Corinna; see the individual introduction to that poet.

2.  There were in fact a few other women poets in addition to Sappho and Corinna, among them Praxilla and Telesilla, but the remains of their work are so scanty that they have been omitted from this volume.

*poetry* in the strict sense—that is, poetry composed to be sung to musical accompaniment. Another term for such poetry is *melic*; in each case the derivation of the word (from *lyra* "lyre" and *melos* "song" respectively) points to the distinguishing characteristic. When, beginning in the third century B.C., the poetic output of earlier centuries was assembled and edited by the great literary scholars of Alexandria, a canon of nine great lyrists (*lyrikoi*) was drawn up, comprising (in alphabetical order) Alcaeus, Alcman, Anacreon, Bacchylides, Ibycus, Pindar, Sappho, Simonides, and Stesichorus. Modern scholars have traditionally divided these nine poets into two groups, writers of *monody* or "solo song" on the one hand and of *choral lyric* on the other. The monodists, on this view, are Alcaeus, Sappho, and Anacreon, each of whom is to be imagined as composing poems for an audience of friends or associates, on topics of immediate interest to the group, and performing them in his or her own person. The other six poets, by contrast, produced poems intended for performance by a group of singer-dancers on occasions of a public nature, the poems themselves falling into such recognized categories as hymns, paeans, dithyrambs, *partheneia* ("maiden-songs"), and *epinikia* ("victory songs"). Although it is certain that both modes of performance, the monodic and the choral, were practiced in archaic and early classical Greece, several scholars have recently questioned whether the poets themselves should be rigidly compartmentalized in such terms, and in fact it seems quite possible that Ibycus or Pindar, say, might have written pieces for solo as well as for choral performance if circumstances so demanded. Nonetheless, the traditional division into two groups can still be justified by certain features of language and metrical form. Alcaeus, Sappho, and Anacreon, on the one hand, wrote in their own native dialects (Aiolic in the case of Alcaeus and Sappho, Ionic in the case of Anacreon) and shared a predilection for comparatively short and metrically simple stanza forms (*strophes*) which they reused from poem to poem.[3] The rest of the canonical lyrists, by contrast, used an "international" poetic dialect of pronounced Doric coloring regardless of their own ethnicity (Simonides and Bacchylides, for example, were Ionian Greeks), and they tended to compose in longer and more complex strophic forms known as *triads*, each pattern unique to a particular poem, in which

---

3. One of these stanza forms is known as the Alcaic, another as the Sapphic, in tribute to the frequency with which they were used by Alcaeus and Sappho respectively.

two metrically identical stanzas (the *strophe* and the *antistrophe*) are followed by a third of a different metrical shape (the *epode*).

The second largest category of poetic composition represented in this volume is that known as *elegy*, a term which implies nothing as to content or tone (unlike "elegy" as applied to English verse) but rather refers exclusively to metrical form. Elegy makes use of a two-line unit called the *elegiac couplet*, comprising a line of a dactylic hexameter (the meter of the Homeric epics) followed by a somewhat shorter line composed essentially of two half-hexameters. Given this metrical commonality between the two poetic forms, it is entirely natural that epic should have exerted a strong influence on elegy in diction and style. Thematically, the elegiac couplet was a versatile instrument, being used (for example) by Tyrtaeus and Callinus for military exhortations, by Mimnermus and Theognis for the treatment of sympotic, erotic, and ethical subjects, and by Solon for some of his poems on the political troubles of his native Athens. It also became the standard meter for verse inscriptions on gravestones and other monuments; a few of such epigrams by Simonides are included in this volume.

The third main category represented in this volume comprises poems in the *iambic* and *trochaic* meters, which resemble one another in their alternation of long and single-short syllables (unlike, say, the dactylic rhythm, which combines long and *double*-short syllables). The commonest measures in this category are the *iambic trimeter* and the *trochaic tetrameter*. According to Aristotle in the *Poetics* (4.18), it was because the iambic trimeter was of all rhythms the closest to ordinary spoken Greek that it became the standard meter of dialogue in fifth-century drama. In earlier poetry, however, it had a particular association with invective and satirical attack, as its name suggests (the original meaning of *iambos* is "lampoon" or "scurrilous abuse") and as can be seen in the work of Archilochus, Hipponax, and Semonides. Yet it is by no means limited to such purposes: Semonides himself uses it not just for his misogynistic satirizing of women but for philosophical reflections on the vanity of human wishes, and Solon uses it in solemn defense of his political reforms. A special subcategory of iambic is so-called *epodic* verse, associated particularly with Archilochus, which combines different lengths of iambic and (often) dactylic meter into brief two- or three-line stanzas.[4]

---

4.  When used in this sense the term "epodic" has nothing to do with the triadic structure of strophe, antistrophe, and epode.

The total quantity of poetry produced during the archaic period—particularly, perhaps, of lyric poetry proper—seems to have been very considerable. In the Alexandrian editions of the major lyricists, for example, the works of Anacreon are reported to have filled five volumes (i.e., five papyrus scrolls); those of Ibycus, seven; those of Bacchylides and Sappho, nine each; those of Alcaeus, ten; and those of Pindar, seventeen. Only a minuscule fraction of this copious material has survived to the present day, and in the case of most of the poets very little of what *has* survived is in the form of complete or even substantially complete poems. The staggering scale of the losses involved can perhaps be epitomized by a single statistic: out of the nine volumes of Sappho's work known to the Alexandrians—and Book 1 alone evidently contained over thirteen hundred lines—only *one* poem is extant in its entirety. Aside from the four books of Pindar's victory odes and the corpus of elegiac pieces attributed to Theognis of Megara, which have been preserved through independent manuscript traditions, the remnants of Greek lyric poetry that we possess we owe either to verbatim quotation by later authors or to damaged scrolls or scraps of papyrus recovered from the sands of Egypt. The quotations, which range in length from substantial extracts all the way down to single words, are to be found in a great variety of sources, among them the philosophical works of Plato and Aristotle (fourth century B.C.); the biographies and essays of Plutarch (c. 100 A.D.); anthologies and miscellanies such as the collection of prose and verse excerpts assembled by John Stobaeus (c. 400 A.D.) or Athenaeus' fifteen-volume *Deipnosophistai* ("Sophists at Dinner") (c. 200 A.D.); rhetorical and literary treatises such as *On Literary Composition* by Dionysius of Halicarnassus (Augustan period) or *On the Sublime*, traditionally attributed to one Longinus (first century A.D.); technical treatises such as that on meter by Hephaestion or that on grammar by Apollonius Dyscolus (both second century A.D.); and the ancient commentaries to standard authors that are known as scholia. Notable among papyrus finds have been that which in 1855 provided more than seventy lines of a maiden-song by Alcman, the extensive remnants of some twenty poems by Bacchylides that came to light in 1896, and the copious papyrus fragments recovered over the years from Oxyrhynchus on the west bank of the Nile, which have yielded extremely important texts by Alcaeus, Sappho, Stesichorus, Ibycus, and Pindar, among others. In recent decades, moreover, additional papyrus fragments have been extracted from mummy wrappings, notably the so-called Cologne Archilochus (Archilochus 39 in this volume) and the Lille Stesichorus (Stesichorus 6). In a field so meagerly stocked as archaic Greek lyric, the smallest increment is welcomed with excitement.

# ARCHILOCHUS

Archilochus probably lived in the first half of the seventh century B.C. He was born on Paros in the southern Aegean (cf. no. 19) and moved from there to Thasos as part of the colonization of that island by Parians and other Greeks (cf. nos. 10 and 16). A soldier as well as a poet (cf. nos. 1 and 2), he seems to have participated in battles between the Thasian settlers and tribes on the Thracian mainland (cf. no. 4); according to one ancient (but perhaps erroneous) tradition, he also served for a time as a mercenary. He wrote in a variety of metrical forms, and his range of theme and tone is very wide, from tender evocations of beauty and erotic longing (cf. nos. 12, 20, 35) to uninhibited coarseness and obscenity (cf. nos. 13, 14, 21), from outbursts of zestful pugnacity (cf. nos. 11, 24, 25) to somber reflections on the limitations and uncertainties of human life (cf. nos. 6, 26, 27). Often he seems to set himself against the conventional norms and beliefs of his day (cf. nos. 4, 7, 18, 29). In later centuries, however, he was particularly famous for his ferocity as a poet of invective and satirical attack. This aspect of his reputation was closely linked with the perhaps apocryphal story of his dealings with the family of one Lykambes (cf. nos. 30–34, 39). According to the traditional account, Lykambes first promised Archilochus the hand of his daughter Neoboule in marriage and then broke off the engagement, whereupon the poet retaliated against the family with verses of such virulent abuse that the victims were driven to commit suicide in order to escape disgrace.

Nos. 1–8 are in elegiac couplets, nos. 9–14 in iambic trimeters, nos. 15–29 in trochaic tetrameters, and nos. 30–39 in various "epodic" systems (see General Introduction, p. xiv).

### 1. (Fr. 1)

I am a servant of Enyalios the battle lord
 and of the Muses also, understanding their lovely gift.

1 **Enyalios** another name for Ares, the god of war.

1

### 2. (Fr. 2)

In my spear is my kneaded barley bread, in my spear is
    my wine
from Ismaros, and I drink it leaning upon my spear.

2 **Ismaros** a town on the coast of Thrace not far from Thasos (see intro-
duction); it was noted for its wines (cf. *Odyssey* 9. 196ff).

### 3. (Fr. 4)

But come now, take the jug and go up and down the benches
    of the swift ship, pulling the stoppers off the hollow jars;
drain off the red wine from the lees. Not even we
    will be able to stay sober on such a watch as this.

### 4. (Fr. 5)

My shield's in the hands of some jubilant Thracian—a
    faultless
    piece of equipment which I left, unwillingly, beside a
    bush.
Myself, I'm safe. What do I care about that shield?
    To hell with it! I'll soon find another one that's no
    worse.

### 5. (Fr. 11)

Neither by weeping shall I bring about any cure, nor shall
    I make
    things worse by pursuing enjoyments and festivities.

Quoted by Plutarch (*How to Study Poetry* 33) as being from a lament for the
death of Archilochus' brother-in-law, who was lost at sea. The lines that fol-
low may be from the same poem.

### 6. (Fr. 13)

Repining at painful sorrows, Perikles, no one among our
    citizens,

no, nor the city itself, will find pleasure in festivities:
such were the men whom the waves of the loud-roaring
    sea
washed over, and we struggle in our distress
5    with swollen lungs. But for evils that have no cure,
    my friend, the gods have ordained stern endurance
as remedy. These things go by turns: now it is to us
    that they have shifted, and we groan at the bloody
    wound,
but soon they will pass to others. Come now, with all
    speed
10    endure, and thrust aside this womanish grief.

### 7. (Fr. 14)

Aisimides, no one who cares about people's censure
    is likely to find many pleasures in life.

### 8. (Fr. 15)

Glaukos, a mercenary is your friend as long as he is
    fighting.

### 9. (Fr. 19)

"I care nothing for the life of Gyges with all his gold,
nor have I ever felt emulous desire; I do not envy
the actions of the gods; I have no craving for a tyrant's
    greatness,
for all such things are distant from my eyes."

According to Aristotle in the *Rhetoric* (3. 17. 16), Archilochus put these lines
into the mouth of "Charon the carpenter," about whom, however, we know
nothing. **Gyges** was a Lydian king of the eighth century B.C.

### 10. (Frs. 21 + 22)

. . . like the backbone of an ass
this island stands, dense with untamed woodland . . .
    . . . . . . . . . . . .

... for the place has no beauty at all, no charm
or loveliness, unlike the land about the banks of Siris.

These lines describe Thasos (see introduction). The **Siris** was a river in south-
ern Italy, site of an Ionian colony of the same name.

### 11. (Fr. 26)

Lord Apollo, afflict the guilty ones with pain
and bring them to destruction, O destroyer;
but us. . . .

### 12. (Frs. 30 + 31)

She rejoiced, holding a branch of myrtle
and the rose-tree's lovely flower . . .
. . . . . . . . . . .
. . . and her hair
shadowed her shoulders and her back.

### 13. (Fr. 42)

. . . like a Thracian or Phrygian drawing beer
out of a straw, she sucked away, head forward, working
hard. . . .

### 14. (Fr. 43)

. . . his prick, like that of a he-ass from Priene
well-fed with grain, spilled over. . . .

### 15. (Fr. 101)

Seven men fell dead when we overtook them at a run,
though we the killers are a thousand. . . .

### 16. (Fr. 102)

How the miserable dregs of all the Greeks have met
together on Thasos!

17.  (Fr. 105)

Glaukos, look: the waves are already roiling the sea's
depths; around the cliffs of Gyrai a cloud stands straight up,
sign of a storm, and out of the unexpected, fear comes on.

According to the ancient source in which these lines are quoted, they refer
allegorically to impending war. The **cliffs of Gyrai** seem to have been on the
south coast of Tenos, an island in the Cyclades.

18.  (Fr. 114)

I have no love for a commander who's tall or stands
    astraddle,
who's proud of his curling locks or wears his beard neatly
    trimmed.
Instead, I'll take a man who's short and crooked to look at
about the shanks, firmly planted on his feet, full of heart.

19.  (Fr. 116)

Have done with Paros and those figs and the seaman's life!

On Paros, see introduction. According to Athenaeus (3. 76a), who quotes this
line, the island was renowned for the excellence of its figs.

20.  (Fr. 118)

If only in such a way I could touch Neoboule's hand.

On Neoboule, see introduction and cf. 39.

21.  (Fr. 119)

. . . to fall upon a hard-working wineskin and to thrust
belly against belly, thigh against thigh . . .

22.  (Fr. 120)

. . . since I know how to start off the lovely song of lord
    Dionysos,

the dithyramb, when my wits are thunderstruck with
    wine.

The **dithyramb** was a type of song associated with the worship of Dionysos;
see the introductory note to Pindar, Dithyramb 2 and cf. *Olympian* 13. 18–19.

23.  (Fr. 122)

"Nothing is unexpected, nothing can be sworn as
    impossible
or marveled at, since Zeus, the father of the Olympians,
made night out of noonday, keeping back the light
of the beaming sun; and upon mankind came fear.
5    Henceforth all things are to be believed, all things
        expected
by men. None of you should in future be amazed, not even
    to see
the beasts change place with dolphins and go grazing
in the deep, holding the sea's resounding billows
dearer than land, while dolphins love the wooded hills. . . ."

According to Aristotle (*Rhetoric* 3. 17. 16) Archilochus put these lines into the
mouth of "the father speaking about his daughter," a phrase which is usually
understood as referring to Lykambes and Neoboule (see introduction). It has
been suggested that the eclipse alluded to may have been that which oc-
curred in 648 B.C.

24.  (Fr. 125)

I love a fight with you just as, when I'm thirsty,
I love to drink.

25.  (Fr. 126)

There's one big thing I know,
to pay back injury done to me with terrible injuries.

26.  (Fr. 128)

O heart, my heart, churning with unmanageable sorrows,

rouse yourself and fiercely drive off your foes
with a frontal attack, standing hard by them
steadfastly; and neither exult openly if you win,
nor, if you are beaten, fling yourself down at home in
  lamentation.
Instead, rejoice in what is joyful, grieve at troubles,
but not too much: be aware what sort of rhythm rules
  man's life.

### 27. (Fr. 130)

All things are easy for the gods. Often out of misfortunes
they set men upright who have been laid low on the black
  earth;
often they trip even those who are standing firm and roll
  them
onto their backs, and then many troubles come to them,
and a man wanders in want of livelihood, unhinged in
  mind.

### 28. (Frs. 131 + 132)

Glaukos, Leptinos' son, the hearts and minds of mortal
  men
are such as the day which Zeus brings upon them;
their thoughts are such as the happenings they encounter.

### 29. (Fr. 133)

No one enjoys respect among his fellow townsmen or is
  spoken of
once he is dead. Rather, we all pursue the favor of the
  living
while we ourselves are alive, and the dead always have
  the worst of it.

### 30. (Fr. 172)

Father Lykambes, what kind of thing did you imagine this
  to be?

Who is it that has unhinged the wits
with which you once were furnished? Now your neighbors
see in you nothing but one big joke.

This and the following four fragments appear to be from a poem in which
Lykambes (on whom see introduction) was accused of treachery (cf. 31), and
an animal fable was recounted by way of admonishment (cf. 32–34).

### 31. (Fr. 173)

You turned your back on the great oath
you swore by salt and table. . . .

### 32. (Fr. 174)

There is a fable that men tell, which says
that a fox and an eagle entered once
into partnership. . . .

In Aesop's version of this fable, the two animals enter into a pact of friend-
ship, but then the eagle kills the fox's cubs in order to feed its nestlings. Later,
however, when the eagle takes a piece of burning meat from an altar and so
sets its nest on fire, the young birds fall to the ground and are devoured by
the fox.

### 33. (Fr. 176)

"Do you see that lofty rock over there,
    rough and forbidding?
He sits there, preparing easy battle against you."

Some third party is evidently speaking to the fox about the eagle.

### 34. (Fr. 177)

"O Zeus, father Zeus, yours is the rulership of heaven;
    you oversee the deeds of men,
villainous and lawful; you care about
    the outrage and right-doing of beasts."

Presumably the fox is praying for vengeance against the eagle.

35. (Fr. 191)

For such was the passion of love that coiled itself beneath
    my heart
    and poured thick mist across my eyes,
robbing me of my tender senses.

36. (Fr. 193)

In wretchedness I lie here, gripped by longing,
lifeless, with bitter pain by the gods' will
    pierced through the bones.

37. (Fr. 201)

The fox knows many things, the hedgehog only one—but
    big.

The "one big thing" that the hedgehog knows is how to protect itself by
curling up into a ball.

38. (P. Argent. 3 fr. 1)

   ... driven off course by the waves;
and may the top-knotted Thracians most hospitably
    receive him, stripped to the skin,
in Salmydessos—there to endure miseries in full measure,
5    eating the bread of slavery—
frozen stiff with cold, crusted with salt
    and covered thick with seaweed,
his teeth chattering like a dog's, as he lies
    face-down in his helplessness
10   at the edge of the breaking waves ...
    This is what I would like to see
happen to the man who wronged me and trod his oaths
    underfoot,
    that man who was once my friend.

The authorship of this fragment (preserved on a papyrus) has been disputed;
some scholars believe that the lines are by Hipponax rather than Archilochus.

4 **Salmydessos** a place on the Thracian coast notorious both for the
dangers it posed to seafarers and for the rapaciousness with which its
inhabitants plundered shipwrecks.

39.  (196a)

"... refraining altogether.
Endure an equal ...

But if you are in pressing haste and desire drives you on,
there is in our household
5      one who now longs greatly ...

a lovely tender maiden. She has, I think,
a beauty that is faultless.
She is the one whom you should make your own."

So much she said, and to her I replied:
10     "Daughter of Amphimedo,
that noble and wise

woman whom the moldering earth now holds below,
the goddess offers pleasures
of many sorts to young men

15     apart from the divine deed: one of those will suffice.
These things, at leisure,
when darkness ...

you and I shall deliberate, with god's aid.
I shall do as you request;
20     greatly do I ...

beneath the cornice and the gates ...
Do not be grudging, dear one,
for I shall come to a halt in grassy

gardens. Now understand this: let Neoboule
25     be claimed by another man.
Alas, she is over-ripe ...

the bloom has withered from her maidenhood,
and the charm which formerly she possessed;
surfeited, she has not . . .

30  and she has shown, that frenzied woman, the measure of
     her. . . .
    To the crows with her!
    May this not be,

that I, possessing such a wife,
should be a source of joy to spiteful neighbors.
35  I much prefer you . . .

for you are neither unreliable nor two-faced,
while she in turn is too sharp
and makes many men her friends:

I fear that blind and premature results
40  may issue from such eager haste,
    just like the pups of a too-eager bitch."

So much I said; and then I took the maiden
and laid her down
among blooming flowers. Wrapping a soft

45  cloak about her, cradling her neck in my arms,
       . . . fearful . . .
    just like a fawn . . .

and with my hands I gently grasped her breasts
       . . . revealed her youthful
50  flesh, the onset of her prime,

and, fondling all her lovely body,
I released my passion's force,
just grazing tawny hair.

This substantial papyrus fragment (first published in 1974) narrates an en-
counter, both verbal and sexual, between the first-person speaker and a
young woman referred to as the **daughter of Amphimedo** (10), whom some

scholars have identified as a sister of the **Neoboule** mentioned in line 24 (on whom see introduction). Scholarly controversy has raged on many points of text and interpretation, including the specific nature of the sexual act allusively described in the final lines.

1–8  The young woman is speaking.

6  **lovely tender maiden**  presumably Neoboule.

15  **the divine deed**  apparently a reference to full sexual intercourse.

39–41  There was a Greek proverb, "A bitch in haste gives birth to blind pups."

# TYRTAEUS

Tyrtaeus was a Spartan poet of the mid-seventh century B.C. He is said to have written a poem on the Spartan constitution, and several of his surviving fragments (cf. nos. 1 and 2) are indeed on political themes. He was best known, however, for the war poetry in which he exhorted Spartan soldiers to bravery in the field (cf. nos. 5–7). These martial verses appear to have been composed in connection with a conflict known as the Second Messenian War, in which the people of Messenia, a fertile region to the west of Lakonia, attempted unsuccessfully to regain the independence which they had lost to Sparta two generations earlier (cf. nos. 3 and 4).

### 1. (Fr. 2)

For Zeus himself, the son of Kronos and husband of fair-
garlanded
Hera, has granted this city to the descendants of Herakles,
together with whom, abandoning windy Erineos,
we came to the broad island of Pelops.

This fragment and the next are probably from a poem called *Eunomia* ("Good Order" or "Discipline").

2 **the descendants of Herakles** the Herakleidai, sons and grandsons of Herakles by Deïaneira, who according to legend led the Dorian invasion and settlement of the Peloponnesos (see Glossary under "Dorians" and cf. note on Pindar, *Pythian* 1. 62ff).
3 **Erineos** a town in Doris, a small mountainous area in central Greece which the Dorians claimed as their point of origin.
4 **we** i.e., the Spartans. **the broad island of Pelops** i.e., the Peloponnesos.

### 2. (Fr. 4)

Having heard the voice of Phoibos, they brought home
from Pytho

13

oracles of the god and words sure of fulfillment:
that deliberation should originate with the god-honored
    kings,
to whose care the lovely city of Sparta is entrusted,
5      and with the elders who take precedence by birth; and that
    thereafter the people,
answering back in accordance with straightforward
    ordinances,
should say things that are honorable and do all things that
    are right,
and offer this city no crooked counsel;
and that victory and power should attend on the mass of
    the people.
10     Such, in these matters, was Phoibos' revelation to the city.

According to Spartan tradition, important elements in the city's constitution had been promulgated by Apollo's oracle at Delphi (Pytho). The Spartan system of government involved (among other institutions) a dual kingship, a council of elders (the *gerousia*), and a general assembly of adult male citizens.

###     3.  (Fr. 5)

. . . to our king, Theopompos dear to the gods,
    through whom we seized Messenia with its wide
    spaces,
Messenia good for ploughing, good for planting.
For its sake war was fought for nineteen years
5      unceasingly by men with enduring hearts,
    the spearmen fathers of our fathers;
and in the twentieth year the others abandoned their
    fertile fields
and fled from the great mountains of Ithome.

1 **Theopompos** an early king of Sparta and leader of his country's forces in the First Messenian War (c. 735–c. 715 B.C.), the purpose of which was to establish Spartan control of Messenia (on which see Glossary).
7 **the others** i.e., the Messenians.
8 **Ithome** a mountain in central Messenia which served as a rallying point and stronghold for the Messenians in their various attempts to break free of the control of Sparta.

### 4. (Frs. 6 + 7)

... being worn out, like asses, by great burdens,
　bringing to their masters, under dire compulsion,
　　half of all the crops that the land produces ...
　　　. . . . . . . . . . . .
... lamenting for their masters, themselves and their wives
　alike,
　whenever death's unhappy doom overtook one of them.

These two fragments are quoted by Pausanias (4. 14. 5) in illustration of the
sufferings imposed by the Spartans on the Messenians after their defeat in
the First Messenian War.

### 5. (Fr. 10)

To fall and die among the fore-fighters is a beautiful thing
　for a brave man who is doing battle on behalf of his
　　country;
but to abandon his own city and his fertile fields
　and take up the life of a beggar is of all things the most
　　painful,
5　being forced to roam with his dear mother and his aged
　　father,
　with his little children and his wedded wife.
For he will be hateful to all among whom he comes
　in his subjection to want and loathsome poverty;
he shames his lineage and belies the splendor of his looks,
10　attended by every kind of dishonor and distress.
Thus if a man who wanders homeless finds no
　　consideration
　or respect, and neither does his lineage hereafter,
then let us fight for this land with all our heart, and for our
　　children
　let us die without further hoarding of our lives.
15　Do battle then, young men, standing firm one beside the
　　other,
　check every impulse toward shameful flight or fear,
make the spirit within your hearts great and valiant,
　and do not love life too much as you fight the foe.

And the older men, whose knees are no longer nimble,
20      those you must not abandon in flight, aged as they are;
for shameful indeed it is when, fallen among the fore-
            fighters,
        an older man lies dead in front of the young ones,
his head already white and his beard grizzled,
        breathing out his valiant spirit in the dust,
25      clutching his bloody genitals in his hands—
        a sight shameful to look at and worthy of indignation—
his body exposed and naked. But for a young man all
            things are seemly,
        as long as he possesses the splendid bloom of attractive
            youth,
in men's eyes worthy of admiration and attractive to
            women
30      while he is alive, and beautiful too when he falls among
            the fore-fighters.
So let each man hold to his place with legs well apart,
        feet planted on the ground, biting his lip with his teeth.

In this exhortation to Sparta's young soldiers Tyrtaeus emphasizes various negative inducements to courage, namely the poverty, homelessness, and dishonor that result from defeat and the shame that they would bring on themselves by running away from battle or allowing older men to die in their place. Lines 19–30 are an adaptation and expansion of *Iliad* 22. 71–76.


        6.  (Fr. 11)

But come, since you are the race of unconquerable
            Herakles,
        be bold! Not yet has Zeus turned his face away.
Feel no fear before the multitude of men, do not run in
            panic,
        but let each man bear his shield straight toward the
            fore-fighters,
5       regarding his own life as hateful and holding the dark
        spirits of death as dear as the radiance of the sun.
For you know how destructive are the deeds of Ares,
            extorter of tears,
        and you have learned well the temper of grievous war;

       you have been among those who fled and those who
           pursued,
10      O young men, and you have had more than enough of
           both.
       Those who dare to remain in place at one another's side
           and advance together toward hand-to-hand combat and
           the fore-fighters,
       they die in lesser numbers, and they save the army behind
           them;
       but when men flee in terror, all soldierly excellence is lost.
15      No one could ever come to an end in recounting all
          the evils that befall a man if he learns to do shameful
           things:
       grievous it is to be struck from behind in the small of the
           back
          as a man is fleeing in the deadliness of war;
       and shameful is a body lying stretched in the dust,
20      driven through the back from behind with the point of a
           spear.
       So let each man hold to his place with legs well apart,
          feet planted on the ground, biting his lip with his teeth,
       thighs and shins below and, above, chest and shoulders
          covered by the belly of his broad shield.
25      In his right hand let him brandish his mighty spear,
          let him shake the fearsome crest upon his head.
       By performing mighty deeds let him learn the skills of
           warfare,
          and not stand with his shield beyond throwing range,
       but moving in close let each man engage hand-to-hand
30      and, wounding with long spear or sword, let him kill an
           enemy.
       Setting foot beside foot, leaning shield against shield,
          crest ranged against crest, helmet against helmet,
       chest against chest drawn near, let him fight his man,
          with sword hilt or long lance gripped in his hand.
35      And as for you light-armed soldiers, crouching here and
           there
          behind the shields, keep hurling great rocks,
       and fling your smooth javelins against them,
          standing hard by the soldiers in full armor.

In these lines Tyrtaeus appears to be rallying the troops after a temporary
setback. After a compliment to their ancestry (1, **the race of unconquerable
Herakles**, on which see no. 1), he propounds a paradox: the best way for a
soldier to ensure his own safety and that of his fellows is to expose himself to
danger by standing firm in the front line (4–14). The second half of the poem
presents a vivid description of the equipment and fighting method of the
heavy-armed infantry soldier or hoplite.

### 7.  (Fr. 12)

I would neither make mention of a man nor hold him in
    esteem
    either for excellence in the footrace or for wrestling skill,
not even if he had the size and strength of the Cyclopes
    and could outdo Thracian Boreas in running,
5    not if he were more attractive in form than Tithonos
    and had greater wealth than Midas or Kinyras,
not if he surpassed Pelops, Tantalos' son, in kingliness
    and possessed Adrastos' honey-voiced eloquence,
not if he had every claim to glory except impetuous valor;
10    for a man does not prove himself good in war
unless he can endure to gaze upon bloody slaughter
    and, standing close, reach out to strike the foe.
This excellence, this prize is best among human beings
    and noblest for a young man to win.
15    A common good it is for the city and all its people,
    when a man stands astride among the fore-fighters and
    holds firm
unceasingly, and utterly forgets all thought of shameful
    flight,
    staking his life and steadfast spirit,
and speaks heartening words to the man beside whom he
    is stationed—
20    this is the man who proves himself good in war;
he quickly turns aside the enemy's bristling
    ranks and with his zeal stems the wave of battle.
And then the man who gives up dear life by falling among
    the fore-fighters,
    bringing fame and glory to his city, his people, and his
    father,

25     struck many times through chest and studded shield
        and breastplate, each wound received from the front,
    that man is mourned alike by young and old,
        and all the city is troubled with painful longing;
    his burial mound and his children are conspicuous among
        men,
30     and his children's children and his lineage thereafter.
    His good repute never perishes, nor his name,
        but, under earth though he be, he proves immortal,
    since he was doing deeds of prowess and standing firm
        and struggling
        for his city's and children's sake when fierce Ares
        brought him down.
35     But if he escapes the fate of death that brings long
        sorrow
        and in victory with the spear obtains the splendid object
        of his prayers,
    all honor him alike, the young men and the aged,
        and he goes to Hades after enjoying many pleasures:
    as he grows old he stands out among his fellow citizens,
        and not one
40     wishes to cheat him of respect or justice;
    on the benches all yield place to him alike, the young
        and those of his own age and those who are older.
    Of this excellence now let every man endeavor to reach the
        height,
        striving with all his heart, never slacking off in battle.

The opening lines of this poem make use of the rhetorical device known to modern scholars as the priamel, which highlights a point of particular interest by setting it against the background of other (related or contrasting) items to which it is preferred. By surveying various forms of "excellence" (*arete*) that command general respect among human beings (physical prowess, good looks, wealth, political power, eloquence), Tyrtaeus focuses attention on the *one* form of excellence that he regards as supreme, namely "impetuous valor" (9), whose value to the community at large he stresses (15–20). The second half of the poem depicts the rewards that await the man who fights bravely on behalf of his country, whether he dies (23–34) or lives (35–42). For information on the various figures in the initial catalogue of examples (3–8), see Glossary.

# CALLINUS

Nothing is known about Callinus except that he was a native of Ephesus, on the Ionian coast of Asia Minor, and lived in the middle of the seventh century B.C. The one substantial fragment of his verse that survives is in the same tradition of martial elegy as Tyrtaeus' exhortations to the soldiers of Sparta. It is not known whom the Ephesians were fighting when Callinus composed these lines; it may have been the people of Magnesia (cf. Anacreon 1).

1. (Fr. 1)

How long are you lying idle? When will you have brave
        hearts,
    you young men? Do you not feel shame before those
        who live round about,
slacking off in this way? As if in a time of peace you think
    you can sit idle, yet war has the whole land within its
        grip. . . .
            . . . . . . . . . . .
5    . . . and let every man, as he dies, hurl his javelin one
        last time.
For it is a thing of honor and splendor that a man should
        fight
    on behalf of land and children and wedded wife
against the enemy, and death will come at whatever
        moment
    the spinning Fates determine. But let each man go
        forward,
10    holding his spear on high and with his shield protecting
        his valiant heart, when battle first is joined.
For in no way is it fated that a man escape
    death, not even if he is descended from immortal
        ancestors.

Often, after escaping the battle-slaughter and the thud of
  spears,
15 he returns, and in his house death's doom overtakes
  him;
but such a one is in any case not held dear by the
  community nor regretted.
The other sort, though, is lamented by small and great
  alike if anything happens to him;
for the people as a whole feel regret for a stout-hearted
  man
when he dies, and while he lives he is equal in worth to
  demigods,
20 for they fix their eyes on him as on a tower of defense,
doing the deeds of many although he is only one.

# SEMONIDES

It is probable that Semonides lived in the second half of the seventh century B.C. and migrated from his birthplace on Samos to the island of Amorgos in the southeastern Cyclades. He is reported to have written two books of elegies and at least two books of poems in iambic trimeter. In the ancient sources he is frequently confused with Simonides of Keos.

### 1. (Fr. 1)

My son, loud-sounding Zeus holds final power
over all things that are and arranges them as he wishes.
Understanding is not within men's grasp; from day to day
they live like animals, in no way knowing
5    how god will bring each thing to its fulfillment.
But hope and confidence encourage all of them
as they set their thoughts on unachievable things. Some wait
for a day to come, some for the circling of the years;
there is no one of mortals who does not think that next year
10    he will become a friend to wealth and good things.
But one is seized by unenviable old age
before he reaches his goal; others are wasted by the miseries
of sickness; others have been subdued in war
when Hades sends them under the dark earth;
15    others, driven upon the sea by storm
and the churning water's many swells,
meet their death when they can no longer make a living;
others fasten a noose for a wretched doom
and by their free choice leave the light of the sun.
20    Thus nothing is without evils, but rather countless

forms of death await mortals, and undreamed-of miseries
and afflictions. If they heeded my advice,
we would not love our misfortunes, nor torment ourselves
by keeping our hearts fixed on our grievous ills.

As a meditation on the limits of human knowledge and the vanity of human
wishes, these lines bear comparison with the latter half of Solon 7.

### 2. (Fr. 7)

The god made women's minds separately
in the beginning. One he made from the bristly sow:
everything in her house lies in disorder,
smeared with dirt, and rolls about the floor,
5      while she herself, unbathed, in unwashed clothes,
sits upon the dung heap and grows fat.
      Another the god made from the wicked vixen,
a woman who knows all things. Whether bad
or good, nothing escapes her notice;
10    for often she calls a good thing bad
and a bad thing good; her mood keeps changing.
      Another is from the bitch, a mischief-maker just like her
           mother,
who wants to hear all things and see all things.
Peering and roaming everywhere, she yelps
15    even when she sees no person there;
and no man can stop her, either by uttering threats
or, in a fit of rage, by knocking out her teeth
with a stone, or yet by speaking to her gently,
even if she happens to be sitting with guests—
20    no, she keeps up her constant useless howling.
      Another the Olympians fashioned out of earth
and gave to man with wits impaired; for such a woman
understands nothing, bad or good.
The only thing she knows how to do is eat:
25    not even when the god brings on a bad winter
does she feel the cold and draw her stool nearer to the fire.
      Another is from the sea: she has two minds.
One day she smiles and beams with joy;
a stranger, seeing her in the house, will praise her:

30    "There is no woman more estimable than this
      among all humankind, nor one more beautiful."
      The next day, though, she is unbearable to lay eyes on
      or to come near to; at that time she rages
      unapproachably, like a bitch with puppies,
35    proving implacable and repulsive
      to everyone, enemies and friends alike.
      So too the sea often stands in unmoved
      calm, harmless, a great joy to sailors,
      in the summer season; but often too it rages,
40    borne along by loud-thundering waves.
      This is what such a woman most resembles
      in mood; the sea too has its different natures.
          Another is from the ash-gray obstinate ass.
      Under compulsion and rebuke, reluctantly,
45    she puts up with everything after all and does
      acceptable work; meanwhile, she eats in the innermost
              room
      all night and all day, and she eats beside the hearth;
      just so, as her companion in the act of love,
      she also welcomes any man who comes.
50        Another is from the weasel, a wretched, miserable sort.
      She has nothing beautiful or charming
      about her, nothing delightful or lovely.
      She is mad for bed and lovemaking,
      but any man who lies with her she sickens with disgust.
55    Her thieving does great harm to her neighbors,
      and she often eats up offerings left unburned.
          Another the delicate, long-maned mare brought forth.
      She turns away from menial tasks and trouble;
      she won't lay a finger on a mill, nor pick up
60    a sieve, nor throw the dung outside the house,
      nor, being anxious to avoid the soot, sit near
      the oven. Yet she compels a man to be her own:
      every day she washes herself clean
      twice, sometimes three times, and rubs herself with
              perfumes;
65    she wears her mane of thick long hair
      well-combed and shadowy with flowers.
      A beautiful sight indeed is such a woman

to others; to her husband, though, she proves disastrous,
unless he is a tyrant or a sceptered king,
70    whose heart takes pride in such ornaments.
     Another is from the ape. This is, above all others,
the greatest evil that Zeus has given to men.
Her face is ugly in the extreme: when such a woman
walks through the city, everyone laughs at her.
75    She's short in the neck; she moves with difficulty;
she's rumpless, nothing but legs. Pity the wretched man
who holds in his arms a calamity like that!
She knows all arts and wily ways,
just like an ape, and doesn't mind being laughed at.
80    She won't do anyone a kindness; all her attention,
all her planning throughout the day is fixed on this:
how she can do a person the greatest possible harm.
     Another is from the bee. Happy is he who gets her,
for on her alone no censure settles.
85    In her care his property flourishes and prospers;
she grows old loving a husband who loves her,
a mother of noble and illustrious offspring.
She is conspicuous among all women,
and a godlike grace suffuses her.
90    She takes no pleasure sitting among women
in places where they tell tales of lovemaking.
Such women are the best and wisest wives
that Zeus in his graciousness bestows on men.
     All these other kinds, however, Zeus
95    has contrived to be with men and there remain.
No greater plague than this has Zeus created—
women. Even if they may seem to be of some service
to him who has them, to him above all they prove a
          plague.
He who lives with a woman never passes through
100   an entire day in a state of cheerfulness;
nor will he quickly push away Hunger from his house,
that hated housemate, that malevolent god.
Whenever a man means to enjoy himself
at home, by divine dispensation or human favor,
105   she finds a reason to criticize him and arms herself for
          battle.

Wherever a woman is, men cannot give a hearty welcome
even to a stranger who has come to the house.
She who seems to be most self-controlled
turns out to commit the greatest outrages:
110      as her husband stands there open-mouthed, the neighbors
take delight in seeing how yet another has gone astray.
Every man will do all he can to praise
his own wife and find fault with another's,
but we fail to recognize that our lots are equal.
115      No greater plague than this has Zeus created,
and he has bound us to them with unbreakable shackles,
ever since Hades welcomed those
who fought a war for a woman's sake. . . .

In both the *Theogony* (570–589) and the *Works and Days* (60–82) Hesiod tells how Zeus, angered by Prometheus' theft of fire, commanded the rest of the Olympian gods to create the first woman (Pandora) as a punishment for mankind, and how in so doing the different gods contributed different qualities to her nature. While working in the same tradition of Greek misogyny, Semonides here rings changes on Hesiod's account by positing multiple acts of creation producing ten distinct types of women, each fashioned from a different element (earth, sea) or animal (sow, fox, dog, donkey, weasel, horse, ape, bee). Of these only the last, the bee-woman, is portrayed in positive terms.

118 **a war for a woman's sake** i.e, the Trojan War, which was fought for Helen.

# MIMNERMUS

Mimnermus was a native either of Smyrna or of Colophon (the ancient sources differ) and lived during the second half of the seventh century B.C. Although in later antiquity Mimnermus was renowned for his amatory elegies, the extant fragments make it clear that love was by no means his only theme. He is also reported to have written a poem on the history of Smyrna.

### 1. (Fr. 1)

What life, what pleasure is there without golden Aphrodite?
    May I die when I no longer care about such things
as clandestine love and cajoling gifts and bed,
    which are the alluring blossoms of youth
5  for men and women. But when painful old age
    encroaches, which makes a man ugly and base alike,
then dreadful anxieties constantly wear away at his mind,
    and he takes no pleasure in gazing on the radiance of
      the sun,
but is instead hateful to boys, unhonored by women.
10    So grievous a thing have the gods made old age.

### 2. (Fr. 2)

We, like the leaves which come forth in the flowery season
    of spring, when they grow quickly under the radiance
    of the sun,
like them we enjoy the blossoms of youth for a short time
    only,
    merely an arm's span in length, having no knowledge
    from the gods
5  either of evil or of good; beside us stand dark Spirits of
    Doom,

both the one that decrees for us grievous Old Age
and the other that brings Death. The harvest-time of youth
    comes as quickly as the sun at dawn spreads its light
      over the earth.
But as soon as this youthful season has passed by to its
    end,
10     then at once to be dead is better than life,
for many sorrows come to the heart: at times one's
      household goods
    waste away, and a painful life of poverty results;
then again, another man lacks children, and yearning for
    them
    more than all other things he goes down beneath the
      earth into Hades;
15    another is afflicted by spirit-destroying disease. There is no
    one
    of humankind to whom Zeus does not give sorrows in
      plenty.

The comparison of human beings to leaves with which this poem begins is as
old as Homer's *Iliad*; see Simonides 12.


    3.  (Fr. 5)

I break out in a sudden sweat all over my body
    and tremble in dismay when I gaze on my generation's
      flowering,
delightful and lovely alike. If only it lasted longer!
    But short-lived like a dream youth passes
5    in all its preciousness; and, grievous and unsightly,
    old age immediately hangs over our heads,
hateful and dishonored alike, which makes a man
      unrecognizable
    and ruins his eyes and mind as it pours about him.


    4.  (Fr. 6)

May it happen that without disease or grievous troubles
    the fate of death might overtake me at sixty years of age!

For a response to this couplet see Solon 10.

### 5. (Fr. 12)

For the Sun has labor as his portion every day,
    nor does a time of rest ever come
either for his horses or for himself, once rosy-fingered
      Dawn
    leaves the Ocean and climbs up into the sky.
5    For through the waves he is carried in a lovely bed
    intricately wrought by Hephaistos' hands
out of precious gold, fitted with wings, which over the top
    of the water
    rapidly carries him sleeping from the land of the
      Hesperides
to the country of the Ethiopians, where his swift chariot
    and horses
10    stand until early-born Dawn arrives;
    there Hyperion's son steps into another carriage.

On the Sun and his nightly passage over the Ocean cf. Stesichorus 2.

4 **Ocean** according to early Greek conceptions, a fresh-water river running around the circumference of the (flat) earth.
8 **Hesperides** nymphs who supposedly dwelt near the Ocean in the extreme west of the world, as their name ("western") indicates.
9 **Ethiopians** the easternmost of peoples; see Glossary.
11 **another carriage** i.e., the one which will carry him through the day-time sky.

### 6. (Fr. 14)

Not such was the might and manly spirit of that man
    of whom I hear from my elders, who saw him
routing the thick-set ranks of Lydian cavalry
    over the plain of Hermos, wielding his ashwood spear.
5    With him Pallas Athena never found fault at all,
    nor with the keen-edged might of his heart, when
      through the front lines
he used to rush in war's bloody combat,

defying with his force the enemy's bitter arrows;
for no man was better and braver than that one
10          at setting about the work of fierce battle
with the foe, when he moved like the rays of the sun.

These lines are probably part of a poem which Mimnermus wrote on a battle fought by the Greeks of Smyrna (see introduction) against the Lydians under their king Gyges. The **Hermos** (4) was an important river in Lydia.

# ALCMAN

Whether or not Alcman was born in Sparta (according to one ancient tradition he was originally from Lydia), his professional life as a poet was spent in that city, probably in the late seventh and early sixth centuries B.C. Much of his work seems to have been composed for performance at public festivals by choruses of young unmarried women (*parthenoi*), a type of poem known as the *partheneion* or "maiden-song." Although it appears that such poems occasionally included mythical narratives, the extant fragments suggest that they were largely devoted to topics and personalities of immediate local interest. During the Alexandrian period Alcman's poems were collected in six (perhaps seven) books.

1. (Fr. 1)

... Polydeukes ...
I pay no heed to Lykaithos among the dead,
but Enarsphoros and swift-footed Sebros,
and ... ... the violent,
5    and ... ... in his helmet,
and Euteiches and lord Areios
and ... ... the most eminent of demi-gods;

and ... ... the commander
... the great, and Eurytos
10    ... in the battle rout
... those who were bravest,
... shall we pass over.
They were defeated by Destiny
and Contrivance, oldest of all
15    the gods. The valor of humankind
must not, unshod, take wing to heaven,
nor attempt to marry Aphrodite

the Cyprian queen, or some . . .
. . . or a daughter of Porkos
20      . . . but the Graces . . . Zeus's house
. . . with love in their glances.

[six lines missing]
. . . youth perished
[two lines missing]
30      . . . went; one of them by an arrow,
. . . by a marble millstone . . .
. . . Hades . . .
[one line missing]
. . . and unforgettable things
35      they suffered, having devised deeds of wickedness.

There is such a thing as retribution from the gods.
That man is blessed who with cheerful heart
weaves out his day
free from tears. I, for my part, sing
40      of Agido's radiant light; I see
her as the sun, which on our behalf
Agido summons to shine
as witness. But I can neither praise
nor censure her: our illustrious chorus-leader
45      forbids it utterly, for she herself appears
to stand out as supreme, just as if one
were to set among grazing herds a horse
of sturdy build, a prize-winning champion with clattering
          hooves,
one of those winged steeds in dreams.

50      You see her, don't you? The racehorse
is Enetic; but the hair
of my cousin
Hagesichora has a bloom upon it
as of pure gold,
55      and her silvery face—
why do I tell you openly?
Here she is, Hagesichora!
But she who is second to Agido in beauty
will run as a Colaxaian horse with an Ibenian;

60 for while we carry
a plough to Her of the Morning Twilight,
the Pleiades, rising through the ambrosial night
like the star Sirios, fight against us.

No abundance of crimson cloth
65 is great enough to ward them off,
no intricate snake,
all gold, nor headband
from Lydia, ornament
of soft-eyed girls,
70 nor even Nanno's tresses,
nor yet again Areta, like a goddess in looks,
nor Thylakis and Kleësithera;
nor, going to Ainesimbrota's, will you say:
"May Astaphis be mine,
75 may Philylla turn her gaze this way,
and Damareta and lovely Ianthemis"—
no, it is Hagesichora who makes me pine.

For is not the lovely-ankled
Hagesichora present here,
80 remaining near Agido
and praising our festival?
Accept, O gods,
their prayers: for to gods belong fulfillment
and consummation. O leader of the chorus,
85 I would say that alone I am
only a girl screeching at random like an owl
from a rafter, though I also yearn most of all
to please Her of the Dawn, for of our troubles
she has proved herself a healer.
90 But it is through Hagesichora that girls
have set their feet on the paths of lovely peace.

For the trace-horse
in the same way must be . . .
and in a ship as well the helmsman
95 most of all must be heeded.
The Sirens, it is true,
have more songful voices,

for they are goddesses, but set against eleven
she sings like ten young girls;
100      her utterance rings as clear as that of a swan upon the
              streams
         of Xanthos; and she, with her lovely yellow tresses. . . .
                        [4 lines missing]

This lengthy fragment, found on an Egyptian papyrus scroll in the middle of
the nineteenth century, is part of a maiden-song or *partheneion* (see introduc-
tion). The text presents a large number of interpretive difficulties, among
them the nature of the religious festival for which it was written and the roles
and interrelations of the various individuals who are named; the suggestions
made in the following notes are merely tentative.

  1–35  These highly fragmentary lines appear to deal with the death in
battle of the sons of Hippokoon, a legendary Spartan king, perhaps at the
hands of their cousins Kastor and Polydeukes. The moralizing in lines 13–
19 suggests that the cause of the conflict may have been rivalry in court-
ship. The relevance of the story to the rest of the poem is unclear.
  19 **Porkos**  apparently a Lakonian sea god.
  44 **our illustrious chorus-leader**  presumably Hagesichora, whose name
literally means "she who leads the chorus."
  50 **The racehorse**  apparently a reference to Agido. The precise signifi-
cance of **Enetic** as an epithet for horses (as of **Colaxaian** and **Ibenian** in
line 59) is not known.
  61 **a plough**  perhaps "a cloak"; the interpretation is uncertain. **Her of
the Morning Twilight**  The identity of the goddess is uncertain; cf. **Her of
the Dawn** in line 88.
  62 **the Pleiades**  The reference may be to Hagesichora and Agido, whose
beauty is so overwhelming that the rest of the choir admit defeat before it.
A less likely alternative is that the Pleiades are another choir with whom
Hagesichora and the rest of her group are competing.
  70–76  The names may be those of the other members of Hagesichora's
choir.
  84 **O leader of the chorus**  cf. note on line 44.
  91 **on the paths of lovely peace**  possibly a reference to victory in choral
competition.
  92–95 Hagesichora is apparently being compared, in her role as chorus
leader, to the **trace-horse** which leads the way for the other horses in a
chariot team and to the **helmsman** who steers a ship.
  96 **the Sirens**  legendary singers whose voices were said to cast an
irresistible spell on listeners.
  98–99 **set against eleven she sings like ten**  The significance of the

numbers is not clear; perhaps Hagesichora's skill at singing is such that
she is, as it were, a choir in herself.
101 **with her yellow tresses** cf. lines 51–54.


   2. (Fr. 3)

Muses of Olympos, fill my heart
with yearning for a new song:
I am eager to hear
the maidenly voice
5     of girls singing a lovely tune to the sky
             [one line missing]
    . . . will scatter sweet sleep from my eyelids,
and leads me to go into the assembly . . .
where I shall shake my yellow hair. . . .

10          . . . tender feet . . .
          [lines 11–60 missing]
. . . with desire that loosens limbs, and more meltingly
than sleep or death she casts her glances:
not to no purpose is she sweet.


But Astymeloisa offers me no answer;
65    rather, holding the garland,
like a star flashing through
the radiant heavens,
or a golden sapling, or soft down . . .
        [one line missing]
70    . . . she stepped through on tapered feet;
making her locks beautiful, the moist charm of Kinyras
sits on the maiden's flowing hair.


   . . . through the crowd Astymeloisa
makes her way as the people's darling . . .
75     . . . taking . . .
    . . . I say . . .
    . . . if only a silver cup . . .
     [one line missing]
   . . . to see if she might love me . . .
80   . . . coming closer, she might take my tender hand,
immediately I would become her suppliant . . .

Another (and even more fragmentary) *partheneion*, in which Astymeloisa appears to be the focus of attention much as Hagesichora is in no. 1.

71 **the moist charm of Kinyras** i.e., perfumed ointment. Kinyras was a legendary king of Cyprus, an island famous for the incense and perfume that it produced.
74 **the people's darling** a play on the literal meaning of Astymeloisa's name, "she whom the city cares about."

### 3. (Fr. 26)

No longer, maidens of honeyed speech and holy voice,
  do my limbs have power to carry me. If only, ah, if only I
      were a *kerylos*,
which wings its way with the halcyons over the
      blossoming waves,
fearless at heart, that holy sea-purple bird.

2–3 The *kerylos*, like the **halcyon** with which it was often associated, was a mythical sea bird later identified with the kingfisher. Halcyons were thought to nest on the sea waves at the time of the winter solstice.

### 4. (Fr. 27)

Come, Muse, Kalliope, daughter of Zeus,
start the lovely verses; imbue the song
with desire and make the choral dancing graceful.

### 5. (Fr. 56)

Often upon the mountain peaks, when
the gods find pleasure in the torch-lit festival,
holding a golden vessel, a large drinking cup
of the sort that shepherds hold,
5       and with your hands putting into it the milk of lions,

you made a cheese, large and firm, for the Slayer of Argos.

The "you" addressed in these lines is apparently a bacchant, a female worshipper of Dionysos. For the association of torches and lions with Dionysos, cf. Pindar's Dithyramb 2. The **Slayer of Argos** (6) is Hermes, to whom Zeus entrusted the infant Dionysos immediately after his birth.

6. (Fr. 59a + b)

Love once again, by the will of Kypris,
pours down in sweetness and melts my heart.
· · · · · · · · · · · ·
This gift of the sweet Muses
was shown forth by one blessed among maidens,
the fair-haired Megalostrata.

1 **Kypris** Aphrodite (see Glossary).

7. (Fr. 89)

Slumber holds the mountains' peaks and chasms,
the headlands and the torrents,
the woods and all the creeping things that the black earth
      nurtures,
the beasts in their mountain lairs, the race of bees,
the monsters in the depths of the churning sea;
and slumber holds the long-winged birds in all their
      kinds. . . .

# ALCAEUS

Alcaeus was a native of Mytilene, the most important city on the island of Lesbos. A contemporary of Sappho, he was probably born around 620 B.C. The aristocratic family to which he belonged was deeply involved in the city's factional struggles, and Alcaeus himself appears to have endured periods of exile as a consequence (cf. nos. 6 and 7). The rough-and-tumble of Mytilenean political life is one of several frequent themes in the extant fragments (e.g., nos. 1, 5–9, 18); others are wine and the joys of the *symposion* or drinking-party (e.g., nos. 3, 13–17, 20–22) and episodes from heroic legend (e.g., nos. 4, 10, 11). It is likely that most if not all of Alcaeus' poems were composed for performance amid a circle of friends and associates. The Alexandrian edition of his poetry comprised at least ten volumes.

Alcaeus makes frequent use of two particular stanzaic forms, the Alcaic and the Sapphic, on which see the General Introduction, note 3. Examples of the former are nos. 1, 6, 9, 11, 14, and 15; of the latter, nos. 2, 4, 10, 12, and 20.

### 1. (Fr. 6)

This wave in turn, like the earlier one,
comes on, and it will give us much labor
3    to bail out once it enters the ship's . . .
[one line missing]

[two lines missing]
Let us strengthen the ship's sides as quickly as possible,
and make a run to a safe harbor;

and let no craven hesitation seize
10    any of us, for clear before us stands a great ordeal.
Remember our previous trouble;
now let every man prove himself reliable,

and let us not put to shame by cowardice
our noble fathers lying under the earth. . . .

This fragment is probably intended as an allegorical representation of politi-
cal conflict on Lesbos (the "Ship of State"); cf. no. 9 and Theognis 15.


### 2. (Fr. 34)

Come to me here, leaving the island of Pelops,
you mighty sons of Zeus and Leda;
appear with kindly hearts, Kastor
and Polydeukes,

5    you who travel across the broad earth
and all the sea on swift-footed horses,
and easily rescue men from death's
deep chill,

springing upon the tops of well-benched ships,
10   shining afar as you run up the forestays,
in the threatening darkness bringing light
to the black ship. . . .

A prayer of the so-called *kletic* type, i.e., one that "calls" or "summons" a
deity to come to the speaker's assistance. Other examples of the kletic prayer
are Sappho 1 and 2 and Anacreon 4.

1 **the island of Pelops** the Peloponnesos, the southern portion of the
Greek mainland, where Sparta, the home of Kastor and Polydeukes, was
located.
2 **sons of Zeus and Leda** On the parentage and functions of Kastor and
Polydeukes, see Glossary under "Tyndaridai."
9–12 **shining afar** Kastor and Polydeukes were believed to manifest
themselves to ships at sea through the phenomenon of "St. Elmo's Fire,"
an electrical discharge visible on masts and rigging.


### 3. (Fr. 38a)

Drink and get drunk with me, Melanippos. Why do you
suppose
that when you have crossed great Acheron's

eddying stream you will see the sun's pure light
again? But come, do not aim at things so great:

5    for even king Sisyphos, Aiolos' son, who excelled
all men in wit, thought he had mastered death;

but, clever though he was, at fate's command a second
time
he crossed the eddies of Acheron, and Zeus the king,

the son of Kronos, contrived a labor for him to undergo
10   beneath the black earth. But come, put such hopes aside;

now if ever, while youth is ours, we must accept
whatever of these things God gives us to experience. . . .

A noteworthy feature of this fragment is the organization of its thought: (A)
an exhortation to drink and be merry; (B) a warning against vain hopes of
evading mortality; (C) an example proving that such hopes are indeed vain;
(B') the warning repeated; (A') the exhortation restated. Such "concentric
ring-form," as it has been called, is not uncommon in archaic Greek poetry;
for a far more elaborate example cf. Pindar, *Pythian* 3. 1–76. On **Acheron** and
**Sisyphos**, see Glossary.

### 4. (Fr. 42)

As the story tells, because of wicked deeds
bitter grief once came to Priam and his sons
from you, Helen, and Zeus with fire destroyed
holy Ilion.

5    A different sort was she whom Aiakos' noble son,
inviting all the Blessed to the wedding-feast,
led into marriage from the halls of Nereus,
a delicate maiden,

to Chiron's house; he loosed the chaste
10   maiden's girdle, and love blossomed
for Peleus and the best of Nereus' daughters;
and in a year

> she bore a son, mightiest of demigods,
> fortunate driver of tawny horses.
> 15      But they were ruined for Helen's sake,
> the Phrygians and their city.

Alcaeus draws a contrast between the adulterous union of Helen and Paris, whose only fruit was the bloodshed and destruction wreaked by the Trojan War, and the hallowed marriage of Peleus (**Aiakos' noble son**, 5) and Thetis (**the best of Nereus' daughters**, 11), from which sprang Achilles (13–14), greatest of all the warriors who fought at Troy. In beginning and ending with the same topic (Helen and the Trojans) the poem exhibits what is known as "ring-form" (see note on previous poem), one effect of which can be to create a sense of closure.

2 **Priam** king of Troy (**Ilion**). Many of Priam's sons were killed during the Trojan War, and he himself perished during the city's final capture.
6 **the Blessed** i.e., the Olympian gods.
15 **the Phrygians** i.e., the Trojans.

### 5. (Fr. 70)

> . . . making merry, the lyre takes part in
> the drinking-party, feasting with
> worthless charlatans. . . .

> But let *him*, kinsman by marriage to the Atreidai,
> 5      keep on devouring the city just as he did with Myrsilos,
> until such time as Ares chooses to turn us
> to our weapons. This present anger may we put from our
> minds,

> and let us relax from this factional strife that eats our
> hearts,
> this civil warfare which some one of the Olympians
> 10      stirred up among us, bringing the people into ruin,
> but to Pittakos giving delightful glory. . . .

One of Alcaeus' many poems on the factional politics of his native city. The **him** of line 4 is Pittakos, on whom see Glossary; Pittakos had married into an aristocratic family of Mytilene, the Penthilidai, which claimed descent from Agamemnon, son of Atreus. Although at an earlier point he and Alcaeus had been political allies (possibly in opposition to the tyrant **Myrsilos**, 5), Pittakos seems thereafter to have joined forces with Myrsilos and eventually ruled Mytilene himself as an absolute ruler chosen by the people. Alcaeus attacks him in nos. 6 and 18 as well.

### 6. (Fr. 129)

. . . men of Lesbos founded
this precinct, large and conspicuous,
common to all, and in it set
altars of the blessed immortals;

5     and Zeus they titled God of Suppliants,
and you they called Aiolian, Glorious Goddess,
Mother of All, and this third one here
they named Kemelios,

Dionysos, devourer of raw flesh. Come,
10     with friendly spirit listen
to our prayer, and from these hardships
and the pangs of exile deliver us.

But let the son of Hyrrhas be pursued
by *those* men's avenging Fury, since once we swore
15     with solemn sacrifice
never to betray a single comrade of ours,

but either to lie clothed in earth,
dead at the hands of men who at that time got the mastery,
or else, by killing them,
20     to deliver the people from their sufferings.

But those things Potbelly did not take
to heart; without compunction
he trampled his oaths under foot
and now devours our city. . . .

Apparently composed during one of Alcaeus' periods of exile (cf. line 12). The implied setting of the poem is a sanctuary of Zeus, Hera (the **Glorious Goddess** of line 6), and Dionysos.

8 **Kemelios** presumably a cult-title of Dionysos, but its meaning is unknown.

9 **devourer of raw flesh** so called because the eating of raw flesh (*omophagia*) was often part of Dionysiac ritual.

13 **the son of Hyrrhas** Pittakos, the **Potbelly** of line 21; see note on preceding poem.

14 *those* **men** presumably men who died through Pittakos' treachery. According to a Greek belief, the commission of a heinous crime summoned into existence a spirit of vengeance or **Fury** (Erinys), which saw to it that the perpetrator was properly punished.


### 7. (Fr. 130b)

. . . I, poor wretch,
live the life of a rustic,
yearning to hear the Assembly
being summoned, O Agesilaidas,

5      and the Council. The property which my father
and father's father grew old possessing,
among these citizens who wrong one another,
from that I am driven away,

an exile on the very edge of things, and like Onomakles
10     I have settled here alone amid the wolf-thickets
. . . war, for it is ignoble
to give up rebellion against. . . .

. . . to the precinct of the blessed gods . . .
. . . stepping on the black earth . . .
15     . . . gatherings . . .
I dwell, keeping my feet clear of trouble,

where women of Lesbos, being judged for beauty,
go back and forth in their trailing robes, and all around
rings out the wondrous sound
20     of the women's holy cry each year . . .

. . . from many toils when will the gods
of Olympos rescue me? . . .

Another poem from exile, addressed to a friend by the name of **Agesilaidas** (4). If the **precinct of the blessed gods** (13) is identical with the sanctuary of Zeus, Hera, and Dionysos described in no. 6, then the two poems may date from the same period in Alcaeus' life.

3–5 The **assembly** and the **council** were the two chief political bodies of a typical Greek city-state.
9 **Onomakles** evidently a well-known recluse (real or legendary).

### 8.  (Fr. 140)

The great house glitters
   with bronze. The entire ceiling is decorated
with shining helmets, down
   from which white plumes of horsehair
5    nod, the adornments of
   men's heads. Greaves of bronze
conceal the pegs they hang on,
   shining bright, a protection against strong arrows,
while corslets of new linen
10   and hollow shields lie thrown about.
Beside them are Chalkidian swords,
   beside them are many belts and tunics.
These it has not been possible to forget,
   since first we undertook this task of ours.

14 **this task of ours** apparently a reference to the armed struggle which Alcaeus and his political allies have been waging against factional enemies.

### 9.  (Fr. 208a)

I cannot understand the strife of the winds;
from this side one wave rolls in,
from that side another, and we in the middle
are borne along together with our black ship,

5    suffering many hardships in the mighty storm.
The bilge water is over the masthold,
the entire sail lets light through now,
tattered to shreds as it is;

> the halyards are slackening, the rudders . . .
> [two lines missing]
12     . . . both my feet remain caught
>
> in the ropes. This is what saves me,
> this alone; but the cargo. . . .

Probably another "Ship of State" poem, like no. 1.


    10.  (Fr. 283)

> . . . and fluttered the heart of Argive Helen
> in her breast. Maddened with passion for the man
> from Troy, the traitor-guest, she followed him
>      over the sea in his ship,
>
5    leaving her child at home . . .
> and her husband's richly covered bed . . .
> . . . her heart persuaded by desire . . .
>      [line missing]
>
>      [line missing]
10   . . . many of his brothers the black
> earth holds fast, laid low on the Trojan plain
>      for that woman's sake,
>
> and many chariots in the dust . . .
>      . . . and many flashing-eyed . . .
15    . . . trampled, and slaughter . . .

Another treatment of the Helen story (cf. no. 4). Fragmentary though it is, its selection of details and general tone present a striking contrast to Sappho 4. **The man from Troy** is of course Paris, for whose sake Helen abandoned her husband Menelaos and her baby daughter Hermione.


    11.  (Fr. 298)

> . . . disgracing those who committed unjust acts . . .
>      . . . throw a noose about
> their necks . . .     . . . with stoning. . . .

... it would have been much better for the Achaians
5    if they had put to death the man who wronged the gods;
in that way, while sailing past Aigai,
they would have met with a gentler sea.

But in the temple the daughter of Priam
was embracing the statue of Athena,
10   giver of booty in abundance, her hand on its chin,
while the enemy occupied the city ...

... and Deiphobos too
they killed, and wailing from the wall
rose up, and children's cries
15   filled the Dardanian plain.

And Ajax came in the grip of ruinous madness
into the temple of chaste Pallas, who
to sacrilegious mortals is by nature
most terrible of all the blessed gods;

20   and laying hold of the maiden with both hands
as she stood beside the holy statue,
he outraged her, that man from Lokros, and felt no fear
of Zeus's daughter, giver of war,

... but she, frowning fearsomely ...
25   ... livid with anger, over the wine-dark
sea came darting, and out of nowhere
suddenly stirred up gales. ...

Although the first few lines of this piece are too fragmentary to yield certain sense, it seems likely that they refer to the publicly administered punishment that Alcaeus believes Pittakos and his political associates deserve as a consequence of their misdeeds. If so, then Alcaeus apparently intends to draw an analogy between contemporary and legendary events in the stanzas that follow.

5 **the man who wronged the gods** Ajax son of Oileus, from the city of Lokros (cf. line 22), who during the sack of Troy raped Priam's daughter Kassandra even though she had taken refuge in the temple of Pallas

Athena. As punishment for this and other sacrileges, the Greeks suffered storms at sea when they returned home from Troy, passing **Aigai** (6) in southern Euboia on their way.

12 **Deiphobos** one of Priam's fifty sons, with whom Helen was living at the time when Troy was sacked.

15 **the Dardanian plain** Dardania was another name for the region of Troy; see Glossary under "Dardanos."

### 12. (Fr. 308)

Greetings, lord of Kyllene: you are the one
my heart desires to sing of, whom on the utmost heights
Maia bore, having lain with Kronos' son,
    the king of all. . . .

The opening of a hymn to Hermes, on whom see Glossary.

### 13. (Fr. 332)

Now each man must get drunk and drink
with all his might, since Myrsilos is dead. . . .

These lines, along with the four fragments that follow and no. 22, are quoted by Athenaeus (10. 430) in support of his observation that Alcaeus "drinks at all times and in all circumstances." On **Myrsilos**, see no. 5 with note.

### 14. (Fr. 335)

We must not yield our hearts to our misfortunes,
for we shall gain nothing by being distressed,
Bycchis: the best of remedies
is to fetch wine and then get drunk.

### 15. (Fr. 338)

Rain falls from Zeus, and out of the sky a great
winter storm comes; the streams are frozen . . .
        [two lines missing]

5        Defy the storm, lay wood upon
         the fire, mix the honey-sweet wine
         unstintingly, and about your temples
         place a headband of soft wool.


         16.  (Fr. 346)

         Let's drink! Why are we waiting for the lamps? Only an
                 inch of daylight's left.
         Lift down the large cups, my friend, the painted ones;
         for wine was given to men by the son of Semele and Zeus
         to help them forget their troubles. Mix one part of water to
                 two of wine,
5        pour it in up to the brim, and let one cup push
         the other along. . . .

3 **the son of Semele and Zeus** Dionysos, god of wine.
4 The Greeks regularly drank their wine mixed with water. The propor-
tion given here is unusually strong; cf. Anacreon 2.


         17.  (Fr. 347)

         Steep your lungs in wine, for the star is coming around;
         the time of year is cruel, and everything is thirsty under
                 the heat;
         out of the leaves the cicada rings forth sweetly, pouring
                 down from under
         its wings a continuous flood of piercing song, whenever
                 summer
5        blazes . . .
                         [one line missing]
         and the golden thistle is in bloom. Now women are at their
                 foulest,
         but men are weak, since they are parched in head and
                 knees
         by Sirius. . . .

These lines are an adaptation of Hesiod, *Works and Days* 582–88: "When the
golden thistle is in bloom and the ringing cicada, / sitting on a tree, pours
down piercing song / continuously from under its wings, in the season of
toilsome summer, / at that time goats are fattest and wine is at its best, / but

women are most wanton and men are at their feeblest, / since Sirios parches their heads and knees, / and their skin is withered by the heat. . . ." The heliacal rising of Sirius (**the star**, 1) in midsummer signaled the season of most intense heat.

### 18.  (Fr. 348)

. . . that base-born
Pittakos they have set up as tyrant of that spiritless
and ill-fated city, praising him loudly all together. . . .

On Pittakos see Glossary and note to no. 5.

### 19.  (Fr. 350)

You have come from the ends of the earth, your sword
boasting a hilt of ivory bound with gold. . . .
. . . . . . . . . . . .
While fighting as an ally of the Babylonians you
        performed
a great exploit: you rescued them from hardships
5    by killing a warrior who came no more
than a single palm's breadth short of five
royal cubits. . . .

Addressed to Alcaeus' brother Antimenidas, who seems to have served as a mercenary in the Babylonian army. Lines 3–7 derive from a prose paraphrase by Strabo (13. 617). The height of the warrior described in lines 5–7 is approximately 8 ft. 4 in.

### 20.  (Fr. 362)

But about our necks let a servant
put plaited garlands of dill,
and let him pour sweet perfume
        over our chests.

### 21.  (Fr. 366)

Wine, dear boy, and truth.

22.  (Fr. 367)

I heard the coming of flowery spring . . .
. . . . . . . . . . . .
and mix the honey-sweet wine as quickly as possible
in the mixing-bowl. . . .

# SAPPHO

Sappho was a contemporary of Alcaeus (c. 600 B.C.) and, like him, lived in the city of Mytilene on the island of Lesbos. Next to nothing is known about her life, although the extant fragments refer to a brother (no. 3) and perhaps to a daughter (no. 25). She is said to have spent time in exile, which suggests that her family (or her husband's family) was involved in Mytilene's factional politics. Sappho's poetic concerns, however, are almost entirely private. Her chief theme is erotic passion as experienced within the context of a close-knit circle of female friends (cf. nos. 1, 4, 6, 9–11, 14, 15, 24); in addition, a number of fragments (e.g., nos. 18–23) appear to be from wedding songs (*epithalamia*). In later centuries Sappho was much admired for the grace, charm, and passion of her poetry; an epigram attributed to Plato hails her as the tenth Muse. In the Alexandrian period Sappho's poems were arranged into nine books, largely according to metrical form. Nos. 1–7 are all in the stanza form known as Sapphic (see General Introduction, note 3).

### 1. (Fr. 1)

Immortal Aphrodite on your richly crafted throne,
daughter of Zeus, weaver of snares, I beg you,
do not with sorrows and with pains subdue
    my heart, O Lady,

5    but come to me, if ever at another time as well,
hearing my voice from far away,
you heeded it, and leaving your father's house
    of gold, you came,

yoking your chariot. Graceful sparrows
10   brought you swiftly over the black earth,
with a thick whirring of wings, from heaven down
    through the middle air.

Suddenly they were here, and you, O Blessed,
with a smile on your immortal face
15    asked me what was wrong *this* time, and why
      I called you *this* time,

and what in my maddened heart I wanted most
to happen. "Whom shall I persuade *this* time
to welcome you in friendship? Who is it,
20    Sappho, that wrongs you?

For if she flees now, soon she shall pursue;
if she refuses presents, she shall give them;
if she does not love, soon she shall love
      even against her will."

25    Come to me now as well; release me from
      this agony; all that my heart yearns
      to be achieved, achieve, and be yourself
            my ally in arms.

Dionysius of Halicarnassus, a literary critic of the first century B.C., quotes this poem in his treatise *On Literary Composition* (173–79) as an example of what he calls the "polished and exuberant" style. It is the only one of Sappho's poems to have survived in its entirety; it may have stood as the first poem in the first book of the Alexandrian edition. In formal terms it is a prayer (of the kletic type; see note on Alcaeus 2), and most of the standard elements of the prayer are present: (a) an invocation (1–2), including such conventional elements as genealogy and honorific epithets; (b) an initial statement of the request (3–5); (c) a lengthy "reminder" of previous assistance rendered by the goddess (5–24); and (d) a second and fuller statement of the request (25–28).

3 **with sorrows and with pains** The poem as a whole makes it clear that the suffering here alluded to is that which arises from unrequited passion.

### 2. (Fr. 2)

Come to me here from Crete, to this holy
temple, where you have a delightful grove
of apple trees, and altars fragrant
      with smoke of incense.

5 Here cold water babbles through apple
 branches, and roses keep the whole place
 in shadow, and from the quivering leaves
  a trance of slumber falls;

 here a meadow, where horses pasture, blooms
10 with flowers of spring, and the breezes
 gently blow. . . .
   [one line missing]

 In this place, Kypris, take up garlands,
 and gracefully, in golden cups,
15 pour out nectar that has been mingled
  with celebration. . . .

A kletic prayer like the previous poem, addressed once again to Aphrodite (**Kypris**, 13). The description of the place to which the goddess is being summoned exemplifies the sensitivity to natural beauty and the vivid evocation of mood that seem to be hallmarks of Sappho's style.


  3. (Fr. 5)

 Kypris and you Nereids, grant
 that my brother arrive here unharmed
 and that everything his heart wishes
  be perfectly achieved;

5 grant too that he atone for all his past errors
 and that he prove a source of joy to his friends
 and sorrow to his enemies; and to us may no one
  ever again bring trouble.

 May he be willing to give his sister
10 her share of honor, and grievous sorrow . . .
  . . . formerly in distress . . .

A prayer that Sappho's brother may have a safe journey home. Named Charaxos, he reportedly spent considerable time in Egypt and there became entangled with a notorious courtesan called Rhodopis; the reference to **past errors** (5) may pertain to this episode.

1 **Kypris** Aphrodite. Being born from the sea (at least according to one tradition), Aphrodite had marine associations and was frequently invoked as a protector of seafarers. The **Nereids** were likewise sea goddesses, being the daughters of Nereus, the Old Man of the Sea.

### 4. (Fr. 16)

Some say a host of horsemen is the most beautiful
    thing
on the black earth, some say a host of foot-soldiers,
some, a fleet of ships; but I say it is
    whatever one loves.

5    Wholly easy it is to make this intelligible
to everyone, for she who by far surpassed
all humankind in beauty, Helen,
    forsook her husband,

noblest of men, to sail away to Troy;
10   neither of child nor of beloved parents
did she take thought at all, being led astray by . . .
    [one line missing]

    . . . for pliant . . .
    . . . lightly . . .
15   . . . now has brought Anaktoria to my mind,
    though she is absent:

I would rather see her lovely step
and the glancing brightness of her face
than Lydian chariots and foot soldiers
20    arrayed in armor.

This poem takes the form of an argument in which Sappho addresses the question, "What is the most beautiful thing in the world?" Her procedure is methodical: a brief priamel (see introductory note to Tyrtaeus 7) which serves to highlight her own general definition (1–4); a mythological paradigm or example to confirm the validity of that definition (5–14); the substitution of a *particular* person for the general category "whatever one loves" (15–18); and a final return to the thought of the opening lines (ring-form), thus creating an effect of closure (19–20).

5.  (Fr. 17)

Close at hand appear to me as I pray,
queenly Hera, in your graceful form,
you whom the sons of Atreus besought
    with supplication, kings renowned:

5    having brought many trials to fulfillment,
first of all around Ilion, then upon the sea,
they set forth to this island, but could not
    complete their journey

until they called on you and on Zeus of Suppliants
10   and on Thyone's charming son.
Now to me as well be gentle and give aid,
    according to that ancient usage. . . .

Another prayer for divine assistance. In place of the "reminder" of past assistance rendered by the deity (cf. introductory note to no. 1), Sappho cites a historical precedent for calling upon Hera in time of need.

3 **the sons of Atreus** Agamemnon and Menelaos (see Glossary).
7 **this island** i.e, Lesbos, where the Greek fleet stopped off on its return homeward after the capture of Troy (**Ilion**, 6).
10 **Thyone's charming son** i.e., Dionysos; Thyone is another name for Semele. The same "trinity" of Hera, Zeus, and Dionysos appears in Alcaeus 6. 5–9.

6.  (Fr. 31)

He seems to me equal to the gods,
that man who sits across from you
and listens close at hand
    to your sweet voice

5    and lovely laughter. Truly it sets
my heart to pounding in my breast,
for the moment I glance at you, I can
    no longer speak;

         my tongue grows numb; at once a subtle
10      fire runs stealthily beneath my skin;
         my eyes see nothing, my ears
            ring and buzz,

         the sweat pours down, a trembling
         seizes the whole of me, I turn paler
15      than grass, and I seem to myself
            not far from dying.

         But everything can be endured, because . . .

Quoted in Ch. 10 of *On the Sublime*, a work of literary criticism that probably
dates from the first century A.D. The author of this work (traditionally known
as Longinus) remarks that Sappho "wants to display not a single emotion,
but a whole complex of emotions. Such things are what happens to all lovers,
but it is in selecting the most important of them and then arranging them into
a single whole that she demonstrates her excellence." The implied situation
in the poem, the identity of "that man" and his relation to the young woman
addressed as "you," and the exact nature of the speaker's "complex of emo-
tions" have all been matters of extensive scholarly debate. Although its text
and meaning are uncertain, the inclusion of line 17 in Longinus' quotation
seems to indicate that the poem was not complete in four stanzas (as other-
wise might be surmised on formal grounds).

     7.  (Fr. 34)

Around the beautiful moon the stars
withdraw the radiance of their form
whenever, at her fullest, she shines
    over earth. . . .

     8.  (Fr. 44)

. . . the herald came . . .
. . . Idaios, the swift messenger . . .   . . . these words:
          [one line missing]
". . . and of the rest of Asia . . .    . . . fame imperishable;
5     Hektor and his companions are bringing a flashing-eyed
     maiden from holy Thebe and from fair-flowing Plakia,
     graceful Andromache, in their ships over the salt
     sea; and there are many golden bracelets and robes

10  of crimson . . .    . . . trinkets of cunning make,
    and silver drinking cups unnumbered, and ivory."
    Thus he spoke; and Hektor's dear father leapt up
        nimbly;
    and the news reached his friends throughout the spacious
        city.
    At once Ilos' descendants hitched up mules
    to the smooth-running carriages, and onto them the whole
        crowd climbed,
15  women and slender-ankled girls together;
    but separately the daughters of Priam . . .
    and young men yoked horses to chariots . . .
        . . . and greatly . . .
        . . . charioteers . . .
            [several lines missing]
        . . . like gods . . .
        . . . holy . . . all together . . .
    set out . . .    . . . to Ilion,
    and the flute's sweet music and . . .    . . . were mingled,
25  and the clatter of castanets, and clear-voiced girls
    sang a holy song, and a wondrous echo
    reached the sky . . .
    and everywhere in the streets were . . .
    bowls and cups . . .
30  myrrh and cassia and frankincense were mingled.
    The older women all raised a joyful shout,
    and all the men sent forth a lovely high-pitched cry,
    calling on Paian the far-shooter, skilled in the lyre,
    and they praised in song the godlike Hektor and
        Andromache.

This fragment, which describes how Andromache was brought to Troy as a
bride by the Trojan prince Hektor (see Glossary), is the only example of
Sappho's narrative poetry that has survived. It has been suggested that the
poem may have been intended for performance at a wedding celebration.

2 **Idaios** a Trojan herald; he appears as a minor character in the *Iliad*.
4 **Asia** i.e., Asia Minor.
6 **Thebe, Plakia** According to *Iliad* 6. 395–97, Andromache was the
daughter of Eëtion, king of Thebe "under wooded Plakos."

13 **Ilos' descendants** i.e., the Trojans. Ilos was the mythical founder of
Troy (Ilion).
33 **Paian** another name for Apollo.

### 9. (Fr. 47)

Love shook
my mind like a wind falling on oak-trees on a mountain.

### 10. (Fr. 48)

You came, and I was yearning for you;
you plunged my heart into coolness when it flamed with
    longing.

### 11. (Fr. 49)

I loved you, Atthis, once long ago . . .
a small child you seemed to me, and graceless. . . .

Atthis is also mentioned in nos. 15 and 24. These lines are quoted by two
different sources and may not belong together.

### 12. (Fr. 55)

But when you die you will lie there, and no memory of
    you
will linger in later time, for you have no share in the roses
that come from Pieria. Unnoticed in Hades' house as well,
you will range among the shadowy dead, flown from our
    midst.

According to Plutarch in his *Table Talk* (3. 1. 2), the poem from which these
lines are quoted was addressed "to some uncultivated and ignorant woman."
By **the roses that come from Pieria** (2–3) Sappho means poetry; see Glossary
under "Pieria."

### 13. (Fr. 81)

Place lovely garlands, Dika, around your hair,
twining together shoots of dill with your tender hands;

for the blessed Graces too prefer things decked with
    flowers
to gaze upon, and turn aside from those that are
    ungarlanded.

14.  (Fr. 94)

. . . honestly I wish I were dead.
She wept as she was leaving me,

shedding many tears, and said to me:
"Oh, what terrible unhappiness is ours!
5      Sappho, I swear I'm leaving you against my will."

And to her I made this answer:
"Go, and fare well, and remember me,
for you know how we cared for you.

If not, why then I want
10    to remind you . . .
      . . . and the happiness we had.

Many the wreaths of violets,
of roses and crocuses together . . .
      . . . you put on beside me,

15    many woven garlands,
fashioned from flowers,
you put around your tender neck;

with much costly perfume
fit for a queen
20    you anointed yourself,

and on soft beds . . .
      . . . tender . . .
. . . you assuaged your longing. . . .

There was neither . . .
25      . . . nor shrine . . .

from which we were absent,

no grove . . . or dance . . ."

The temporal scheme in this fragment is a complex one, involving three distinct stages linked (implicitly or explicitly) by memory: (1) the present moment in which Sappho "wishes she were dead" as she remembers (2) the earlier time when the young woman was going away and she tried to comfort her by recalling (3) the still earlier times of happiness that they shared. It should be noted, however, that some scholars attribute the first line not to Sappho herself but to the young woman whose past departure Sappho is describing (ancient Greek texts used no quotation marks).

15.  (Fr. 96)

. . . Sardis . . .
. . . often turning her mind in this direction . . .

. . . she regarded you
as a goddess made manifest,
5      and in your song she took most delight.

But now among Lydian women she shines forth
as sometimes, after sunset,
the rosy-fingered moon

surpasses all the stars; its light is
10     spread alike over salt sea
and fields of many flowers;

the dew is shed in loveliness;
roses bloom, and tender chervil,
and flowery melilot;

15     and often, pacing to and fro,
she remembers gentle Atthis with yearning;
doubtless her delicate heart is heavy for your fate.

To go there . . .
. . . much . . .
20     . . . sings . . .    . . . in the middle.

It is not easy for us to equal
goddesses in attractiveness
of form, but you have . . .

Addressed to a young woman named Atthis (cf. 16), whom Sappho wishes to console by assuring her that she has not been forgotten by an absent friend, a young woman who is now living in Lydia (cf. 1, 6). Atthis is mentioned in nos. 11 and 24 as well.

1 **Sardis** the capital of Lydia.
2 **in this direction** i.e., toward Lesbos (presumably), where Sappho and Atthis are to be imagined.

### 16. (Fr. 102)

I tell you, sweet mother, I cannot weave at the loom,
subdued by longing for a boy through slender Aphrodite.

### 17. (Fr. 104)

Hesperos, bringing all things back which bright Dawn
    scattered,
you bring the sheep, you bring the goat, you bring the
    child back to its mother.

1 **Hesperos** the Evening Star.

### 18. (Fr. 105a)

Like the sweet apple that reddens on the highest bough,
high on the highest bough, and the apple gatherers have
    forgotten it—
no, they have not forgotten it completely, but they could
    not reach it.

This and the following five fragments appear to be from wedding songs (*epithalamia*).

### 19. (Fr. 105b)

Like the hyacinth which shepherds on the hillsides

trample underfoot, and on the ground the crimson
   flower. . . .


### 20.  (Fr. 110)

The doorkeeper has feet seven fathoms long,
and his sandals are made from five ox-hides;
it took ten cobblers to fashion them.


### 21.  (Fr. 111)

Up, up with the roof—
Hymenaios—
raise it high, you carpenters—
Hymenaios!
5    The bridegroom is coming, Ares' equal,
larger by far than a large man.

2, 4 **Hymenaios** the god of marriage, frequently invoked in wedding
songs. He was also known as Hymen.


### 22.  (Fr. 114)

Virginity, virginity, where have you gone and left me?
"Never again shall I return to you, never again shall I
   return."


### 23.  (Fr. 115)

To what, dear bridegroom, may I fittingly compare you?
To a slender sapling most of all do I compare you.


### 24.  (Frs. 130)

Once again Love drives me on, that loosener of limbs,
bittersweet creature against which nothing can be done.
            . . . . . . . . . . . .
But to you, Atthis, the thought of me has grown
hateful, and you fly off to Andromeda.

25. (Fr. 132)

A beautiful girl is mine, her form like that
of golden flowers, beloved Kleïs,
for whom not even all Lydia would I take, or lovely. . . .

Kleïs has traditionally been taken to be Sappho's daughter, but it is possible
that she was another beloved friend like Atthis in nos. 11 and 24.

26. (Fr. Adesp. 976)

The moon has set,
and the Pleiades; it is
midnight, and time is passing;
and I lie alone.

The ancient source that quotes these lines does not name their author. Some
scholars believe that they are by Sappho, others emphatically deny it.

# SOLON

Solon of Athens was born c. 640 B.C. and died c. 560. A politician and statesman as well as a poet, he served as chief magistrate (archon) in 594–93, at a time when Athenian society was polarized between a small and wealthy aristocracy and a common people oppressed by poverty and disenfranchisement. Much of his surviving poetry deals with this state of crisis (cf. nos. 2, 3) and with the various political, social, and economic reforms that he carried out in an effort to resolve it (cf. nos. 4, 13–17); the defensive tone of the latter pieces indicate that they were composed some time after his archonship when the measures he had taken were under political attack. He lived long enough to see Peisistratos make himself tyrant of Athens (cf. nos. 5 and 6). Not all of his poetry, however, was political in character; a number of fragments (e.g. nos. 7, 8, 12) treat topics of more general philosophical and/or ethical interest.

Nos. 1–12 are in elegiac couplets, nos. 13–15 in trochaic tetrameters, and nos. 16 and 17 in iambic trimeters.

1.  (Frs. 1, 2, 3)

I myself have come as a herald from lovely Salamis,
  having arranged words into song in place of a public
    speech.
      . . . . . . . . . . . .
At that time I would rather hail from Pholegandros or
    Sikinos
  than be an Athenian, giving up my country in exchange,
5  for quickly among men this remark would become current:
    "That man is from Attika, one of those who let Salamis
      go."
      . . . . . . . . . . . .
Let us go to Salamis in order to fight for the lovely
  island and to thrust away harsh disgrace.

These three fragments are from a poem in which, according to Plutarch (*Solon* 8. 1–2) and Diogenes Laertius (1. 47), Solon urged his fellow Athenians not to give up their war with Megara over possession of the island of Salamis (on which see Glossary).

3 **At that time** i.e. at such a time as Salamis shall have been lost to Megara. **Pholegandros** and **Sikinos** were two small and insignificant islands among the southern Cyclades.

### 2.  (Fr. 4)

Our city will never be destroyed by Zeus's
    ordinance and the purposes of the blessed immortal
      gods:
such is the great-hearted guardian who holds her hands
    over it,
    Pallas Athena, she whose father is mighty.
5    No, it is the citizens themselves who in their witlessness
    are bent on ruining their great city, putting trust in
      money;
and the leaders of the people are unjust in mind. In their
    case it is certain
    that out of great arrogance many griefs must be
      endured;
for they do not know how to keep excess under restraint,
    nor how
10    to order the present joys of their feasting in
    tranquillity. . . .
    . . . . . . . . . . .
. . . they grow wealthy, putting trust in unjust deeds. . . .
    . . . . . . . . . . .
Neither sacred nor public property
do they spare, each stealing and plundering from a
    different source,
    nor do they guard the holy foundations of Justice,
15    who is aware in silence of what is happening and what
    was before,
    and who in time assuredly comes to exact payment.
This is already coming upon the entire city as an
    inescapable wound,

and it has quickly entered into base servitude,
which rouses civil discord and war from sleep—
20          war that destroys the lovely youth of many.
For by its enemies the surpassingly lovely town is quickly
     worn away, amid conspiracies dear to those who do
     injustice.
These are the evils that range at large in the community;
     but of the poor,
many make their way to foreign lands,
25     having been sold off in bondage, fettered by shameful
     chains. . . .
               . . . . . . . . . . . .

In this way public calamity comes to each man's home,
     and the doors of the courtyard no longer can hold it
     back;
over the high wall it leaps, and assuredly it finds
     even one who flees to the innermost corner of the room.
30     This is the lesson that my spirit urges me to teach the
     Athenians,
     how many evils Unlawfulness brings about for the city,
while Lawfulness puts all things into good order and
     makes them sound,
     and often places shackles about those who are unjust.
She smooths what is rough, puts an end to excess,
     enfeebles arrogance;
35     she withers the flowers of ruin as they spring up;
she straightens crooked judgments, and overbearing acts
     she turns to gentleness; she puts an end to acts of
     dissension,
puts an end to the bitterness of painful strife: beneath her
     hand
     all things among mankind are sound and prudent.

A diagnosis of the political and social ills besetting Athens in the years lead-
ing up to Solon's archonship.

17 **This** i.e., the misconduct of the city's leaders.
22 **conspiracies** literally, "gatherings"; probably a reference to the clubs
(*hetaireiai*) that were a common feature of political life in Greek city-states.
25 **sold off in bondage** a reference to debt-slavery, an institution whereby

men who borrowed money on the security of their own persons would, if they defaulted, be sold into servitude in satisfaction of their debts. Debt-slavery was abolished as part of the reforms carried out by Solon during his archonship (on which see introduction).

### 3. (Frs. 4a + 4c)

I understand, and sorrows lie within my heart
    when I behold the oldest land of Ionia
foundering. . . .
      . . . . . . . . . . . .

But you must bring the strong hearts within you to
    quietness,
5      you who have pushed your way to a surfeit of good
    things,
and set your great minds on moderate aims; for neither
    shall *we*
    be submissive, nor will *you* find everything to your
    liking.

Quoted by Aristotle in the *Constitution of the Athenians* (5. 2–3) as part of a poem in which Solon argued that reconciliation between rich and poor was necessary for the common good of Athens.

2 **the oldest land of Ionia** Athens, regarded by the Athenians as the mother city of all Ionian Greeks.
6–7 As Aristotle notes, Solon here appears to exclude himself from the class of the wealthy.

### 4. (Frs. 5, 6, 7)

For to the people I gave as much privilege as sufficed
    them,
    neither taking away honor nor holding out still more.
As for those who had power and were admired for wealth,
    I took care that they too should have no unseemly share.
5    I stood holding my strong shield about both parties,
    allowing neither to gain victory unjustly.
      . . . . . . . . . . . .
The people are likely to follow their leaders best under
    these conditions,

that they be neither given too much rein nor held too
    much in constraint.
For excess gives birth to arrogance, whenever great
    prosperity attends
10    on those among human beings whose minds are not
    sound.
       . . . . . . . . . . .

In actions of great importance it is difficult to please
    everyone.

Lines 1–10 are quoted by Aristotle in the *Constitution of the Athenians* (12. 1–
2) in illustration of Solon's determination to favor neither the poor nor the
rich but to strike a balance that would do justice to the claims of both sides.
These themes recur in nos. 15, 16, and 17.


    5.  (Fr. 9)

From the clouds comes the power of snow and hail,
    and thunder arises from the brilliant lightning flash;
from great men destruction comes on the city, and under
    one man's rule
    the people through witlessness fall into servitude.
5    Having once raised a man too high, it is not easy to hold
    him in check
    afterwards: now is the time to think of all these things.

In these lines (according to Diodorus 9. 20. 2, who quotes them), Solon pre-
dicted the impending tyranny of Peisistratos as a consequence of the political
and social turmoil in Athens which he had attempted (without success) to
ameliorate through his reforms.


    6.  (Fr. 11)

If you have suffered miseries through your own baseness,
    do not shift the blame for your lot to the gods,
for you yourselves strengthened these men by giving them
    guards,
    and for this reason you incurred base servitude.
Each one of you walks with the footsteps of a fox,
    but all of you alike have empty minds within you,

for you look to the tongue and the words of a wheedling
    man
and pay no heed to his acts as they unfold.

According to Diodorus (see note on previous fragment), Solon wrote these
lines after Peisistratos had made himself tyrant of Athens.

3 **by giving them guards** According to Herodotus (1. 59), Peisistratos
persuaded the Athenians to give him bodyguards by pretending that
enemies of his had attacked him; he then used the guards to seize the
Acropolis—and with it, control of Athens.


    7.  (Fr. 13)

Splendid children of Memory and of Olympian Zeus,
    Muses of Pieria, harken to my prayer.
Grant me prosperity from the blessed gods, and from all
    men may I always receive esteem and honor;
5     and in this way may I be sweet to my friends and bitter to
        my enemies,
        to the ones an object of reverence, to the others a
            fearsome sight.
As for money, I long to have it, but to possess it unjustly
    is not my wish: assuredly Justice comes at a later time.
Wealth that is given by the gods remains at a man's side,
10     firmly planted from its lowest root to its crown;
but that which men pursue out of arrogance does not come
        to them
    in orderly fashion. Instead, yielding to acts of injustice,
it follows unwillingly and is quickly entangled with ruin,
    which from a small beginning arises like fire,
15     insignificant at first, but a source of pain in the end.
    Not for long do acts of arrogance persist among mortals:
Zeus watches over the end of all things, and suddenly,
    as a wind quickly scatters the clouds
in spring, stirring the billows of the unwearied sea
20     to their very depths and over the wheat-bearing land
ravaging well-worked fields, till it reaches the gods'
        dwelling-place, steep
    heaven, and brings clear weather once again into view,

and the sun's force blazes over the fertile earth
    in beauty, and not one cloud is still to be seen—
25  such is the retribution of Zeus. Not at each single thing,
    like a mortal man, does he prove quick to anger,
yet he is aware unceasingly of anyone whose heart
    is wicked, and he assuredly is revealed as such in the
        end.
But one man pays immediately, another later, while to
        those who escape
30      themselves and are not overtaken by doom from the
            gods,
it assuredly comes hereafter: their deeds are paid for by
        the guiltless,
    either their children or their posterity in time to come.
This is the way we mortals think, noble and base alike:
    each has the notion that he himself is thriving
35  before something happens to him, and then he laments in
        turn. Till then, however,
    with mouths agape we take pleasure in insubstantial
        hopes.
Whoever is pressed hard by cruel diseases
    imagines that he will be sound in health;
another, though a coward, believes that he is a brave man,
40      and he who lacks grace of form thinks he is handsome;
if someone is needy and has the conditions of poverty
        forced upon him,
    he thinks that assuredly he will acquire plentiful money.
Each man seeks gain from a different source: one roams
        over the sea
    in ships, desiring to bring profit home,
45  tossed here and there over swarming fish by the cruel
        winds,
    with no thought of sparing his life;
another, breaking well-wooded land, the whole year
        through
    labors for hire, his attention fixed on crooked plows.
Another, learned in the works of Athena and Hephaistos
50      of many crafts, gathers together a livelihood with his
            hands;
another, instructed in the gifts of the Olympian Muses,

does so by knowing the measure of lovely skill;
another is made a seer by the far-shooting lord Apollo,
   and perceives the evil that comes on a man from a
     distance,
55  if the gods are at his side, though what is fated assuredly
   neither omen nor sacrifice will ward off.
Others, who claim the task of Paian of many medicines,
   are doctors—for them also there is no end at hand,
for often out of some small ache great anguish arises,
60    and one cannot loosen its grip by giving soothing
     medicines;
but a man disquieted by dire and cruel diseases
   is made sound in health through a laying on of
     hands.
But it is Fate, of course, that brings mortals evil as well as
   good,
   and the gifts of the immortal gods prove inescapable.
65  Risk is present in all activities, and no one knows
   where he will put ashore when an enterprise is
     starting:
the man who attempts to act correctly unawares
   falls into great ruin that is difficult to bear,
while to the man who acts wrongly god gives in all
   matters
70    a favorable outcome and so releases him from his
     folly.
No limit to wealth is clearly set for men,
   since those of us whose means of livelihood are now
     most plentiful
are twice as eager in pursuit. Who could satisfy everyone?
   Gains are granted to mortals by immortals,
75  but out of them ruin comes to light, whenever Zeus
   sends it as retribution to one man first and then another.

Quoted by Stobaeus (3. 9. 23) under the heading "About Justice." Although justice—or perhaps more to the point, *in*justice, with its various consequences—is indeed the chief theme of the first thirty-two lines, the second half of the poem is a more general meditation on human action as conditioned by the limitations of human knowledge. This latter section bears comparison with Semonides 1.

57  In the Homeric poems **Paian** is a god of healing distinct from Apollo,
while in later Greek the name is often used as one of Apollo's epithets (cf.
Sappho 8. 33). The fact that Apollo has already been mentioned in line 53
suggests that Solon intends the name to be understood in its Homeric
sense.

### 8.  (Fr. 15)

Many bad men are wealthy, and many good men are poor;
    but we shall not exchange with them
our goodness for their wealth, because the one is sure
      forever,
    while money belongs to different men at different times.

### 9.  (Fr. 18)

I grow old, always learning many things.

### 10.  (Fr. 20)

But if you will still heed me, even at this late date, remove
    that phrase,
    and don't hold it against me that I have thought things
    out more clearly.
Rewrite your verse, Ligyastades, and sing it in this fashion:
    "May the doom of death overtake me at eighty years of
    age."

A response to Mimnermus 4, in which the poet expresses a wish for death at
the age of sixty.

3 **Ligyastades** apparently coined by Solon as a name for Mimnermus; it
may be formed from elements meaning "clear" and "singer."

### 11.  (Fr. 21)

And may death not come upon me unbewailed, but for my
    friends
    may I leave behind grief and moaning when I die.

Probably from the same poem as the previous fragment.

## 12. (Fr. 24)

Equally rich are the man who possesses much silver
    and gold and acres of wheat-bearing land
and horses and mules, and he who has only these things at
    hand:
    the means for comfort in belly and flanks and feet,
5    and the blooming beauty of boy or woman, when the time
    for this too comes, and youth's prime is present in all its
    fitness.
This is wealth for mortals: all goods above and beyond it
    no one can take along when he goes to Hades,
nor by offering ransom can he escape death, or
    burdensome
10    diseases, or the approach of foul old age.

## 13. (Fr. 32)

. . . But if I spared my native
country, and did not lay my hands on tyranny
and implacable violence, staining and disgracing my
    reputation,
I feel no shame at this; for I believe that in this way I shall
    far outdo
all of mankind.

Plutarch in his *Life of Solon* (14. 8) quotes this and the following passage in
illustration of Solon's attitude toward those who found fault with him for not
having seized absolute power in Athens when he had the chance.

## 14. (Fr. 33)

"Solon was by nature a man neither intelligent nor wise,
    for when the gods offered him good things, he refused of
    his own accord.
Though his net was cast about the quarry, he was too
    stunned to draw
its great folds in, falling short alike in courage and in
    sense.
5    I would be willing, if I could come to power amid
    abundant wealth

and hold sole rule in Athens for a single day,
to be flayed thereafter and turned into a wineskin and
    have my posterity rubbed out."

These lines articulate what Solon imagines to be the popular view of his
refusal to establish himself as tyrant (see note to previous fragment).


### 15. (Fr. 34)

But those who came for plunder were rich in hopes,
and each of them thought that he would find great
    prosperity
and that despite my smooth coaxing I would reveal a
    harsh intention.
Their thoughts and plans at the time were empty, and now
    in anger
5    they all look askance at me as if I were their enemy.
This is not right; for with the gods' aid I accomplished
    what I said I would,
and did not do other things without good reason; nor did
    it please me
to act in any way with tyrannical force, or to allow the base
    to hold
an equal share of their country's fertile soil with the noble.

Probably from the same poem as the two previous fragments, although this
excerpt is quoted not by Plutarch but by Aristotle in the *Constitution of the
Athenians* (12. 3). The following two fragments are preserved in the same
work as well; see note on no. 4.

1 **those who came for plunder** a reference to the poor and dispossessed
(the **base** of line 8), who had hoped that Solon's reforms would include a
redistribution of land in Attika.


### 16. (Fr. 36)

But as for me, which of the things for which I called
the people together did I not attain before I stopped?
In support of this before the court of Time
the supreme mother of the Olympian powers,

5    black Earth, can best bear witness. From her I once
took up the boundary stones that were fixed in many
        places,
so that she who was once in servitude is now free.
And to Athens, their god-founded homeland,
I brought back many men who had been sold off, some
        unjustly,
10   others justly, still others sent into exile by
the compulsive power of need, none of whom still spoke
the speech of Attika, wandering as they were in many
        places.
And as for those who here at home endured the shame
of servitude, in terror of their masters' ways,
15   I made them free. These things through power,
by fitting together force and justice,
I brought to pass, and so came through as I promised.
Laws too, however, alike for the base man and the noble,
fitting straightforward justice to each one's case,
20   I set down in writing. Another man who took up the goad
        as I did,
one who was ill-intentioned and greedy for possessions,
could not have restrained the people. For if I had been
        willing
to do what pleased their opponents at that time,
and then again what the other party had in mind for them,
25   this city would have been widowed of many men.
For these reasons, mounting a defense in every quarter,
I turned and twisted like a wolf among many hounds.

6 **boundary stones** markers (*horoi*) set up on the lands of indebted
farmers to indicate that the property was mortgaged to creditors. These
markers were removed as a consequence of the cancellation of debts that
was part of Solon's reforms.
9 **I brought back many men** a reference to Solon's emancipation and recov-
ery of debt-slaves who had been sold abroad (see note to no. 2, line 25).

### 17. (Fr. 37)

As for the people, if it is right to censure them openly,
the things that they now possess they never could

have seen in dreams . . .
And those of the greater sort, superior in force,
5    may praise me and regard me as their friend.
For if some other man had gained this honor,
he would not have restrained the people, nor would he
     have stopped
his churning until he had extracted the rich fat from the
     milk.
As for me, in the middle ground between the two parties
10   I stood like a boundary stone.

# STESICHORUS

Stesichorus seems to have been active as a poet in the first half of the sixth century B.C., making his home in the city of Himera, on the northern coast of Sicily. He specialized in the composition of long narrative poems on such heroic subjects as the Trojan War, the adventures of Herakles, and the Theban cycle; in the words of the Roman rhetorician Quintilian (10. 1. 62), Stesichorus "sustained on the lyre the weight of epic song." Although these poems are triadic in form (see General Introduction, pp. xiii–xiv), it is not clear whether they were intended for performance by a chorus or by a solo singer.

    1.  (Fr. S15)

    ... bringing loathsome
      death to pass,
  with ... doom about its head, defiled
      by blood ...    ... and gall,

5    the torments of the man-destroying
    Hydra with its shifting necks; and in silence and with
      cunning he thrust it into his brow,
    and it split the flesh and bones by the dispensation
      of divinity;
10   and the arrow held its course straight through
      to the top of his head
    and stained with crimson blood
      his breastplate and his gory limbs.

    Then Geryon's neck drooped
15     to one side, like a poppy
    which, disfiguring its tender beauty,
      suddenly sheds its petals. ...

This and the following fragment are from the *Geryoneis*, a poem of more than thirteen hundred lines which narrated Herakles' quest to obtain the cattle of Geryon (on which see Glossary under "Herakles" and "Geryon"). A number of brief papyrus fragments of the *Geryoneis* have been recovered from Oxyrhynchus (see General Introduction, p. xv).

1–6 Herakles' arrows were poisoned with the blood and gall of the **Hydra**, a many-headed monster whose slaying constituted the second of Herakles' twelve labors.
15 **like a poppy** This simile is adapted from *Iliad* 8. 306–8.

### 2.  (Fr. S17)

... Thereupon Hyperion's mighty son
stepped down into the all-golden cup, so that,
    passing across the Ocean,
he might come to the depths of dark
5      and holy Night
and to his mother and wedded wife
    and beloved children.
But the other, Zeus's son, went into the grove that laurels
    shaded ...

On the Sun and his golden transport over the waters of Ocean, cf. Mimnermus 5.

1 **Hyperion** one of the Titans (see Glossary), father of Helios the Sun god.
8 **Zeus's son** Herakles; the **grove** may be the garden of the Hesperides (on which see note to Mimnermus 5).

### 3.  (Fr. 187)

Many Kydonian apples they threw about the chariot of
    their lord,
many myrtle leaves
and crowns of roses and garlands twined from violets.

These lines are from a poem called the *Helen*; they presumably refer to the marriage of Helen and Menelaos. **Kydonian apples** are quinces (cf. Ibycus 2).

### 4. (Fr. 192)

That story is not true:
you did not go on the well-benched ships,
nor did you reach Troy's citadel.

According to Plato, who quotes these lines in the *Phaedrus* (243A), Stesichorus was stricken with blindness as a punishment for speaking ill of Helen in his poetry; recognizing his error, however, he then composed a recantation (*palinodia*) and so recovered his eyesight. In fact, there was a countertradition to the Homeric version of events (found, e.g., in Euripides' *Helen*) according to which only a *phantom* of Helen went to Troy, while Helen herself spent the duration of the war in Egypt.

### 5. (Fr. 210)

Muse, thrust wars aside and, in my company,
celebrate the marriages of gods, men's banquets,
and the festivities of the Blessed. . . .

### 6. (Fr. 222b)

". . . to our sorrows do not add cruel anxieties,
and stop revealing to me
grievous pains to be feared hereafter.

For not through all of time alike                          [Ep.]
205       have the immortal gods decreed that on the holy earth
strife shall remain fixed for mortals—
no, nor friendship either: day by day, men's minds
are as the gods dispose them.
As for your prophecies, may lord Apollo who works from
afar
210     not bring them all to fulfillment.

But if to behold my sons laid low each by the other's   [Str.]
hand
is my destiny, and the Fates have spun it so,
at once may I find an end in loathsome death,
before I ever gaze upon these things,
215       heaping groans and tears on present sorrows:

my sons dead within
  the palace or the city captured.

But come, my sons, dear children, heed my words;     [Ant.]
  for thus do I reveal to you the outcome.
220    One of you must possess the house and dwell here . . .
  the other must depart with all
    the livestock and the gold of your dear father—
  whichever of you, when the lots are shaken,
    is first to obtain his portion by the Fates' decree.

225    For this, as I believe,                                [Ep.]
    is what may set you free from evil doom
  as the divine prophet has warned,
  if in truth Kronos' son means to protect the race
      and city
  of lord Kadmos,
230    postponing for many years the evil fortune which
      is fated
  for the royal line."

So said the noble lady, speaking with gentle words,     [Str.]
  trying to check her sons from strife within the palace,
  and with her Teiresias, reader of omens. And the young
      men obeyed. . . .

These lines represent the legible portion of a papyrus text recovered from a
mummy case in the early 1970's (another twenty-five lines at the beginning
and seventy lines at the end are too fragmentary to yield consecutive sense).
They are evidently part of a poem (of unknown title) dealing with the for-
tunes of the house of Oedipus (on which see Glossary under "Oedipus" and
"Polyneikes"). The **noble lady** (232) who speaks through most of the frag-
ment is probably Iokaste, Oedipus' mother and wife, although some scholars
believe that she is to be identified as Euryganeia, whom (according to one
tradition) Oedipus married after the death of Iokaste. As the fragment be-
gins, she is addressing the prophet **Teiresias** (cf. 234), whom she rebukes for
his dire predictions of strife between her sons Polyneikes and Eteokles; she
then turns to the young men themselves, urging them to settle their differ-
ences by peaceably dividing their inheritance through the casting of lots.

229 **Kadmos** the legendary founder of Thebes.

7. (Fr. 223)

. . . because, when Tyndareos
once sacrificed to all the gods, he forgot one only, giver of
     gentle gifts,
the Cyprian; and she in her anger made
Tyndareos' daughters twice-wed and thrice-wed
and deserters of their husbands.

1 **Tyndareos** See Glossary.
3 **the Cyprian** Aphrodite (see Glossary).
4 **twice-wed and thrice-wed** Klytaimnestra was married to Agamemnon
and, after his murder, to Aigisthos, while Helen (according to some
accounts, at any rate) was married in succession to Theseus, Menelaos, and
Paris.

# THEOGNIS

Nearly fourteen hundred lines of elegiac verse have come down to us under the name of Theognis of Megara. The authorship and date of the corpus have been subjects of extensive scholarly debate: a number of poems in it are elsewhere attributed to other poets, and some contain apparent allusions to historical events considerably later than the middle of the sixth century B.C., the period to which Theognis has traditionally been assigned. Although the most frequently treated themes in the corpus are political (e.g. nos. 4, 5, 9, 15) and ethical (e.g. nos. 7, 8, 13, 16), there are sympotic (e.g. nos. 14 and 20) and erotic (e.g. nos. 22–26) pieces as well, the latter being grouped together at the end of the collection. Many of the poems are addressed to a young man named Kyrnos, the son of Polypaos, toward whom Theognis adopts the role of preceptor and adviser.

### 1. (Lines 1–4)

O lord, son of Leto, child of Zeus, you I shall never
    forget, either beginning or coming to an end,
but always, first and last and in the middle,
    I shall sing of you. And you, hear me and grant good
      things.

1 **son of Leto** i.e, Apollo.

### 2. (Lines 5–10)

Lord Phoibos, when the goddess, lady Leto, bore you,
    clasping a palm tree in her slender hands,
you the most beautiful of immortals, beside the wheel-
    round lake,
    then all of boundless Delos was filled
5    with an ambrosial scent; the huge earth laughed,
    and the deep waters of the hoary sea rejoiced.

3–4 A palm-tree and a small lake were among the sacred landmarks to be found on the island of **Delos**, Apollo's reputed birthplace.

### 3. (Lines 19–30)

Kyrnos, as I work my craft let a seal be set upon
    these words of mine, and they will never be stolen
    unremarked,
nor will anyone change the good that is there to something
    worse;
    and this is what everyone will say: "These are the lines
    of Theognis,
5    the man from Megara"—famous throughout all peoples.
    But all my fellow citizens I have not yet been able to
    please.
This is nothing to wonder at, son of Polypaos, for not even
    Zeus
    pleases everyone, whether he rains or holds it back.
To you with kindly intent I shall offer such advice as I
    myself,
10    Kyrnos, heard from noble men when I was still a child.
Be intelligent, and do not at the cost of shameful or unjust
    deeds
    attempt to draw to yourself honors or merits or
    wealth.

On **Kyrnos**, see introduction. What precisely the **seal** is to which Theognis refers has been a matter of scholarly debate; possibilities include (a) Theognis' name, (b) Kyrnos' name, and (c) the poetic excellence of Theognis' verses themselves.

### 4. (Lines 39–52)

Kyrnos, this city is pregnant, and I fear that it may give
    birth to a man
    who will chastise and correct our wicked arrogance.
For though the citizens here are still of sound mind, their
    leaders
    are on a fixed course to fall into great wickedness.
5    No city yet, Kyrnos, has ever been destroyed by noble men;

but when it pleases the base to grow arrogant,
and they corrupt the people and grant judgments to the
    unjust
for the sake of their own private gain and power,
do not expect that city to enjoy unshaken calm for long,
10    not even if it lies now in great quietness,
once base men set their hearts on things like these,
    gains that come with hurt to the people.
For from these things come factions, the internecine
    slaughter of men,
and tyrants—may they never be pleasing to *this* city.

On the political ills of Megara, Theognis' city. The piece shows similarities in theme to Solon 2 and 5.

5. (Lines 53–68)

Kyrnos, this city is still a city, but its people now are
    different,
being those who earlier knew neither judgments nor
    laws
but instead wore goatskins to tatters about their sides
    and grazed like deer outside of this city.
5    And now they are noble, son of Polypaos, while those who
    before had merit
now are worthless. Who could endure to look upon
    these things?
They cheat one another while laughing at one another,
    lacking the wit to distinguish bad from good.
Son of Polypaos, make none of these citizens your
    friend
10    from the heart, not for the sake of any need;
instead, seem from your speech to be a friend to all,
    but share with none of them any business whatsoever
of a serious sort. You will come to know the minds of
    wretched men,
how in their actions there is no place for trust,
15    since they have come to love tricks and deceits and
    cunning snares
in the manner of men who are beyond all rescue.

Another complaint about conditions in Megara, specifically about a new class of citizens that has risen to power at the expense of the established aristocracy.

6. (Lines 173–78)

Of all things it is poverty that most subdues a noble man,
  more even than hoary old age, Kyrnos, or fever;
indeed, to avoid it one should even throw oneself into the sea's
  deep gulfs, Kyrnos, or off sheer cliffs.
5 For the man subdued by poverty can neither say
  nor do anything, because his tongue is tied.

7. (Lines 183–92)

Among rams and asses and horses, Kyrnos, we look for those
  of noble breeding, and a man wants them to mate
from worthy stock. Yet a noble man does not mind marrying
  a base woman of base birth if she brings him money in abundance,
5 nor does a woman shrink from becoming the wife of a base man
  with wealth; she prefers a rich husband to a worthy one.
Money is what they honor; the noble weds a base man's daughter,
  the base a worthy man's: wealth mixes stock.
Thus do not be amazed, son of Polypaos, that the citizens' stock
10 is growing feeble, for what is noble is being mixed with what is base.

8. (Lines 213–18)

My heart, display toward all your friends a changeful character,
  adding into it the disposition that each one has.
Adopt the disposition of the octopus, crafty in its
  convolutions, which takes on

the appearance of whatever rock it has dealings with.
5    At one moment follow along this way, but at the next
        change the color of your skin:
you can be sure that cleverness proves better than
        inflexibility.


### 9. (Lines 219–20)

Do not distress yourself too much at the turbulence of
        your fellow citizens,
Kyrnos, but walk down the middle of the road, as I do.


### 10. (Lines 237–54)

To you I have given wings, on which you may fly aloft
        above the boundless sea and all the earth
with ease. At feasts and banquets you will be present
        on all occasions, lying in the mouths of many,
5    and to the clear-toned sound of pipes young men
        with seemly grace and loveliness, their voices fair and
        clear,
will sing of you. And when beneath the hollows of the
        murky earth
you go to Hades' halls ringing with lamentation,
not even then, though dead, will you ever lose your fame;
        instead, you will be known
10    to people of all time, your name imperishable,
Kyrnos, roaming through mainland Hellas and up and
        down the islands,
        passing over the restless fish-swarming sea,
not mounted on the backs of horses, but sent abroad
        by the radiant gifts of the Muses, violet-crowned:
15    to all who care for them, even to those who are not yet
        born, you will be
        alike a theme of song, so long as earth and sun exist.
From you, however, I get scant respect;
        instead, you cheat me with words as if I were a little
        child.

The idea that poetry can confer a kind of immortality on its subjects is found also in Sappho 12 (although there it is formulated negatively) and very frequently in Pindar and Bacchylides.

### 11. (Lines 255–56)

The noblest thing is justice; the most advantageous, health;
  but what gives greatest delight is to gain the object of
   one's desire.

According to Aristotle (*Eudemian Ethics* 1. 1) this couplet was inscribed over the entrance to the temple of Leto on the island of Delos (on which see no. 2).

### 12. (Lines 425–28)

Not to be born is the best of all things for those who live
  on earth,
   and not to gaze on the radiance of the keen-burning
   sun.
Once born, however, it is best to pass with all possible
  speed through Hades' gates
   and to lie beneath a great heap of earth.

For the sentiment cf. Bacchylides, Ode 5. 160–162.

### 13. (Lines 429–38)

To beget and rear a man is easier than to put good sense
  inside him. No one yet has ever contrived a way
to make the senseless sensible and good men out of bad.
  If the sons of Asklepios had this gift from the god,
5   to work a cure on badness and men's infatuate wits,
   many and great would be the fees they earned.
And if understanding could be fashioned and placed in a
  man,
   never would a good man's son have turned out bad,
  by heeding the words of sensible counsel. But as it is, no
   teaching
10   will ever serve to make the bad man good.

4 **the sons of Asklepios** i.e., doctors; see Glossary under "Asklepios."

14.  (Lines 467–96)

Of those now here with us, do not detain anyone who is
        unwilling to remain,
    nor show the door to anyone who does not wish to go,
nor wake anyone who is sleeping, Simonides, should one
        of us,
    well fortified by wine, be gripped by gentle slumber,
5   nor bid the wakeful man to sleep against his will;
    for everything that is forced is by nature painful.
For the one who wants to drink, let the boy stand close
        and pour;
    not on all nights is it possible to enjoy delights like
        these.
But as for me, since I have reached my limit of honey-
        sweet wine,
10      I shall think of sleep that loosens cares, going home.
I have reached the point when a man feels most pleasure
        in drinking wine,
    being neither sober at all nor yet excessively drunk.
Whoever goes beyond the limit of drinking, that man no
        longer
    is master of his own tongue or of his mind;
15  he talks recklessly, saying things which the sober find
        disgraceful,
    and feels no shame in any action when he is drunk,
a man of sound sense before, and now a fool. But you,
    understanding these things, should not drink to excess,
but either stand up and leave before you get drunk—don't
        let your belly
20      overpower you as if you were a base laborer hired by
        the day—
    or else stay put and refrain from drinking. But no, "Pour
        me another"
    is what you keep idly chattering, and that's why you get
        drunk.
For one cup comes around in the name of friendship,
        another on a bet;
    another you pour out as a libation for the gods, another
        you keep on hand,

25      and you do not know how to refuse. That man is truly
            invincible,
        who though he has drunk many cups says nothing
            foolish.
        As for the rest of you, take care in what you say as you
            linger around the wine bowl,
        steering well clear of quarrels with one another,
        speaking in a way that any may hear, whether you address
            one or all together.
30      Conducted in this way, a drinking-party proves far from
            unpleasant.

The importance of maintaining decorum during a drinking-party (*symposion*)
is a theme treated also in Anacreon 2 and 3 and Xenophanes 1. The Simonides
addressed in this and the following poem may be the famous poet of that
name; both poems are attributed by some scholars to Euenos of Paros, a poet
of the fifth century B.C., rather than to Theognis.


        15.  (Lines 667–82)

        If I had money, Simonides, I would not feel such pain
            as I do now when in the company of the noble.
        As it is, wealth recognizes me but passes by, and I am
            speechless
            out of want, although it would seem that I know better
                than most
5       that now, with our white sails lowered, we are being
            carried
            out of the Melian Sea through the murky night,
        and the men refuse to bail, although the sea sweeps over
            both sides of the ship. Indeed, only with great difficulty
                is anyone likely to be
        saved, acting as they are: they have stopped the
            helmsman,
10      good though he was, who kept watch skillfully;
        and they are plundering the cargo by force. Discipline has
            perished,
            and fair division is no longer carried out in an open
                fashion;
        the deckhands are in control, and the base have the upper

hand over the noble.
I am afraid that the waves may swallow up the ship.
15    Let this, well hidden, be my riddling message for the
         noble,
      though a base man too may understand it, if he is
         clever.

This piece begins as one of Theognis' characteristic complaints about poverty (cf. no. 6) and then turns into an allegorical representation of political disorder through the figure of the "Ship of State" (cf. Alcaeus 1 and 9).

16.  (Lines 699–718)

For the majority of human beings there is but a single
         virtue:
      to be wealthy. Nothing else, it seems, is of any use,
   not even if you should have the prudence of
         Rhadamanthys himself
      and know more things than Sisyphos, Aiolos' son,
5    who through his cunning even came up from Hades,
         after his wheedling words won over Persephone,
      who gives forgetfulness to mortals and harms their wits—
         no other man has yet contrived this feat,
      when once the dark cloud of death has closed about him,
10      and he goes to the shadowy region of the extinguished
      and passes through the blue-black gates that keep
         the souls of the dead fenced in, however much they
            may resist;
      but even from there, it seems, the hero Sisyphos came back
         into the light of the sun by his own inventiveness—
15    nor if you could form falsehoods similar in kind to truths,
         having the able tongue of godlike Nestor,
      and were swifter on your feet than the rushing Harpies
         or Boreas' sons, whose feet are speedy.
      But every man must lay this sentiment to heart:
20      wealth has the greatest power for every purpose.

In using the priamel form (and a catalogue of mythological examples) to argue for the primacy of a particular quality or value, this poem resembles Tyrtaeus 7; see the introductory note to that poem.

3–4 **Rhadamanthys, Sisyphos** See Glossary. Sisyphos' escape from death
is put to a different paradigmatic use in Alcaeus 3.
17 **Harpies** winged demons possessed of superhuman speed; the name
means "snatchers."
18 **Boreas** the North Wind; see Glossary.

### 17. (Lines 769–72)

A servant and messenger of the Muses, if he has any unusual
  knowledge, must not be stingy with his wisdom,
but rather seek out one thing, reveal another, invent still
  more.
  What use are they to him if he alone has knowledge of
  them?

### 18. (Lines 773–82)

Lord Phoibos, you yourself built high the towers of the city,
  showing favor to Alkathoos, Pelops' son;
and you yourself, I pray, keep the arrogant army of the Medes
  away from this city, in order that its people in merriment,
5 when spring approaches, may give you splendid hecatombs
  as they take pleasure in the lyre and lovely feasting
and paeans danced and sung by choruses around your altar.
  For truly I am afraid when I look on the witlessness
and ruinous discord of the Greeks; but you, Phoibos,
10  in gracious spirit guard this city of ours.

A prayer to Apollo that Megara be protected from harm during the Persian
invasion of mainland Greece in 480 B.C.; if the traditional dating of Theognis
to the mid-sixth century is correct, it is difficult to see how these lines can
actually be his. **Alkathoos** (2) was a legendary king of Megara.

### 19. (Lines 783–88)

Yes, I went once to the land of Sicily too,
  I went to Euboia's vineyard-covered plain,
and to Sparta, that splendid city on Eurotas' reedy banks;
  and everywhere I went they welcomed me with kindness.
5 But no pleasure came to my heart from any of them:

so true is it, after all, that nothing is dearer than one's
homeland.

## 20.  (Lines 983–88)

Let us devote our hearts to merriment and feasting
while the enjoyment of delights still brings pleasure.
For quick as thought does radiant youth pass by,
nor does the rush of horses prove to be swifter
5    when carrying their master to the labor of men's spears
with furious energy, taking joy in the plain that brings
forth wheat.

## 21.  (Lines 1197–1202)

I heard, son of Polypaos, the voice of that loud-crying bird
which comes to mortal men as a messenger
of timely plowing, and it set my darkened heart to
pounding,
because my fertile fields are in others' hands,
5    and not for me do the mules drag the curving plow,
because of this most hateful voyage.

1 **that loud-crying bird** the crane, whose southward passage overhead
signaled the time for autumn plowing; cf. Hesiod, *Works and Days* 448–51.
6 The text and meaning of this line are doubtful; it may refer to exile.

## 22.  (Lines 1267–70)

A boy and a horse are alike in mind, for the horse does not
weep for its rider when he lies in the dust,
but, fed full with barley, it carries the next man;
and in just this way the boy too loves whoever is at
hand.

## 23.  (Lines 1327–34)

My boy, as long as your cheeks and chin are smooth, I shall
never
cease to praise you, not even if I am fated to die.

For you, the giver, it is still honorable, and for me as lover
    it is not shameful
  to ask. But I beseech you, in the name of my parents:
5    show me respect, my boy, and grant me favor. If in time to
    come,
  craving in your turn the gift of the violet-crowned
Cyprian, you shall approach another, then may the gods
    grant that you meet with just such words as I hear now.

6–7 **the violet-crowned Cyprian** i.e., Aphrodite (see Glossary).

### 24. (Lines 1337–40)

No longer do I love a boy. I have kicked aside harsh
    torments;
  from grievous hardships I have gladly escaped;
I am set loose from longing by fair-wreathed Kythereia.
    As for you, my boy, you have no attractiveness in my
    eyes.

3 **Kythereia** another name for Aphrodite, derived from her association
with the island of Kythera, which lies off the southern coast of Lakonia.

### 25. (Lines 1341–50)

Alas, I am in love with a soft-skinned boy, who to all my
    friends
  reveals that this is true, though he does so against my
    will.
I shall endure without concealment the many outrages
    done in my despite,
  for not ill-favored is the boy whose conquest I am
    shown to be.
5    The love of boys has given delight ever since Ganymede
    was loved by Kronos' son himself, king of the
    immortals,
who seized and brought him up to Olympos and made
    him
  divine, possessing as he did the lovely bloom of
    boyhood.

So do not be amazed, Simonides, that I as well have been
10       shown to be conquered by love for a handsome boy.

5 **Ganymede** See Glossary, and cf. Pindar, *Olympian* 1. 44.


26.  (Lines 1353–56)

Bitter and sweet, alluring and tormenting:
    such, till it be fulfilled, Kyrnos, is love to the young;
for if one finds fulfillment, it proves sweet; but if,
        pursuing,
    one fails of fulfillment, then of all things it is most
        painful.

# IBYCUS

Ibycus was active as a poet in the second half of the sixth century B.C. According to later tradition, he was born in Rhegion, a Greek city on the southwestern tip of Italy, but later took up residence (like Anacreon) at the court of Polykrates, tyrant of Samos. His compositions appear to have been of two distinct types, long lyric narratives after the manner of Stesichorus and personal poems on erotic (particularly homoerotic) themes. In the Alexandrian period Ibycus' poems were collected into seven books.

1. (Fr. S 151)

... who brought Dardanian Priam's great     [Ant.]
city, far-famed and prosperous, to destruction,
setting out from Argos
by the counsels of great Zeus,

5    involved, over fair-haired Helen's beauty,     [Ep.]
in a struggle glorified by many songs,
a war that led to tears
when ruin scaled long-suffering Pergamos
through Aphrodite of the golden tresses.

10    Now, however, neither Paris the traitor-guest     [Str.]
nor Kassandra of the slender ankles
do I desire to celebrate in song,
nor Priam's other children

or the unspeakable day on which     [Ant.]
15    Troy's high gates were captured. Nor shall I recount
the magnificent prowess
of the heroes who sailed

in hollow ships made tight with many nails,                    [Ep.]
bringing calamity to Troy, those noble heroes.
20      Commanding them was lord Agamemnon,
descendant of Pleisthenes, king and leader of men,
son of a noble father, Atreus.

Such themes the Muses of Helikon, whose skill          [Str.]
is great, might embark upon in speech;
25      but by himself no man
alive could tell in detail

how many ships were launched from Aulis              [Ant.]
and over the Aegean Sea from Argos
came to Troy,
30      the nurse of horses, and with them men

bearing bronze shields, the sons of the Achaians.      [Ep.]
Of them the most outstanding with the spear
were swift-footed Achilles
and Telamon's valiant son, great Ajax . . .
35          . . . of fire . . .

. . . from Argos . . .                                          [Str.]
. . . to Ilion . . .
[2 lines missing]

40          . . . whom golden-belted                         [Ant.]
Hyllis bore. To him was Troilos
compared, like gold
already thrice refined to brass,

by Trojans and Danaans, for in attractiveness          [Ep.]
45      of form they found them very much alike.
These two have a share in beauty for all time;
you also, Polykrates, will enjoy imperishable fame
to the extent that song and my own fame can give it.

Most of this fragment (preserved without attribution on a piece of papyrus) consists of a lengthy *praeteritio* ("passing over"), the rhetorical maneuver by which a speaker introduces various topics while saying that he is not going to talk about them. The themes that are "passed over" all pertain to aspects of the Trojan War; the theme that is apparently preferred (although in the end next to nothing is said about it) is **Polykrates** (lines 47–48), the Samian tyrant at whose court Ibycus is known to have spent time. Some scholars have argued that the piece is not in fact by Ibycus.

1 **Dardanian** i.e., Trojan; see Glossary under "Dardanos."

8 **Pergamos** another name for Troy.

9 **Aphrodite** brought ruin to Troy through the erotic attraction that Helen exerted on Paris.

21 **Pleisthenes** It is not clear precisely where this figure belongs in Agamemnon's family tree.

23 **Helikon** the highest mountain in Boiotia (cf. Corinna 1), closely associated with the Muses; there was a sanctuary dedicated to them on its eastern slopes.

27 **Aulis** a port on the eastern coast of Boiotia where the various contingents of the Greek army gathered before setting sail to Troy.

40–41 **whom gold-belted Hyllis bore** probably a reference to Zeuxippos, who was king of Sikyon (a town not far from Corinth) at the time of the Trojan War.

41 **Troilos** the youngest of Priam's sons by his wife Hekabe.

44 **Danaans** Greeks.

## 2. (Fr. 286)

In spring the Kydonian
apple trees, watered by flowing
streams there where the Maidens
have their unravished garden, and vine buds,
5     growing under the shadowy branches
of the vines, bloom and flourish. For me, however,
       love
is at rest in no season,
but like the Thracian north wind
ablaze with lightning,
10     rushing from Aphrodite with scorching
fits of madness, dark and unrestrained,
it forcibly convulses, from their very roots,
my mind and heart.

1–2 **Kydonian apple trees** i.e., quince trees (cf. Stesichorus 3).

3 **the Maidens** presumably nymphs of some sort.

3. (Fr. 287)

Once again Love darts me a melting
    glance from under dark eyelids
and by magical charms of all sorts entangles me
    in Aphrodite's endless nets.
5    I swear that at his approach I tremble,
    like a prize-winning horse still under the yoke in old age
who against his will draws the swift chariot to the contest.


4. (Fr. 288)

Euryalos, offshoot of the gray-eyed Graces, favorite
of the Seasons with their lovely locks, you are one whom
        Aphrodite
and Attraction with her tender eyelids
    nursed among blooming roses.

# ANACREON

Anacreon was born in Teos, a city on the Ionian coast of Asia Minor, probably around 570 B.C. He spent a number of years at the court of Polykrates, tyrant of Samos, and after Polykrates' death (c. 520) he was brought to Athens by Hipparchos, the younger brother of the Athenian tyrant Hippias. His poetry is characterized by wit, stylistic polish, and careful craftsmanship; his favorite themes are wine (cf. nos. 2, 3, 15) and love (cf. nos. 4–9, 12–14). The Alexandrian scholar Aristarchus edited Anacreon's poems in five books.

### 1. (Fr. 348)

I entreat you, shooter of deer,
fair-haired daughter of Zeus,
   Artemis, mistress of wild beasts,
who now somewhere beside the eddies
5   of the Lethaios look down upon
a city of bold-hearted men
with pleasure, since not untamed
   are the citizens you shepherd. . . .

The opening of a prayer to Artemis, who had a temple on the **Lethaios** river in western Asia Minor, not far from the city of Magnesia (the **city of bold-hearted men** in line 6). See the introductory note to Sappho 1 for an outline of the typical prayer form; here the fragment ends before the actual request is made, but it may have pertained to Magnesia's political well-being.

### 2. (Fr. 356a)

Come now, bring us a wine bowl,
my boy, so I can drink it down
in one long swallow. Pour in ten
ladles of water to five of wine,

5        so that without unseemly wildness
         I can revel once more in Bacchic fashion.

With this and the following fragment, on the importance of maintaining de-
corum during the *symposion* or drinking-party, cf. Theognis 14 and
Xenophanes 1.

### 3.  (Fr. 356b)

Come, let us no longer in this way
with uproar and with shouting
conduct our carousal in Scythian style,
but instead let us drink in moderation
5        to the accompaniment of lovely hymns.

3 The **Scythians**, a barbarian people living in what is now southern
Russia, were notorious for the uncontrolled violence of their drinking
habits.

### 4.  (Fr. 357)

O lord, for whom Love the subduer,
the dark-eyed Nymphs,
     and Aphrodite of the rosy skin
are companions in play as you wander
5        over the mountains' lofty peaks,
I entreat you, come to me
in a kindly mood, and with approval
     listen to my prayer:
to Kleoboulos offer good
10       counsel, O Dionysos, so that he
     may accept my love.

A prayer of the kletic type (see note on Alcaeus 2), asking Dionysos for assis-
tance in a love affair. A pun on Kleoboulos' name ("famed for counsel") may
be intended in line 10.

### 5.  (Fr. 358)

Once more tossing a purple ball

at me, Love with the golden hair
points to a girl in embroidered sandals
   and challenges me to play.

5     But she (she comes from illustrious
Lesbos) laughs at my hair in scorn
(it's turning white) and goes off gaping
   after another—girl.

8 **another—girl** The interpretation of the Greek text here is disputed.
Anacreon may instead mean "another (head of) hair," i.e. one belonging to
another (and presumably younger) man.

#### 6.  (Fr. 359)

For Kleoboulos I long,
On Kleoboulos I dote,
At Kleoboulos I gaze.

#### 7.  (Fr. 360)

O boy whose glance is girlish,
I pursue you, but you pay no heed,
not knowing that you hold my soul's
   reins in your hand.

#### 8.  (Fr. 373)

I lunched on a small piece broken off from a honey-cake,
but I drained a cask of wine. Now I delicately pluck
my lovely lyre as I sing a serenade to my beloved girl.

#### 9.  (Fr. 376)

Lifted up once again, from Leukas'
cliff I leap into the gray waves, drunk with love.

**Leukas** was an island off the northwest coast of Greece. To leap from the high
cliffs at its southern tip was apparently regarded as a cure for love.

10.  (Fr. 388)

Before, he used to go about in an old cap, a hood tied
        tightly,
with wooden knucklebones in his ears, and around
        his ribs
    the hairless hide of an ox,
the unwashed covering of a worthless shield,
        consorting
5      with bread-women and willing whores, that scoundrel
        Artemon,
        contriving a fraudulent livelihood;
    often he had his neck in the stocks, often on the wheel;
    often his back was scourged with a leather whip, his hair
        and beard plucked out.
10     But now he rides in a carriage wearing golden earrings,
       that son of Kyke, and he carries an ivory parasol
           just the way the ladies do.

A satirical attack on one Artemon and his "speedy rise from poverty to
luxury," according to Athenaeus (12. 534a), who quotes the lines.


11.  (Fr. 395)

My temples have already
gone gray, my head is white,
the grace of youth is no longer
at hand, my teeth are old,
5      and of sweet life no longer
does any large span remain.

Therefore I weep and sob
often, in fear of Tartaros;
for Hades' inner chamber
10     is terrible, and full of grief
       the road down. One thing is certain:
       once down there, no one comes back up.

Included by Stobaeus (4. 51. 12) in the section of his anthology entitled "On
death and its inevitability." On **Tartaros** and **Hades**, see Glossary.

### 12. (Fr. 396)

Bring water, boy, bring wine, and fetch us flowers
twined into garlands, so that I may box a round with
    Love.

### 13. (Fr. 413)

Once again Love has beaten me like a blacksmith
with a great hammer and dipped me into a wintry torrent.

### 14. (Fr. 417)

My Thracian filly, tell me, why
    do you look at me askance
and stubbornly shun me, thinking
    that I have no skill at all?
5    I could, I assure you, deftly
    put the bridle on you
and, reins in hand, then guide you
    around the turning post of the racetrack.
But as it is, you graze in the meadows
10    and frisk and frolic with light heart,
for you have no expert in horsemanship
    to ride you handily.

Quoted by an ancient authority as an example of allegory (i.e. extended
metaphor) directed against a young woman with a "frisky disposition."

### 15. (Eleg. 2)

I don't like the man who, while drinking wine beside the
    full mixing bowl,
    talks about quarrels and warfare with its tears,
but rather one who mingles the Muses' and Aphrodite's
    splendid gifts
    together and so keeps the charms of festivity in mind.

On themes of violence and bloodshed as being inappropriate to the
*symposion*, cf. Xenophanes 1. 19–23.

# HIPPONAX

Hipponax was a native of Ephesus, an Ionian city on the coast of Asia Minor, and lived during the second half of the sixth century B.C. In later antiquity he was renowned as a poet of invective and satirical attack; as in the case of Archilochus, it was said that several of his victims—one of them a sculptor by the name of Boupalos (cf. no. 8)— were driven to suicide by the violence of his abuse. Another of his favorite themes, it would seem, was his own poverty (cf. nos. 3–6). Most of his extant fragments are in a meter known as choliambic ("limping iambic"), a variation of the iambic trimeter which ends haltingly with three long syllables.

    1.  (Frs. 3 + 3a)

. . . shouting, he called on Maia's son, the Sultan of
    Kyllene . . .
    . . . . . . . . . . . .

"Dog-throttling Hermes, called Kandaules in the Maionian
    tongue,
companion of burglars, come here and lend a hand."

1 **Sultan** The word thus translated (*palmys*) is not Greek but Lydian; Hipponax seems to have made fairly frequent use of foreign words. On Hermes' connection with Mt. **Kyllene**, see Glossary.
2 The name **Kandaules** apparently means "dog-throttler" in Lydian (**the Maionian tongue**). Maionia was a region in eastern Lydia.

    2.  (Frs. 26 + 26a)

For one of them, at his ease and lavishly,
dined every day on tuna and spicy cheesecake,
just like some eunuch from Lampsakos,
and ate up his estate. So now he has to dig

5      rocks on the hillside, nibbling a modicum of figs
       and barley bread, the fodder of slaves . . .
                    . . . . . . . . . . .
       . . . not gobbling partridges and hares,
       not seasoning griddle cakes with sesame,
       nor dipping fritters into honeycomb.

On a glutton and spendthrift. **Lampsakos** (3) was a town on the Asian shore
of the Hellespont; the point of the comparison is not clear.

### 3. (Fr. 32)

Hermes, dear Hermes, Maia's son, Kyllenian,
I call upon you, for I am shivering terribly with cold,
my teeth chattering. . . .
Give Hipponax a cloak, and a tunic,
5      and sandals, and felt-lined overshoes, and gold,
       some sixty staters of it, hidden by the inner wall.

6 **staters** a type of coin.

### 4. (Fr. 34)

To me you have not yet given a thick
cloak as a remedy for winter's cold,
nor thick felt-lined overshoes to cover
my feet and stop chilblains from breaking out.

### 5. (Fr. 36)

In my case the God of Wealth—he is completely blind—
has never walked into the house and said, "Hipponax,
I'm giving you three thousand silver drachmas,
and much, much more." No, he's too feeble-witted.

### 6. (Fr. 39)

I'll hand over my much-lamenting soul to sorrows
unless you send me, right away, a bushel
of barley, so that I can make myself a potion
of groats to drink as a remedy for my miserable state.

7. (Fr. 68)

Two days in a woman's life are sweetest:
when someone marries her and when he carries her out
        dead.


8. (Frs. 120 + 121)

Hold my jacket, people; I'm going to punch Boupalos in
        the eye.
I'm ambidextrous, and my punches never miss.


9. (Fr. 128)

O Muse, tell me of Eurymedon's son, that sea-swallowing
        gulf,
that knife-in-the-belly, who eats in no decorous fashion,
that he may perish by stoning, a vile fate for a vile man,
after a public vote, beside the shore of the barren sea.

Quoted by Athenaeus (15. 698c) as an example of parody. Hipponax's model
for this satirical attack on **Eurymedon's son** (who is otherwise unknown to
us) is the epic invocation such as is found at the beginning of the *Iliad* ("Sing,
goddess, of the wrath of Achilles son of Peleus, that destructive wrath which
caused countless sorrows for the Achaians . . .") and the *Odyssey* ("Tell me,
Muse, of the man of many turnings, who wandered far and wide . . ."). The
lines are in the meter of epic, dactylic hexameter.

# XENOPHANES

Xenophanes was born c. 570 B.C. in the Ionian city of Colophon. At age twenty-five (cf. no. 4) he left Colophon and embarked on a life of wandering, much of which he spent in southern Italy and Sicily; he evidently lived well into the fifth century. His surviving fragments deal chiefly with ethical and philosophical themes, often taking issue with the conventional beliefs of his time. Nos. 1–4 are in elegiac couplets, Nos. 5–13 in dactylic hexameters.

### 1. (Fr. 1)

Now the floor is clean, and so too are everyone's hands
    and cups. One person sets the plaited wreaths on
      people's heads,
while another passes around sweet-smelling myrrh in a
    dish;
    the mixing bowl stands full of merriment,
5    and other wine is ready, promising never to give out,
    a gentle vintage in the jars that is redolent of flowers.
In the midst of things frankincense sends forth its holy
    scent,
    and there is water, cold and sweet and pure.
Nearby lie golden loaves and an estimable table
10    heavily burdened with cheese and rich honey;
the altar in the middle is covered with flowers all over,
    and song and festivity encompass the house.
The first duty of men who are merry is to hymn divinity
    with decorous stories and pure speeches,
15    once they have poured libations and prayed for the
    capacity
    to do what is right; for that indeed is what lies closer to
    hand.
There is no outrage in drinking as much as you can hold

and still make your way
    home without an attendant, unless you are very old
      indeed.
Praise that man of men who when he has drunk brings
    worthy things to light
20      as his memory and his zeal for virtue enable him;
he does not narrate the battles of Titans or of Giants,
    nor yet of Centaurs, the fictions of earlier men,
or violent civil discord; in such themes there is nothing
    useful.
    It is good always to have consideration for the gods.

The theme of the decorous drinking-party is treated as well in Anacreon 2, 3, and 15 and in Theognis 13. On the **Titans, Giants,** and **Centaurs** (21–22), see Glossary.


## 2. (Fr. 2)

If a man were to win a victory by speed of foot
    or by performing the pentathlon, there where Zeus's
      precinct is
beside Pisa's stream at Olympia, or by wrestling
    or by sustaining boxing's painful bouts
5      or that terrible contest that they call the pankration,
    he would, in that case, be more glorious for his
      townsmen to gaze upon,
and he would win the right to sit in the front row in full
    view at assemblies,
    and he would be given meals at public expense
by the city, and a gift that would be for him as an
    heirloom—
10      even if he won in the chariot race, all these things
    would fall to his lot,
though he would not be my equal in worth; for superior to
    the strength
    of men and of horses is the expertise that *I* lay claim to.
But thought on this point is very haphazard, and it is not
    right
    to give preference to strength over serviceable
      expertise.

15      For neither if the people should have a good boxer among
them,
nor a man good at the pentathlon or at wrestling,
nor yet again in speed of foot, which is most honored
of all the deeds of strength which men perform in
contests,
not for that reason would the city be any better
governed.
20      Small is the joy that a city would get from such a man
if he should be victorious in the games beside the banks of
Pisa,
for not in this way are the city's storehouses fattened.

Xenophanes criticizes the adulation accorded to victorious athletes by their
cities, contrasting their minimal contribution to the common welfare with
the value of his own "expertise" or *sophia*, a term which here seems to encom-
pass both poetic skill and philosophical intelligence.

2 **pentathlon** a combination of five different events: footrace, discus,
javelin, long jump, and wrestling. The word means "five-contest."
3 **Pisa's stream** i.e., the Alpheos river, upon which Olympia, site of the
Olympic games, was situated; Pisa was a town in the vicinity of Olympia.
5 **pankration** an event combining elements of boxing and wrestling, and
the most violent of the Greek combat sports; its name means literally "all
strength." Victorious pankratiasts are celebrated in Pindar's *Nemean 5*,
*Isthmian 6*, and *Isthmian 7* and in Bacchylides' Ode 13.


   3. (Fr. 7a)

. . . and once, passing by as a puppy was being treated
with abuse,
they say that he took pity and uttered the following
words:
"Stop! Don't keep on thrashing, because this is in truth a
friend's
soul, which I recognized when I heard it giving voice."

Diogenes Laertius quotes these lines in his *Life of Pythagoras* (8. 36). The sub-
ject of the anecdote is Pythagoras himself, whose doctrine of metempsychosis
(the reincarnation of the soul from one body to another) Xenophanes would
seem to be satirizing.

4.  (Fr. 8)

Up to the present moment sixty-seven years have sent
    my mind restlessly tossing throughout the land of Hellas.
From birth until that point there were twenty-five years to
    be added in,
        if indeed I know how to reckon correctly in these matters.

Diogenes Laertius quotes these lines (9.19) in illustration of the poet's ex-
treme longevity; in them Xenophanes claims to have lived a life of wander-
ing for sixty-seven years after leaving his native Colophon at age twenty-
five.

5.  (Fr. 11 D-K)

Both Homer and Hesiod ascribed to the gods all things
that evoke reproach and blame among human beings,
theft and adultery and mutual deception.

In this and the next three fragments Xenophanes reflects in critical fashion on
the traditional anthropomorphism of Greek religion, i.e., its representation
of gods as human both in appearance and in behavior. Cf. note to no. 10.

6.  (Fr. 14 D-K)

But mortals believe that gods are begotten
and have clothing, voice, and body like their own.

7.  (Fr. 15 D-K)

But if oxen and horses and lions had hands
and so could draw and make works of art like men,
horses would draw pictures of gods like horses,
and oxen like oxen, and they would make their bodies
in accordance with the form that they themselves severally
    possess.

8.  (Fr. 16 D-K)

Ethiopians say that their gods are snub-nosed and black;
Thracians say that theirs have blue eyes and red hair.

9. (Fr. 18 D-K)

The gods have not, of course, revealed all things to mortals
     from the beginning;
but rather, seeking in the course of time, they discover
     what is better.


10. (Fr. 23 D-K)

There is one god, greatest among gods and human beings,
not at all like mortals in form nor yet in mind.

In this and the next three fragments Xenophanes proposes a conception of
divinity radically different from the anthropomorphism attacked in nos. 5–8.


11. (Fr. 24 D-K)

All of him sees, all of him thinks, all of him hears.


12. (Fr. 25 D-K)

But, far from toil, with the thought of his mind he puts all
     things in motion.


13. (Fr. 26 D-K)

Always he remains in the same place, moving not at all,
nor does it befit him to go at different times in different
     directions.

# SIMONIDES

Simonides was born c. 556 B.C. on Keos, a small island in the western Cyclades. Like Anacreon, he moved to Athens at the invitation of the tyrant Hipparchos, and he found other patrons among the princely families of Thessaly, the Aleuadai and the Skopadai. After the Persian Wars he composed a number of poems celebrating the exploits (and commemorating the losses) of various Greek states. He is said to have spent his final years at the court of Hieron, tyrant of Syracuse; he died in Sicily in 468. According to later tradition, Simonides was the first poet to charge fees for his services. He wrote poems of various types, including hymns, odes for victorious athletes, and laments or dirges (*threnoi*), for which he was particularly famous. He also wrote a number of epigrams in elegiac couplets for inscription on stone (cf. nos. 14–17).

### 1. (Fr. 506)

Who indeed of men now alive has so many times bound
    up his hair
with myrtle leaves or crowns of roses,
having gained victory in competition with those who
    dwell nearby?

This and the next fragment are from odes composed for victorious athletes (*epinikia*), on which see the introduction to Pindar.

### 2. (Fr. 507)

Krios was shorn in no unseemly fashion
when he came to Zeus's well-wooded, splendid
precinct. . . .

1 **Krios** The name means "ram" in Greek; hence the play on words.

2 **Zeus's well-wooded precinct** presumably either Nemea or Olympia; Panhellenic contests in honor of Zeus were held in both places.

### 3. (Fr. 520)

Small is men's
strength, and without effect their cares;
in a brief span of life there is toil on toil.
Inescapable, death hangs over all alike,
5    for an equal portion of it falls both to the noble
and to the man who is base.

This and the next two fragments appear to be from poems of lamentation (*threnoi*). Naturally enough, in such poems the transience and instability of human life and the universality of death were common themes.

### 4. (Fr. 521)

Being human, never say what is going to happen
    tomorrow,
nor, when you see a prosperous man, how long he will be
    so;
for even the long-winged fly is not so quick
in shifting its position.

### 5. (Fr. 522)

For all things come to a single dread Charybdis,
great excellences and wealth alike.

1 **Charybdis** a legendary whirlpool that swallowed everything that came near it. Here the name is applied metaphorically to death.

### 6. (Fr. 531)

Of those who died at Thermopylai
glorious is the lot, noble the doom.
Their tomb is an altar; in place of lamentation,
    remembrance; for pity, praise.
Such a funeral gift as this neither mould

·5 nor time that conquers all shall make obscure.
This precinct of brave men has claimed the glory
of Hellas as its inhabitant; and to this Leonidas too bears
   witness,
the king of Sparta, who has left behind a great
ornament of his valor and everlasting fame.

Written in honor of the Spartan king **Leonidas** and the three hundred Spartan soldiers under his command who, in 480 B.C., died fighting at the pass of **Thermopylai** in north-central Greece, in an unsuccessful attempt to prevent the invading Persian army from making further progress southward. Cf. no. 17.


   7.  (Fr. 542)

To become a truly good man
is difficult, in hands and feet and mind
   four-square, fashioned without reproach. . . .
            [7 lines missing]

11 Nor does the saying of Pittakos
have, in my view, the ring of truth, though spoken by
   a wise man: he said that it is difficult to be good.
Only a god could possess that prize; for a man it is
15    impossible not to be bad
when irresistible misfortune grips him.
If he fares well, every man is good;
but he is bad, if badly. . . .
and for the most part the best
20    are those whom the gods love.


For this reason I shall never cast away
my allotted span of life on an empty, unrealizable hope
   by searching for something that cannot come into
      existence:
a human being altogether blameless among all of us
25    who take the fruits of the broad earth for our use.
If I find one, though, I shall send you word.
I praise and love all those
who of free will commit

30     no shameful act; but against necessity
       not even the gods do battle.

                    [2 lines missing]
       I am not prone to fault-finding; I am satisfied
       with anyone who is not bad nor too shiftless, who
35         at least understands justice and its benefits to his city,
       a sound man. With such a one
       I shall not find fault, for when it comes to fools,
       the stock is limitless.
       All things are honorable in which
40     the shameful is not mingled.

This fragment of a poem addressed to one Skopas, a Thessalian prince, is quoted by Socrates in Plato's *Protagoras* (339A–346D; the content of lines 19–20 and 33–34 is reconstructed from Plato's prose paraphrase). Simonides' intention in the poem as a whole, and in particular the apparent contradiction in sense between lines 1–3 and 10–12, is the subject of extended discussion in the dialogue and has remained controversial among modern scholars. On **Pittakos** (11), see Glossary.

          8. (Fr. 543)

       . . . when in the chest,
       intricately fashioned,
       the blowing wind
       and the sea stirred into motion
5      cast her down in fear, with cheeks not free from tears
       she put her loving arm around Perseus
       and said: "My child, what pain and trouble I have!
       But you are asleep, and in your milk-fed
       baby's way you slumber
10     in this cheerless brass-bound box
       gleaming amid the night,
       stretched out under the blue-black gloom.
       The thick spray that looms over
       your curly head as the wave
15     passes by means nothing to you, nor the wind's
       clamorous voice, as you lie wrapped
       in a crimson cloak, with only your lovely face showing.

If to you what is fearsome were truly fearsome,
then you would turn that delicate ear
20      to hear my words.
But I tell you: sleep, my baby!
Let the sea sleep, let this unmeasured evil sleep!
May some shift in purpose appear,
father Zeus, from you;
25      and if I pray too boldly here,
or ask for other than what is right,
forgive me. . . ."

A fragment of a lyric narrative on Danaë and the infant **Perseus** (6), her son
by **Zeus** (24). When Perseus was born, mother and child were cast out to sea
in a large wooden chest on the orders of Danaë's father Akrisios (see Glos-
sary), who had been warned by an oracle that his daughter would produce a
son who would kill him.

### 9. (Fr. 579)

There is a saying
that Excellence dwells on cliff ledges difficult to climb
and there tends, close to the gods, a hallowed spot.
Not to all mortals' eyes
5      is she visible, but only to one upon whom heart-rending
            sweat
comes from within,
and who in that way reaches the height of manliness.

An adaptation of Hesiod, *Works and Days* 289–92: "In front of excellence the
immortal gods have placed sweat. / Long and steep is the way to it, / and
difficult at first; but once one reaches the height, / then it becomes easy,
though difficult before."

### 10. (Fr. 581)

What man who relies on his understanding could praise
            Kleoboulos, inhabitant of Lindos,
who against the ever-running rivers and the flowers of
            spring,
against the flame of the sun and the golden moon

and the eddies of the ocean wave has set the force of a
    gravestone?
5    All things are weaker than the gods; but a stone
even mortal hands can shatter. A fool
was he who planned this.

These lines are a comment on an epitaph attributed to one Kleoboulos, who was tyrant of Lindos on the island of Rhodes c. 600 B.C. The epitaph runs: "I am a maiden of bronze, and I am set on the tomb of Midas. / As long as water flows and trees grow tall, / and the rising sun shines bright and the shining moon, / and rivers run and the sea washes up against the shore, / here I shall remain on this much-lamented tomb / and announce to passersby that Midas is buried here."

11. (Fr. 584)

Without pleasure, what mode
    of life is desirable to mortals, or
        what royal power?
If that is lacking, not even the gods' existence is worth
    coveting.

12. (Eleg. 19 + 20)

. . . . . . . . . . . .

One thing the Chian poet said very well indeed:
"Like the generation of leaves is the generation of men."
    Yet few among mortals who hear this with their ears
lay it away in their hearts, for each man has Hope,
5    Hope which grows by nature in the hearts of the young.
So long as a man possesses the much-desired flower of
    youth,
    his spirit is light and foolish, and he thinks to no
        purpose;
for he has no expectation of growing old or of dying,
    nor, while he is healthy, does he entertain thoughts of
        pain.
10   Childish and vain are those who think thus and do not
    know
    how brief is the time of youth and life

for mortals. But *you*, heed what I say as you move toward
  life's boundary:
stand firm in endurance, taking delight in all good
  things.

Attributed to Simonides by Stobaeus (4. 34. 28); some scholars have argued
that it is the work of Semonides. For a different treatment of the comparison
of human beings to leaves, see Mimnermus 2. The **Chian poet** (1) is Homer;
the island of Chios was one of many places that claimed to be his birthplace.
The line quoted is *Iliad* 6. 146.


    13.  (Eleg. 11)

     . . . you were conquered by no mortal man:
   it was Apollo's hand that struck you down.
       . . . being nearby . . .
       . . . angry at Priam's children . . .
5    because of Alexandros whose thoughts were wicked . . .
       . . . brought down by the chariot of divine justice.
   Having sacked the city of which songs tell, they came
     home,
     mightiest of heroes, Danaans foremost in battle,
   on whom undying glory has been shed, thanks to a man
10     who received from the dark-haired maidens of Pieria
   the whole truth, and brought renown in the eyes of
     younger generations
     to the race of demigods whose doom came swiftly.
   But now hail and farewell, O son of a glorious goddess,
     daughter of briny Nereus. But as for me,
15   I summon you to assist me, Muse of great renown,
     if indeed you care about men's prayers:
   now also help to set in order this pleasing song
     of mine, that later ages may remember
   the men who on behalf of Sparta . . .
20       . . . warded off . . .
   nor did they forget valor . . .    . . . as high as heaven,
     and their fame among humankind will be undying.
   Leaving behind the Eurotas and the town of Sparta,
     they marched out with the sons of Zeus, those horse-
       taming

25       heroes the Tyndaridai, and with strong Menelaos,
             . . . captains of the city of their fathers.
         And it was Kleombrotos' valiant son who led them
             forth,
                                         . . . Pausanias.
         . . . they came to the famous fields of Corinth . . .
30           . . . of Pelops, Tantalos' son . . .
             . . . and the city of Nisos, where the others . . .
             . . . contingents from neighboring lands . . .
         . . . putting trust in divine omens, and with . . .
         they reached the lovely plain of Eleusis . . .
35           . . . driving the Medes from Pandion's land . . .

A fragment of what seems to have been a substantial elegy on the Battle
of Plataia (479 B.C.), where the Greek alliance under Spartan leadership
decisively defeated the Persian land forces. Although the fragment breaks
off before the account of the battle itself begins, Simonides' intention in
what remains appears to be twofold: to establish the Trojan War as a he-
roic prototype of the struggle between Greeks and Persians, and to draw
a parallel between himself and Homer as divinely inspired poets capable
of conferring immortality through fame on those who do great deeds of
valor. The first fourteen lines (cf. 1–2, 13–14) are cast in the form of a
hymnal address to Achilles, the greatest of the Greek warriors who
fought at Troy.

5 **Alexandros** another name for Paris (on whom see Glossary).
9 **a man** i.e., Homer.
10 **maidens of Pieria** i.e., the Muses.
13 **a glorious goddess** i.e., Thetis.
23 **the Eurotas** the chief river of Sparta (cf. Theognis 19. 3, Pindar,
*Isthmian* 5. 33).
24–25 Both the **Tyndaridai** and **Menelaos** (see Glossary) were revered in
Sparta as tutelary heroes.
27–28 The commander in chief of the Spartan forces at Plataia was
**Pausanias** (cf. no. 15), nephew of King Leonidas (cf. no. 6) and son of
Leonidas' brother **Kleombrotos**.
29–35 The stages of the Spartan advance from the Peloponnesos into
Boiotia are summarized.
31 **the city of Nisos** i.e., Megara (cf. Pindar, *Nemean* 5. 45 with note).
35 **Pandion's land** i.e., Attika; Pandion was a legendary king of Athens
(cf. Bacchylides, *Dithyramb* 18. 15).

### 14.  (Epigr. 11)

Stranger, we dwelt in Corinth once, that well-watered city,
      but now the island of Ajax holds us, Salamis.

A sepulchral epigram commemorating a contingent of Corinthians who
fought and died in the Battle of Salamis (see Glossary) and were buried on
that island. On the connection between **Salamis** and **Ajax**, cf. Pindar, *Isthmian*
5. 48.

### 15.  (Epigr. 17)

As commander of the Greeks, after he destroyed the army
      of the Medes,
Pausanias set up this memorial in Phoibos' honor.

On **Pausanias** and his role in the Battle of Plataia, see no. 13, lines 27–28 with
note.

### 16.  (Epigr. 21)

Fighting in the forefront of the Greeks, the Athenians at
      Marathon
laid low the power of the Medes arrayed in gold.

An epigram commemorating the Athenians who died fighting at Marathon
in 490 B.C., when the first attack launched by Persia against mainland Greece
was decisively repulsed.

### 17.  (Epigr. 22b)

Stranger, report to the Lakedaimonians that in this place
      we lie, obedient to that people's precepts.

On the Spartan dead at Thermopylai; see note on no. 6.

# CORINNA

Corinna was a native of Tanagra, a town in Boiotia. Her date is a matter of controversy: in later antiquity she was thought to have been a contemporary (and rival) of Pindar, but some modern scholars have argued that she lived instead in the third century B.C. Her poems were largely narrative in content and dealt, it would seem, exclusively with local Boiotian legends in a style of artless simplicity.

1. (Fr. 654 col. i)

". . . the Kouretes
hid the goddess's holy
infant in a cave, unbeknownst
15    to Kronos of the crooked counsels,
when blessed Rhea stole him

and from the immortals won
great honor." That was what he sang;
and the Muses at once directed
20    the blessed ones to drop their secret
voting pebbles into the urns
of gleaming gold. They all rose up together,

and Kithairon won the larger number;
and Hermes speedily declared,
25    shouting, that he had won the victory
which he desired, and with garlands . . .
    . . . he was adorned
by the blessed ones; and his mind rejoiced.

But Helikon, in the grip
30    of cruel torments,
tore out a bare rock,

shaking the mountain, and groaning
pitiably he dashed it from on high
into innumerable stones. . . .

This fragment describes a singing contest between two mountains in Boiotia,
**Kithairon** (23) and **Helikon** (29), in which the Olympian gods (**the blessed
ones,** 20) served as judges. The first song is missing; the second—whether
Kithairon's or Helikon's is not clear—concerns the birth of Zeus (12–18). The
**Kouretes** (12) were semidivine beings who helped **Rhea** (16) to protect her
newborn son from the hostility of his father **Kronos** (15) by drowning out the
infant's cries with noisy dancing.

2. (Fr. 654 col. iii)

". . . and of your daughters, three are now
with Zeus the father, king of all;
three are wedded to the ruler of the sea,
15     Poseidon; two of them have
Phoibos as master of their beds;

and one belongs to Maia's noble
son, Hermes. For thus did Eros
and Kypris persuade them, that they should
20     enter your house in secret
and take your nine daughters,

who one day shall give birth
to a race of heroes, demigods,
and shall be scattered about the earth
25     and ageless—such, from the oracular
tripod, is what I learned.

This privilege came to me
among fifty mighty brothers,
to be the preeminent spokesman
30     of the holy shrine, with truthfulness
allotted to me at birth—to me, Akraiphen.

For first the son of Leto
gave to Euonymos the gift

of uttering oracles from his tripods;
35  expelling him from the land, Hyrieus
was second to acquire the honor,

Poseidon's son; next was
Orion, our begetter,
after he had regained possession of his own land;
40  and he now dwells in heaven,
while I hold this honor.

Therefore . . .   . . . and I utter
oracles of the strictest accuracy.
Come then, yield to the immortals
45  and free your heart from grief,
being father-in-law to gods."

So spoke the seer, much-revered;
and Asopos, joyfully
taking hold of his right hand
50  and shedding tears from his eyes,
answered him in this way. . . .

This fragment concerns the Boiotian river god **Asopos** (48) and his nine daughters, whose disappearance has prompted him to consult the prophet **Akraiphen** (31). Akraiphen first reveals the present condition and future glory of the daughters (12–25) and then proclaims both the truthfulness and the history of his prophetic office (27–43).

19 **Kypris** Aphrodite (see Glossary).
32 **the son of Leto** Apollo, here in his function as the god of prophecy.
35 **Hyrieus** father of Orion (38) and hence grandfather of Akraiphen and his forty-nine brothers.

### 3. (Fr. 655)

Terpsichore calls upon me
to sing beautiful tales
for the women of Tanagra in their white robes;
and greatly does the city take pleasure in
5  my voice, clear and coaxing;

for whatever ... great ...
false ...
    ... the earth with its wide spaces.
Stories from our fathers' time
10     I have embellished ...
and I recite them for maidens.
Often it has been our founder Kephissos
that I have embellished with my words,
but often too the great Orion
15     and the fifty sons of lofty strength
whom, while mingling with the nymphs,
he begot; and beautiful Libya. ...

1 **Terpsichore** one of the nine Muses (see Glossary).
3 **Tanagra** See introduction.
12 **Kephissos** a river in Boiotia (cf. Pindar, *Olympia* 14. 1).
14f On **Orion** and his **fifty sons**, see previous fragment.

4.  (Fr. 664a + b)

... and I find fault as well with the clear-voiced
Myrtis because, though being a woman,
she entered into competition with Pindar. ...
     . . . . . . . . . . .
... but as for me, the glorious deeds of heroes
and heroines are my themes ...

The Boiotian poet **Myrtis** was said to be the teacher of both Corinna and
Pindar.

# PINDAR

Pindar (518–c. 438 B.C.) was born in Kynoskephalai, a village near Thebes. He is said to have spent time as a youth studying music in Athens. He received his first commission for a victory ode (*Pythian* 10) at the age of twenty, while the latest extant poem that can be dated with reasonable certainty (*Pythian* 8) was composed in 446; thus his professional career as a poet spanned more than fifty years. In Alexandrian times his works were collected in seventeen books comprising all the major choral genres, including hymns, paeans, dithyrambs, victory odes, maiden-songs, and *enkomia*.

Of these only the four books of victory odes (*epinikia*) have survived intact (or virtually so), arranged according to the various athletic festivals for which they were written (Olympian, Pythian, Nemean, Isthmian). Victors in the games (or their families) would commission such odes to commemorate their achievements in a variety of athletic disciplines, including footraces of various distances, combat sports like boxing and wrestling, and equestrian events, most notably the four-horse chariot race. Epinicians usually contain three main types of material: factual data pertaining to the victor and his family, stories drawn from the storehouse of Hellenic myth and legend, and general reflections on the conditions and issues of human life (what the Greeks called *gnomai* or "maxims"). Of these the only truly indispensable element is the factual information, which typically comprises the victor's name, his father's name, his city or homeland, where and in what sport the current victory was won, and (often) a list of previous victories won by the athlete, by other members of his family, or by his clan as a whole. Mythic material, which ranges in scale from brief allusions to extended narratives, is regularly *paradigmatic* in function, offering heroic prototypes, models, or exemplars for the character and achievements of the victor, his family, and/or his city. Extended mythical narratives usually (but not invariably) occupy the central portion of the ode.

## *Olympian* 1:

for Hieron son of Deinomenes, from Syracuse,
victor in the horse race

Best is water, and gold, like blazing fire by night,     [Str. 1]
shines forth preeminent amid the lordliness of wealth.
But if it is contests that you wish
to sing of, O my heart,
5    do not look further than the sun
for warmth and brilliance in a star
     amid the empty air of day,
nor let us herald any games as superior to Olympia's,
from which comes glorious song to cast itself about
the intellects of skillful men, to celebrate
10   the son of Kronos when they have arrived, amid
          abundance,
at the blessed hearth of Hieron,

who wields his scepter lawfully amid the fruitful     [Ant. 1]
          fields
of Sicily. He culls the foremost of all excellences,
and he is made resplendent too
15   by music's choicest strains,
such songs as we men often sing
in playful fashion around his friendly table.
     But from its peg take down
the Dorian lyre, if both Pisa's grace and Pherenikos'
have placed your mind beneath the spell of sweetest
          thoughts,
20   recalling how beside the Alpheos he rushed,
giving his body's strength ungoaded to the race,
and so infused his lord with mastery,

the Syracusan king whose joy                          [Ep. 1]
     is horses. Bright for him shines fame
in the brave-hearted settlement of Lydian Pelops,
25   with whom the mighty Earthholder fell in love,
Poseidon, when from the pure cauldron
     Klotho took him out,
his shoulder marked with gleaming ivory.

Truly, wonders are many, yet doubtless too men's talk,
28b     tales embellished beyond the true account
    with lies of cunning pattern,
       cheat and lead astray.

30     And Charm, which fashions all that pleases       [Str. 2]
       mortals,
    by adding her authority makes even what outstrips belief
    be frequently believed.
    But future days remain
    the wisest witnesses.
35     It is fitting for a man to say good things
       about the gods, for so the blame is less.
    Son of Tantalus, contrary to earlier accounts I shall
       proclaim
    how when your father called the gods to that
    most orderly of feasts at his dear Sipylos,
    offering them a banquet in return,
40     then it was that he of the splendid trident snatched you up,

    his mind subdued by longing, and on golden       [Ant. 2]
       horses
    brought you aloft to the house of august Zeus,
    where at a later time
    Ganymede came as well,
45     to render Zeus the selfsame service.
    But when you disappeared, and those who sought you long
       failed to return you to your mother,
    at once some envious neighbor told a tale in secret,
    how into water brought to the fullest boil by fire
    they cut you with a knife, limb by limb,
50     and then among the tables, as the final course,
    they portioned out your flesh and ate.

    For me, however, it is impossible to call       [Ep. 2]
       any of the blessed gods a glutton: I stand apart.
    Often a lack of profit falls to slanderers.
    But truly, if the watchers of Olympos ever held a mortal man
55     in honor, Tantalos was he—but all
       in vain, for he could not digest

his great good fortune. In his greed he gained
excess of ruin, for the Father
57b     hung over him a mighty rock,
and being always eager to cast it from his head,
        he strays exiled from merriment.


He has this helpless life of lasting toil,                       [Str. 3]
60      a fourth trial with three others, since he cheated the
                immortals
by sharing with his drinking friends and age-mates
the nectar and ambrosia
with which they had made him
free from decay. But if in any action any man
        hopes to elude divinity, he is in error.
65      Therefore the immortals sent his son back once again
to dwell among the short-lived race of men.
And when, toward the time of his youth's flowering,
his chin and jaw were darkening with soft hair,
he set his thoughts upon the ready marriage


70      that might be his by wresting fair-famed                 [Ant. 3]
                Hippodameia from her father,
the king of Pisa. Drawing near the white-flecked sea, alone
                in dark of night,
he hailed the loud-resounding
god of the trident, who close by
the young man's feet revealed himself.
75      To him he said: "Come, if in any way the Cyprian's
                affectionate gifts lay claim, Poseidon,
to gratitude, then shackle Oinomaos' brazen spear;
dispatch me on the swiftest of all chariots
to Elis; draw me near to mastery.
For thirteen men, all suitors, he has killed,
80      and so puts off the marriage


of his daughter. Great risk does not place               [Ep. 3]
        its hold on cowards.
Since we must die, why sit in darkness
and to no purpose coddle an inglorious old age,
without a share of all that's noble? But for me,

this contest is a task that I
85 must undertake; may *you* bring to fulfillment that which I
hold dear."
Thus he spoke, and the words that he laid hold of
86b were not without effect. Exalting him, the god
gave him a golden chariot and a team
of tireless winged horses.

He took strong Oinomaos down and took the [Str. 4]
maiden as his bride,
begetting six sons, leaders eager to excel.
90 But now he has a share
in splendid acts of sacrifice,
reclining by the course of Alpheos,
in his well-tended tomb beside the altar
that many strangers visit. Fame
gleams far and wide from the Olympic races
95 of Pelops, where the speed of feet contends,
and utmost strength courageous to bear toil.
Throughout the rest of life the one who wins
enjoys a honeyed calm,

at least as regards games. That good, however, [Ant. 4]
which comes day by day
100 is always uppermost for every mortal. As for me, to crown
that man with music in the Aiolian mode,
a tune fit for a horseman, is
my duty. I am confident that no host
exists who can lay claim to deeper knowledge
of noble ends or yet to greater power,
105 at least among those living now, to be embellished with
loud folds of song.
Having this as his special care,
a guardian god takes thought
for your ambitions, Hieron. Unless he should leave
suddenly,
I hope to honor a still sweeter victory

110 with a swift chariot, discovering [Ep. 4]
a path of words to lend assistance

as I approach the sunny hill of Kronos. Now for me
the Muse fosters in her reserves of force the mightiest
    arrow:
in different matters different men show greatness, but
    the utmost peak belongs
to kings. Extend your gaze no further.
115    May your lot be to walk on high throughout the time you
    have;
may mine be to keep company with those who win
on each occasion, foremost in poetic skill
    among Greeks everywhere.

On Hieron, tyrant of Syracuse, see Glossary. This ode, like Bacchylides' Ode 5, was commissioned to celebrate a victory won by Hieron's racehorse Pherenikos in 476. It seems to have been placed first among Pindar's *Olympians* because of the praise of the Olympic Games with which it begins and because Pelops' chariot race against Oinomaos, the subject of the central myth, can be regarded as a mythical prototype of Olympic competition. Also noteworthy in the ode is the poet's emphatic rejection of a traditional story pertaining to Pelops' youth (28–53) as false and disrepectful toward the gods.

10 **the son of Kronos** Zeus, the divine patron of the Olympic games.
18 **Pisa** i.e., Olympia (see Glossary). On Hieron's racehorse **Pherenikos** ("Bringer of Victory"), cf. also *Pythian* 3. 73–74 and Bacchylides, Ode 5. 36–49.
20 **Alpheos** the river on which Olympia was situated.
24 **settlement of Lydian Pelops** i.e., Elis, the region in the western Peloponnesos in which Olympia was located. Poseidon brought the hero Pelops to Elis from his home in Lydia in order that he might win a bride for himself, as is told in lines 67ff. According to a traditional story that Pindar rejects in lines 52ff, when Pelops was a boy his father **Tantalos** (36), the king of **Sipylos** (38), cut him up, cooked him, and served him to the assembled gods, although only Demeter actually ate any of the flesh. Subsequently the pieces of Pelops' body were returned to the cauldron in which they had been cooked, and he miraculously reemerged in good health, with an ivory shoulder to replace what Demeter had eaten.
25–27 It is not certain whether these lines are to be interpreted as part of the rejected or the "purified" version of events. In the former case the **pure cauldron** is that in which the dismembered Pelops was reconstituted and the **ivory shoulder** is that which was substituted for the shoulder that had been eaten; in the latter, the cauldron must be the vessel of water in which Pelops was washed as a newborn baby and the ivory shoulder merely a

mark of beauty with which he was endowed from birth. The presence of **Klotho,** one of the Fates (see Glossary), is equally appropriate whether birth or rebirth is at issue.

40 **he of the splendid trident** Poseidon.

44 **Ganymede** See Glossary and cf. Theognis 25. 5–8.

54 **watchers of Olympos** i.e., the Olympian gods.

57 **the Father** Zeus.

60 **a fourth trial with three others** The meaning of this phrase is uncertain. One possibility is that Pindar is alluding to three other *trials* endured by Tantalos in addition to the suspended rock; another is that he is alluding to three other *sinners* in whose company Tantalos undergoes his eternal punishment.

70 **Hippodameia** the daughter of **Oinomaos** (76), king of Pisa in Elis. Oinomaos challenged any man who wished to marry Hippodameia to compete with him in a chariot race. Since his own horses were of divine origin, he was able to overtake and kill each suitor that presented himself—until he encountered Pelops.

75 **the Cyprian** i.e., Aphrodite (see Glossary). Pelops is invoking the prior love relation between himself and Poseidon.

90–91 **he has a share in splendid acts of sacrifice** an allusion to the active hero cult that Pelops enjoyed at Olympia in historical times.

101 **the Aiolian mode** one of several distinct "modes" or styles of tuning in ancient Greek music; cf. *Olympian* 14. 17.

103 **no host** Epinician poets frequently speak of their patrons in terms of the Greek social institution of "guest-friendship" (*xenia*), which bound host and guest together in an enduring relationship of mutual respect and obligation; cf. *Pythian* 3. 69, *Pythian* 10. 64–66, *Isthmian* 6. 18, Bacchylides, Ode 5. 12, 13. 225–27.

109 **a still sweeter victory** i.e., one gained in the four-horse chariot race, which had greater prestige than the race for horse and jockey alone which Pherenikos had won. The hope expressed here was finally fulfilled for Hieron in 468, but on that occasion Bacchylides, not Pindar, was commissioned to celebrate the victory (see Bacchylides, Ode 3).

111 **hill of Kronos** a small hill near the Olympian game site.

## *Olympian* 2:

### for Theron son of Ainesidamos, from Akragas, victor in the chariot race

O songs that rule the lyre,                                    [Str. 1]
what god, what hero, and what man are we to celebrate?
In truth, Pisa belongs to Zeus; and Herakles

   established the Olympian festival
   as the first fruits of war;
5   but it is Theron, victor in the four-horse chariot race,
   who must with loud voice be proclaimed, just in his
         reverence for strangers,
      bulwark of Akragas,
   his city's savior, flower of an illustrious line,

   men who, steeling their hearts to labor,                 [Ant. 1]
   won sacred soil to be their home beside the river, and
         proved themselves
10   the eye of Sicily. Unfolding in its destined form,
      life brought both wealth and glory
   to crown their native virtues.
   O Kronian child of Rhea, you who guard Olympos' seat,
   the summit of all games, and Alpheos' crossing,
         cheered by song,
   preserve with gracious spirit their ancestral land

15   for their posterity. Once deeds are done,               [Ep. 1]
   for good or ill, just or unjust, not even
   Time, the father of all things,
         has power to undo the end.
   Forgetfulness, however, may with kindly fortune come.
   Under the weight of noble joys, pain dies,
20   its fierce resistance mastered,

   when Destiny, which come from god, propels               [Str. 2]
   prosperity aloft. This truth applies to Kadmos'
   regal daughters, who suffered hugely: grief
         falls heavy to the ground
   when blessings gain the upper hand.
25   One lives among the Olympians, having died
   amid the thunder's roar, Semele of the streaming hair;
         she is held dear by Pallas
   and father Zeus, but chiefly by her son, the ivy-crowned.

   And then they say that in the sea as well,               [Ant. 2]
   among the briny Nereids, imperishable life
30   has been ordained for Ino through the whole of time.

In truth, to mortals no fixed bound
of death has been allotted,
nor can we know, when sunrise brings each day to birth,
whether it will close peacefully, with good unblemished.
    Different currents flow
at different times, bearing delights and troubles to
    mankind.

35 Thus Destiny, which holds in hereditary trust     [Ep. 2]
this family's benevolent fate, along with heaven-sent
prosperity brings pain too in some measure,
    itself reversible with time.
This has been so since Laios' destined son stepped out
across his path and killed him, and so brought the prophecy
40 spoken of old at Pytho to fulfillment.

A sharp-eyed Fury marked the deed     [Str. 3]
and slew his warlike progeny with mutual slaughter;
and yet, though Polyneikes fell, Thersandros still
    lived on, in young men's games
and in the brunt of war
45 much honored, scion and savior of Adrastos' house.
Deriving thence his stock and seed, it is becoming that
    Ainesidamos' son
meet with the lyres and revel songs of triumph.

For at Olympia he himself     [Ant. 3]
has won a prize, while to the brother whose lot he shares
50 the Graces have conjointly brought,
    at Pytho and the Isthmus, flowers of victory in
the twelve-turn chariot race. To find success,
attempting competition, frees one from the charge of folly.
Wealth, when adorned with virtues, brings due measure
    of diverse ends within one's grasp,
sustaining deep ambitions eager at the chase,

55 a star conspicuously bright, the truest source     [Ep. 3]
of lasting radiance for men. If one who has it knows the
    future—
knows that the dead

whose souls are reckless forthwith pay
penalty here, while crimes committed in this realm of Zeus
are judged beneath the earth by one whose sentence
60      resounds with grim necessity;

but always under equal nights                          [Str. 4]
and equal days of shining sun, the good
are granted life with little labor, not
        troubling the soil with strength of hand
nor yet the sea's expanse
65      to earn an ineffectual livelihood. Instead, beside
                revered
divinities sit those who found their joy
        in keeping oaths; existence without tears
is theirs, while what the rest endure bears no beholding.

But those who have the hardihood,                      [Ant. 4]
sojourning thrice on either side, to keep their souls apart
70      from all injustice, pass along the road of Zeus
        to Kronos' tower, there
where ocean breezes blow
about the Island of the Blessed. Golden flowers blaze,
some on dry land, from shining trees,
while others grow in water;
with such wreaths do they deck both hand and head

75      as Rhadamanthys, upright judge, decrees.        [Ep. 4]
He sits in readiness beside the mighty father,
husband of Rhea, goddess
        whose throne is over all.
Both Peleus and Kadmos have a place among them,
and there Achilles too was brought, once Zeus's heart
80      had yielded to his mother's pleas—

the man who leveled Hektor, Troy's                     [Str. 5]
unswervable, unconquerable pillar, and brought death to
        Kyknos,
and to the son of Dawn, the Ethiopian prince.
        Many swift arrows lie in store within
the quiver crooked beneath my arm,

85      having a voice that speaks to experts; but to grasp their gist
         requires interpreters. That man is wise who knows many
               things
             by nature; but let those whose skills are learned,
         like boisterous crows, fling futile, indiscriminate
               chatter

         against the divine bird of Zeus.                    [Ant. 5]
         Come, aim the bow now at the target, O my heart! Who is
               the one
90      against whom darts of fame are launched
             once more with mild intent?
         Drawing at Akragas,
         I shall proclaim on oath straightforward truth:
         no city has within a hundred years produced
             a man who toward his friends is more
         beneficent in thought or free of hand

95      than Theron. And yet praise is trampled by excess,    [Ep. 5]
         not guided by a sense of right but, in the hands of greedy
               men,
         ready to babble on and so
             obscure the noble deeds
         of good men. For as sand escapes all counting,
         so all the joys which that man has bestowed on others
100     who has the power to make clear?

Theron ruled as tyrant of Akragas, a large and wealthy city in southwestern
Sicily, from 488 until his death in 472; the chariot victory which this ode cel-
ebrates was won in 476. Theron's family, the Emmenidai, traced their descent
from the royal house of Thebes (cf. 38–47), and the checkered history of that
line contributes largely to one of the ode's central themes, the vicissitudes of
fortune. Another such theme is the proper use of wealth (53–56), as exempli-
fied by Theron's generosity toward others (89–100). Reinforcing this theme is
the lengthy excursus on the afterlife (57–83), which sets forth both the gen-
eral principle that human actions, for good or ill, have lasting consequences
and the specifically relevant corollary that posthumous rewards await the
virtuous and noble (such as Theron). The details of this eschatological pas-
sage, which appears to show the influence of the Pythagorean doctrine of
metempsychosis (reincarnation), have been of great interest to historians of
Greek religious thought.

3 **Pisa belongs to Zeus** i.e., Olympia and the Olympic festival are under the patronage and protection of Zeus; see Glossary under "Pisa."

4 **as the first fruits of war** Herakles founded the Olympic games using booty gained from his war against Augeas, the king of Elis.

9 **their home beside the river** The city of Akragas was situated on a river of the same name.

10 **the eye of Sicily** i.e., its greatest glory.

12 **Kronian child of Rhea** i.e., Zeus (see Glossary).

13 **Alpheos** the river on which Olympia was situated.

22–23 **Kadmos' regal daughters** See Glossary under "Kadmos," "Semele," and "Ino."

27 **her son, the ivy-crowned** Dionysos, to whom ivy (like the vine) was sacred.

29 **Nereids** daughters of the sea god Nereus (see Glossary).

38 **Laios' destined son** Oedipus; for story see Glossary.

40 **Pytho** Delphi, site of a famous oracle of Apollo (see Glossary).

42 **mutual slaughter** The two sons of Oedipus, **Polyneikes** and Eteokles, killed one another during the attack of the Seven against Thebes (on which see Glossary under "Adrastos").

43 **Thersandros** Polyneikes' son by his wife Argeia, the daughter of **Adrastos** (45).

49 **brother** Xenokrates, whose victories at the Pythian and Isthmian games are celebrated in Pindar's *Pythian* 6 and *Isthmian* 2 (not included in this volume).

57–60 Pindar appears to be saying that misdeeds committed in the world below are punished here on earth (through reincarnation) and vice versa. The passage is highly controversial, however, and has been variously interpreted.

75 **Rhadamanthys** See Glossary and cf. Theognis 16. 3.

77 **husband of Rhea** i.e., Kronos (see Glossary).

78 **Peleus and Kadmos** On these two exemplars of human felicity see Glossary and cf. *Pythian* 3. 86ff.

80 **his mother** the sea goddess Thetis.

81–83 On **Hektor, Kyknos,** and Memnon (**the son of Dawn**) as victims of Achilles' valor, see Glossary and cf. *Isthmian* 5. 39–41.

83–95 The poet declines any further treatment of the posthumous rewards awaiting the righteous in favor of a straightforward assertion that Theron's philanthropic use of wealth is unsurpassed.

88 **the divine bird of Zeus** the eagle. For its association with Zeus cf. *Pythian* 1. 6–10, *Isthmian* 6. 49–50.

95–100 I.e., to particularize Theron's many acts of beneficence would defeat the purpose of praise by burying it under a plethora of detail.

## *Olympian* 12:

for Ergoteles son of Philanor, from Himera,
victor in the long race

|  | I beseech you, daughter of Zeus the Deliverer, | [Str.] |
|---|---|---|
|  | stand by Himera and make her strong, O saving Fortune! |  |
|  | For you are she by whom swift ships at sea |  |
|  | are guided, and on land both sudden turns of war |  |
| 5 | and policies in council. So men's hopes and fears, |  |
|  | tossing now up, now down, |  |
| 6a | cleaving through vain illusions, ride and roll. |  |

|  | Not one of those on earth has yet discovered, | [Ant.] |
|---|---|---|
|  | through god, a trustworthy token of events to come: |  |
|  | the mind's eye finds the future dark. |  |
| 10 | For mankind many things fall out against expectation, |  |
|  | at times contrary to delight, but there are those |  |
|  | who, having come upon fierce squalls, |  |
| 12a | change in a moment anguish for deep good. |  |

|  | Son of Philanor, truly, like the cock | [Ep.] |
|---|---|---|
|  | that only fights at home, beside your native hearth |  |
| 15 | the glory of your racing feet would have shed its leaves |  |
|  | unsung, |  |
|  | had Faction that sets men against their fellows |  |
|  | not robbed you of your fatherland in Knossos. |  |
|  | But as it is, having crowned yourself at Olympia, |  |
|  | in Pytho twice, and at the Isthmus, you, Ergoteles, |  |
|  | touch and lift high in fame the warm baths of the Nymphs, |  |
|  | in company, at home amid your fields. |  |

Ergoteles was a native of Knossos on Crete, but when factional conflict forced him into exile (a truly dire calamity for a Greek), he emigrated to Sicily, where he obtained citizenship at Himera, a city on the island's northern coast that was famous for its hot springs (cf. **the warm baths of the Nymphs**, 19). Although Ergoteles evidently began his career as a long-distance runner while still on Crete, Pindar suggests that it was only after he had settled in Himera that opportunities for Panhellenic competition and success opened up to him. By beginning the ode with a hymn to the power of Fortune (Tyche in Greek), Pindar presents the unexpectedly happy outcome of Ergoteles' troubles as an illustration of the paradoxical role—at times deleterious, but at

other times profoundly beneficent—which apparently random chance plays
in human life.

## *Olympian* 13:

for Xenophon son of Thessalos, from Corinth,
     victor in the stade race and the pentathlon

Three times victorious at Olympia,                         [Str. 1]
gentle toward townspeople and attentive to the needs
of strangers—praising such a family, I shall come to know
prosperous Corinth, foreporch
5    of Isthmian Poseidon, splendid for its youths.
For there dwell Good Order and
     her sisters, steady base of cities,
Justice and Peace her twin,
     who deal out wealth to men,
the golden daughters of wise Themis.

And there they are resolved to keep at bay              [Ant. 1]
10   Arrogance, bold-mouthed mother of Excess.
I have fine themes to set forth, and the daring
that prompts my tongue to speak of them outright:
it is a losing fight to stifle inborn nature.
To you, descendants of Aletes, many times
     the radiance of victory has been granted,
15   when in the sacred games you have
     excelled through acts of utmost prowess;
and many times also into your men's hearts

the Horai rich in flowers have of old cast clever       [Ep. 1]
     inventions. Every work belongs to its discoverer.
Whence did the graceful songs of Dionysos come to light,
the dithyramb that wins an ox as prize?
20   Yes, and who set the bit in horses' harness as due measure,
or placed twin pediments—those outstretched eagles'
          wings—
upon the temples of the gods? There too the Muse breathes
          sweetly,
there Ares blooms in young men's deadly spears.

Lord supreme of Olympia,                              [Str. 2]
25   you who rule far and wide, be unbegrudging
toward my words for all time, Father Zeus,
and while you keep this people safe from harm,
continue to guide straight the breeze of Xenophon's good
        fortune.
Accept as well the crown which, by the custom of
        the victory revel, he brings here from Pisa's plains,
30   being victorious at one time in both
        pentathlon and stade race, thus gaining
what never yet befell to mortal man before.


Two wreaths of parsley                                [Ant. 2]
were laid on him when he appeared
at Isthmian festivals, and Nemea offers no denial.
35   As for his father Thessalos, beside the streams
of Alpheos the glory that his feet have earned lies
        treasured up;
at Pytho he has honor, having won both stade and double
        stade race in
the compass of one sun, and then within
that very month, in rocky Athens,
        a swift-footed day
set three most lovely prizes round his hair;


40   and at the Hellotia seven times; but at            [Ep. 2]
        Poseidon's games established between two seas
longer songs will attend on him, together with
his father Ptoiodoros, and on Terpsias too, and Eritimos.
As for the excellence your family has displayed at Delphi
and in the pastures of the lion, I contend with many
45   about the full sum of their exploits, since indeed I know
        no way
to number with exactitude the pebbles of the sea.


In everything due measure                             [Str. 3]
applies; to observe the right degree is best.
I myself, sailing as a private citizen on a public mission
50   and singing of the craft of men born long ago
no less than of heroic deeds in warfare,

shall tell no lies concerning Corinth—neither Sisyphos,
    whose wiles were of surpassing shrewdness, like a
        god's,
nor yet Medeia, who against her father's will
    arranged a marriage for herself
and saved the Argo, ship and crew alike.

55      And then again, in fighting                  [Ant. 3]
      before the walls of Dardanos, they gained the
        reputation
of bringing battles to decision on both sides,
some striving hard with Atreus' dear sons
to carry Helen back, and others doing all they could
60      to ward that off. When Glaukos came from Lykia,
      the Danaans trembled. To them he
proclaimed with pride that in the city of
    Peirene were the kingship
and rich estate and palace of his father,

who once, because he yearned              [Ep. 3]
    to harness Pegasos, the snaky Gorgon's son,
endured long pain indeed beside the springs,
65      until the maiden Pallas brought to him
a golden bridle: dream then suddenly
was waking truth. She spoke thus: "Are you sleeping,
    royal scion of Aiolos?
Come, take this charm of horses
and, offering a white bull, reveal it to the One Who Tames,
    your father."

70      Her aegis gleaming darkly in the night,      [Str. 4]
      the Maiden said this much to him in sleep,
or so it seemed; and he sprang upright to his feet.
The marvel that lay by him he took up,
and gladly seeking out the local prophet,
75      he made known to the son of Koiranos the whole
      outcome of the affair, how on the altar of the goddess
he slept the night through at
    that expert's bidding, and how she herself,
daughter of Zeus whose spear is thunder, gave him

the spirit-taming gold.                                               [Ant. 4]
The seer urged him with all speed to obey
80      the dream and, having slaughtered a stout-footed bull
in honor of the Earthholder whose sway is wide,
forthwith to raise an altar to Athena of the Horses.
The power of the gods with ease brings to fulfillment
    things far beyond what one would swear to or expect.
Truly, the strong Bellerophon
    through eager striving made his capture,
85      stretching that gentle remedy about the jaw

of the winged horse; and mounting, he at once         [Ep. 4]
    began
    to play war games in brazen armor.
With him the hero later slew the Amazons,
from the chill hollows of the empty air
striking the host of women armed with bows,
90      and brought the fire-breathing Chimaira and the Solymoi
    to death.
About his fate I shall keep silent;
the other, though, in Zeus's ancient mangers on Olympos
    still finds shelter.

But I must not, while whirling javelins                [Str. 5]
on their straight course, impart such power to them
95      that in great numbers they fly past the mark.
For it is to the Muses on their splendid thrones
and to the Oligaithidai that I have come to offer willing
    aid.
Their victories at the Isthmus and at Nemea with few words
    I shall make known together, and the truth of what
      I say
will find its warrant in the sweet-tongued cry which, sixty
    times
100    in either place, was uttered under oath by noble heralds.

Their triumphs at Olympia                              [Ant. 5]
already, it would seem, have been recounted earlier;
of those to come I would speak clearly at that time.
For now, I have my hopes, but it is god that grants

105    the outcome. If their family's guardian spirit stays the course,
       to Zeus and Enyalios we shall hand this task
           for its accomplishment. Their victories beneath
               Parnassos' brow
       are six in number, but how many won at Argos and
           in Thebes, and those to which the altar of Lykaian Zeus
       will offer lordly witness in Arkadia;

       Pellene too, and Sikyon;                                    [Ep. 5]
           Megara and the well-fenced precinct of the Aiakidai;
110    Eleusis and resplendent Marathon;
       the cities, rich and lovely, under the high crest
       of Aitna, and Euboia—through the length and breadth
       of Hellas, if you search, you will find more than any eye
           could compass.
       Come now, with nimble feet swim clear.
115    O Zeus, Fulfiller, grant respect and sweet enjoyment of
           delights.

Xenophon's family, the Oligaithidai, were phenomenally successful in ath-
letic competition, amassing numerous victories not only in all four of the
major Panhellenic contests but also in a wide range of local games. The
double victory at Olympia that provided the occasion for this ode (won by
Xenophon in 464) was in itself an unprecedented achievement. In addition,
Xenophon's hometown of Corinth was one of the most prosperous and pow-
erful Greek city-states, with an illustrious legendary past. In order to deal
with this abundance of poetic material, Pindar methodically shifts the focus
of his attention back and forth between Xenophon's family and its achieve-
ments (1–3, 24–46, 93–115) and the many claims to fame of Corinth as a whole
(4–23, 47–92). The story that he chooses to tell about one particular Corinthian
hero, Bellerophon, is probably intended to have exemplary force: if man's
vaulting aspirations and ambitions (represented by Pegasos) can be mas-
tered and kept under tight control through the exercise of moderation or
"due measure" (represented by the golden bridle) and then directed toward
the proper objects, remarkable exploits become possible—as is evidenced
not only by Bellerophon himself but by Xenophon and the Oligaithidai as
well.

6–7 **Good Order, Justice, Peace** the three Horai (cf. 17); see Glossary.
14 **descendants of Aletes** the people of Corinth, of which Aletes, a
descendant of Herakles, was a legendary king.

18–22 Pindar here attributes three inventions to the Corinthians: the dithyramb (a kind of choral song dedicated to Dionysos); the bit and bridle; and the temple pediment, whose name in Greek (*aetoma*, from *aetos* "eagle") derives from its resemblance in shape to a pair of outstretched wings. The reference to the bit and bridle as an embodiment of "due measure" (*metron* in Greek) invites the paradigmatic interpretation of Bellerophon's taming of Pegasos (63–92) sketched in the introductory note.

29 **from Pisa's plains** i.e., from Olympia (see Glossary).

30 The **stade race** (*stadion*) was the length of the standard stadium (approximately two hundred meters), hence its name. On the **pentathlon** see note on Xenophanes 2. 2.

35–36 **beside the streams of Alpheos** i.e., at Olympia (see Glossary).

38 **in rocky Athens** i.e., at the festival known as the Great Panathenaia.

40 **Hellotia** an athletic festival held in Corinth, dedicated to Athena Hellotis. **Poseidon's games established between two seas** the Isthmian games, held on the Isthmus of Corinth, between the Corinthian and Saronic gulfs.

41–42 **Ptoiodoros, Terpsias, Eritimos** members of Xenophon's family. Ptoiodoros was apparently the father of Thessalos; precisely how the other two were related to Xenophon is not known.

44 **the pastures of the lion** Nemea (see Glossary).

47–48 To justify discontinuing the catalogue of the family's athletic triumphs the poet invokes the principle of "due measure" (*metron*) already alluded to in line 20. To carry on with praise at the present moment would be to fall into reprehensible excess—particularly since the poet has a responsibility not just to Xenophon and his family but to the Corinthian community at large (cf. **sailing as a private citizen on a public mission**, 49).

52 **Sisyphos** See Glossary, and cf. Alcaeus 3 and Theognis 16.

53 **Medeia** daughter of Aietes, king of Kolchis. When Jason and his shipmates on the **Argo** came to Kolchis in quest of the Golden Fleece, Medeia fell in love with him, assisted him with her magical powers, and eventually settled with him in Corinth.

56 **the walls of Dardanos** Troy (see Glossary). Not only were there Corinthians among the contingent of Greeks led to the Trojan War by Agamemnon (who was, with Menelaos, one of **Atreus' dear sons**, 58), but the Lykians, who fought as allies on the Trojan side, were under the command of a man of Corinthian descent, namely **Glaukos** (60), who was either Bellerophon's grandson (according to Homer) or his son (according to Pindar).

61 **Peirene** a spring in Corinth.

63 **Pegasos** See Glossary.

69 **the One Who Tames** Poseidon in his role as god of horses (see Glossary).

75 **the son of Koiranos** Polyidos, a Corinthian seer.

81 **the Earthholder** Poseidon (see Glossary).

87 **With him** i.e., with Pegasos. The killing of the **Amazons**, the **Chimaira**, and the **Solymoi** were all tasks set for Bellerophon by Iobates, king of Lykia (see Glossary under "Bellerophon"). The Amazons were a race of warrior women famed for their skill as archers; the Chimaira was a monster whose bodily form combined elements of lion, snake, and she-goat (*chimaira* in Greek); the Solymoi were a people indigenous to Lykia.

91 **About his fate** Despite Pindar's ostentatiously tactful silence on the point, his audience would have understood precisely what was being hinted at: when Bellerophon tried to join the gods by flying up to Olympos, he was thrown off by Pegasos and direly crippled in his fall to earth. In *Isthmian* 7. 44–48 Pindar cites this incident as a cautionary example of human over-reaching.

92 **the other** i.e., Pegasos.

97 **the Oligaithidai** See introductory note.

99–100 Victors at the games were proclaimed as such by heralds, who announced their names, the names of their fathers, and their cities (cf. *Pythian* 1. 32, *Pythian* 10. 9).

103–6 A suitably circumspect wish that the family may win further Olympian victories.

106 **Enyalios** another name for Ares. **beneath Parnassos' brow** i.e., at the Pythian games (see Glossary).

107 **the altar of Lykaian Zeus** Games sacred to Zeus were held on Mt. Lykaion in southwestern Arkadia.

109 **the well-fenced precinct of the Aiakidai** the island of Aigina (see Glossary under "Aiakidai"). Like **Eleusis** (a town in western Attika) and the other places listed in lines 107–12 (on which see Glossary), Aigina sponsored athletic competitions; cf. *Pythian* 8. 65–66 and 79.

# *Olympian* 14:

for Asopichos son of Kleodamos, from Orchomenos,
victor in the stade race

You who, claiming the waters of Kephissos as          [Str. 1]
    your own,
  dwell in wide pasture land that breeds fair colts,
  O queens of song and rich Orchomenos,
  Graces, who guard the Minyans' ancient stock,
5    listen, because I pray. Through you all pleasure and

all sweetness come to mortals,
whether a man be skilled, have beauty, or gain sudden
  glory.
For even the gods without the august Graces
marshal no dance
  or feast. Attendant upon all
10 activities in heaven, with their chairs set close beside
Pythian Apollo of the golden bow,
they revere the Olympian father's ever-flowing
  honor.

O queenly Aglaia, and you who cherish music,       [Str. 2]
Euphrosyne, daughters of the mightiest
15 of gods, now harken; and you, Thalia,
craver of music, look upon this band that dances with
  light step
in thanks for kindly luck. With Lydian tones and craft
  of words
I have come to sing Asopichos,
because his Minyan land is victorious at Olympia
20 through you. To the black-walled house
of Persephone now go,
    O Echo, bringing his father the resplendent news:
when you see Kleodamos, tell him that his son
in Pisa's valley of fair fame
has crowned with wings of victory his young hair.

Orchomenos, a town in northern Boiotia, was the site of an ancient cult of the Graces (Charites), embodiments of grace and charm who were mythologically represented as the daughters of Zeus and Eurynome. In this poem the celebration of Asopichos and his victory (in an event which the text, most unusually, does not specify) is cast in the form of a prayer to these divinities, addressed first collectively (1–12) and then individually (13–20).

1 **Kephissos** one of the chief rivers of Boiotia, a region of Greece renowned for the fertility of its soil.

4 **Minyans** the ancient inhabitants of Orchomenos (cf. 19).

7 This line specifies three "gifts" that are frequently associated with the Graces in Pindar's poetry: poetic skill, physical beauty, and victory in athletics.

13–15 **Aglaia, Euphrosyne, Thalia** The names of the individual Graces
mean respectively "splendor" or "glory," "cheerfulness," and "abun-
dance."
17 **Lydian tones** an allusion to a particular "mode" or style of Greek
music; cf. the "Aiolian mode" in *Olympian* 1. 101.
21 **Persephone** wife of Hades (see Glossary) and hence queen of the
Underworld; the victor's father Kleodamos is dead.
23 **in Pisa's valley** i.e., at Olympia (see Glossary).

## *Pythian* 1:

for Hieron son of Deinomenes, from Syracuse,
victor in the chariot race

O golden Lyre, possession of Apollo and the          [Str. 1]
   violet-haired
Muses that speaks on their behalf, to whom the dance step
   harkens
   as initiator of festivity,
and whose signals the singers obey
whenever you strike up the preludes that
   lead off the chorus with your throbbing notes—
5    you even quench the warlike thunderbolt
of ever-flowing fire; and as the eagle sleeps
   on Zeus's scepter, his swift wings
   relaxed and folded on each side,

the king of birds, you pour a black-faced cloud      [Ant. 1]
over his curving head to set
   a sweet seal on his eyelids: slumbering,
he undulates his supple back, held fast
10   by your impetuous spells. Indeed, even strong
   Ares, abandoning the rough
violence of spear points, cheers his heart
in utter quiet, while your shafts enchant the minds
   of other gods as well, thanks to the skill
   of Leto's son and the deep-girded Muses.

But those shut out from Zeus's love grow faint       [Ep. 1]
   with terror
on hearing the Pierian maidens' cry, both those on land

and in the irresistible sea,
15 and he who in dire Tartaros lies pinned, foe of the gods,
the hundred-headed Typhos. Once
he grew to strength within the famed Kilikian cave, but
now indeed
the sea-fenced cliffs by Kyme
and Sicily press down upon
his shaggy breast, confined beneath the pillar of the sky,
20 white-mantled Aitna, nurse year-long of biting snow.

Disgorged from its recesses, unapproachable fire       [Str. 2]
wells up in awesome purity. By day the rivers
pour forth a flood of smoke
tinged with a ruddy glow, but in the dark of night
a rolling crimson flame sends boulders plunging down
into the deep
sea's expanse with a roar and crash.
25 Such are the fountains of Hephaistos which that monster
sends up to terrify the world, a portent
wondrous to behold,
a wonder even to hear about from those at hand.

Beneath the heights and plain of dark-leaved       [Ant. 2]
Aitna
he is in chains, stretched on a bed that tears
and goads the whole length of his back.
May it, O Zeus, may it be possible to please you,
30 you who frequent this mountain, forefront of
a fertile land, which gives its name
to the neighboring city glorified by its renowned
founder when at the Pythian games the herald
proclaimed it to the crowd,
announcing Hieron as victor in

the chariot race. For sailors setting out upon a       [Ep. 2]
voyage,
the first of blessings is to have a favorable wind,
since it is likely, then, that in the end
35 they will hit on a smoother homeward voyage too. This
saying

gives reason to expect, in view of these successes,
that in the time to come the city will win glory from its
    crowns and horses
and have a name for sweet-voiced celebrations.
Lykian Phoibos, lord of Delos,
    you who love the Kastalian spring beneath Parnassos,
40    consent to take these hopes to heart and make the country
    strong in men.

For to the gods are owed all resources for mortal    [Str. 3]
    worth;
by them are skill and strength of hand and eloquence
    bestowed at birth. For me that man
is theme of eager praise, and I have hopes
not to launch, as it were, the bronze-tipped javelin
    outside the place of contest, whirling it in my hand,
45    yet still to cast it far and so outstrip my rivals.
May all of time continue thus to guide aright
    his fortunes and the granting of possessions,
    and offer too forgetfulness of troubles.

In truth, it may call up to mind in what fierce    [Ant. 3]
    battles
he stood firm with enduring heart, when he and his
    were gaining, at the gods' hands, honor
such as no Greek has ever culled
50    to be a lordly crown of wealth. Just now, indeed,
    after the fashion of a Philoktetes
he set out on campaign: constrained by necessity,
even one who was proud in spirit fawned on him as friend.
    They say that godlike heroes came
    to fetch from Lemnos, harried by his wound,

the son of Poias, wielder of the bow,    [Ep. 3]
who ravaged Priam's city and brought to an end
    the toils of the Danaans,
55    feeble in body as he walked, but such was fate.
So too for Hieron may god be a preserver
as time draws on, granting due measure of his heart's
    desires.

O Muse, beside Deinomenes as well sound forth a song,
I bid you, to reward the four-horse chariot:
   the joy is not a stranger's when a father wins.
60  Come then, for Aitna's king let us devise a loving hymn.

For him that city was established, built by Hieron   [Str. 4]
    to enjoy
god-crafted liberty according to the laws
   of Hyllos' code. The heirs of Pamphylos,
and those of the Herakleidai too,
though dwelling under Taÿgetos' steep slopes, choose
    always
   to remain within Aigimios' ordinances,
65  Dorians as they are. By fortune blessed, they seized
    Amyklai,
sallying forth from Pindos to become the neighbors,
   high in renown, of the white-horsed Tyndarids,
   their fighting-spirit blooming into fame.

O Zeus, Fulfiller, grant that such a lot be lastingly   [Ant. 4]
    assigned,
beside the river Amenas, to citizens and kings,
   to be a subject of men's truthful speech.
With your aid, certainly, a leader,
70  giving instructions to his son, may through the esteem he
    shows them guide
   his people toward the harmonies of civic peace.
I beg you, son of Kronos, nod consent that now
the Phoenicians and the Etruscans with their battle cry
   may stay at home in meekness, having seen
   how arrogance brought groans upon their fleet at
    Kyme,

and what they suffered when the Syracusan ruler   [Ep. 4]
    beat them down
on their swift-moving ships and hurled
   into the sea the flower of their youth,
75  drawing Hellas out from under slavery's burden. I shall
    win
from Salamis the Athenians' gratitude

as my reward, the Spartans' from the battle fought before
    Kithairon,
struggles in which bow-wielding Medes grew weary.
But by the well-watered banks of Himeras
    it is Deinomenes' sons to whom I render song as tribute,
80    earned when their valor brought the foe to utter weariness.

If in your speech you keep due measure, drawing    [Str. 5]
    many strands
together in brief compass, people's censure will be less,
    for over-fullness blunts
with its relentlessness the quickest expectations,
and citizens are prone to secret heavy-heartedness
    above all when they hear of others' blessings.
85    But nonetheless, since envy is superior to pity,
pass over nothing that is noble. Steer your people
    with justice as your rudder; forge
    your tongue upon the anvil of plain truth:

the slightest spark struck off moves weightily,    [Ant. 5]
coming from you. Your stewardship is great in range, and
    many
    bear trusty witness to your acts of either sort.
In the full flower of your generous impulses stand firm;
90    if you like to take pleasure always in the things you hear
    about yourself, do not grow overweary of expenditures.
Like a man at the helm, let out the sail
free to the wind. Do not be tricked, my friend,
    by the base claims of avarice;
    the vaunting glory that trails after mortals

alone lays bare the lives of the departed    [Ep. 5]
to chroniclers and poets alike. The just benevolence
    of Croesus does not waste and die,
95    while cruel Phalaris, who burned men in a brazen bull,
is everywhere weighed down by hateful speech;
nor do lyres resounding in the hall receive him
in gentle fellowship with boys' soft voices.
Good fortune is the first of prizes;
    good report takes second place; but he who lights on both,

100      and grasps them firmly, has received the loftiest of crowns.

On Hieron, tyrant of Syracuse, see Glossary. In 475 Hieron founded a new
city not far from Mt. Aitna (the highest mountain in Sicily and—both then
and now—an active volcano); as ruler of this city, itself named Aitna, he
installed his son Deinomenes. When, five years later, Hieron won a chariot
victory at the Pythian games, he had himself announced to the spectators not
as Hieron of Syracuse but as Hieron of Aitna, thus doing honor to the new
city. Although that victory provided the occasion for *Pythian 1*, the poem is
chiefly concerned with the triumph of the forces of order and civilization
over the forces of disorder and barbarism. This theme first appears in the
contrasting descriptions of festivity and peace on Olympos (1–12) and the
violence of Typhos, the monstrous "foe of the gods" who is kept imprisoned
under Mt. Aitna by the superior power of Zeus (15–28), and then reemerges
in the portrayal of Hieron as city founder and guarantor of political stability
(61–70) and the key role he played in decisively defeating "barbarian" (i.e.
non-Greek) enemies in the battles of Kyme and Himera (71–80).


  1–2 **O golden Lyre** The lyre was a typical accompaniment for perfor-
mances of dance and song in ancient Greece. Through this hymnal
invocation, however, Pindar seems to cast the lyre in the role of a cosmic
power, source of harmony and peace on Olympos and (by implication) on
earth as well. It is the **possession of Apollo and the violet-haired Muses**
because both he and they are intimately associated with poetry and song;
it **speaks on their behalf** in the sense that it joins with them in praising the
praiseworthy and reprobating those who (like Typhon) are "shut out from
Zeus's love."
14 **the Pierian maidens** the Muses (see Glossary).
18 **Kyme** the earliest Greek colony in Italy, near present-day Naples and
Mt. Vesuvius, which like Mt. Aitna was (and still is) an active volcano. The
vulcanism of both mountains is thus implicitly attributed to the restless
torment of the imprisoned Typhos.
25 **Hephaistos** god of fire.
31 **the neighboring city** Aitna; see introductory note.
39–40 The god Apollo (**Phoibos**) had strong associations with the region
of **Lykia** in Asia Minor, with the island of **Delos** (his reputed birthplace),
and with Delphi on the southern slopes of Mt. **Parnassos**. Not far from
Apollo's temple at Delphi was the **Kastalian spring**, whose waters were
sacred to the god.
42 **that man** i.e., Hieron. Through the image of the javelin throw that
follows the poet expresses his desire to outdo other (real or potential)
encomiasts in his praise of Hieron (45) while successfully avoiding any
irrelevance or excess (44).

48 **he and his** Hieron had three brothers, Gelon, Polyzelos, and Thrasyboulos.

50 **Philoktetes** a Greek warrior, **the son of Poias** (53). When the Greek army, on its way to Troy, stopped off on the island of **Lemnos**, Philoktetes was bitten on the foot by a snake and subsequently abandoned there by his friends, who found his agonized cries and the stench of the wound intolerable. Ten years later, however, the Greeks were compelled to send for Philoktetes when it became clear that Troy (**Priam's city**, 54) could not be captured without the assistance of his bow. According to an ancient commentator, Hieron likewise endured a physical affliction (bladder stones) while out on military campaign.

54 **the Danaans** i.e., the Greeks.

60 **Aitna's king** Hieron's son Deinomenes; see introductory note.

62–66 **Hyllos** was the eldest of the sons of Herakles (the **Herakleidai**) and the ancestor of the Dorian tribe known as the Hylleis. **Aigimios** was a friend of Hyllos and, through his sons **Pamphylos** and Dymas, the ancestor of the two other Dorian tribes, the Pamphyloi and the Dymanes. Moving from their original home near Mt. **Pindos** in northern Greece, the Dorians entered the Peloponnesos and seized control of the town of **Amyklai**, just east of Mt. **Taÿgetos** near what later became Sparta. Syracuse itself was originally founded by Corinth, another Dorian city.

66 **Tyndarids** Kastor and Polydeukes; see Glossary under "Tyndaridai."

68 **Amenas** a small river that flowed through the city of Aitna.

71–75 In 474 B.C. Hieron had defeated an alliance of **Etruscans** and Carthaginians (who were of **Phoenician** origin) in a sea battle off the coast of **Kyme** (cf. 18).

79 **Deinomenes' sons** Hieron and his older brother Gelon, who defeated the Carthaginians in a battle fought near the river **Himeras** in 480. Pindar associates that battle with the victories won in the same year by the Greek alliance against the invading Persians (often referred to as **Medes**) off the island of **Salamis** and in 479 at Plataia, near Mt. **Kithairon** in Boiotia.

80–86 The poet first gives reasons why it might be expedient to curtail further praise of Hieron, then overrides those objections by reflecting that it is better to be envied for one's advantages and achievements than to be pitied for one's insignificance.

86–94 Various admirable qualities in Hieron's style of ruling are praised under the form of a series of exhortations; the implication in each case is that he should *keep on* acting in the prescribed manner.

94–98 On **Croesus**, see Glossary and cf. Bacchylides, Ode 3. 23–62.

**Phalaris** was a tyrant of Akragas (see Glossary) during the sixth century B.C.; notorious for his cruelty, he is said to have put people to death by roasting them in a metal bull so constructed that the screams of the victims issued from its mouth.

99–100 With the sentiment cf. *Isthmian* 5. 12–13.

## *Pythian* 3:

### for Hieron of Syracuse

Would that Chiron, Philyra's son—                    [Str. 1]
  if it is right that from my lips
    this common prayer should fall—
he that is dead and gone, were living still,
offspring of sky-born Kronos, wide in stewardship,
    and ruling in the glens of Pelion, that beast of wood and
      field
5    whose mind was warm toward mankind, as when once
he reared the craftsman of mild remedies
    for pain, Asklepios, whose hero's hands
warded from weary bodies all disease.

Before the daughter of knightly Phlegyas              [Ant. 1]
  could bring him with Eleithyia's aid to birth,
    she was laid low by golden
10    arrows loosed from the bow of Artemis
and sank from bedchamber to Hades' house,
    Apollo so contriving it: the wrath of Zeus's children
proves far from futile. She, adrift from sense,
made light of it and welcomed
    a second union secret from her father,
though she had lain before with Phoibos of the unshorn
      locks

15    and bore the god's pure seed within her.            [Ep. 1]
She would not wait to join the bridal feast
nor hear the clear full sound of marriage hymns, such as
young girls, age-mates and friends, delight
to sing at dusk with soft endearments. No, instead
20    she lusted for what was distant. Many have done so.
There is a kind among human beings, random, rash,
who scorn all things at hand and gaze afar,
stalking illusions out of empty hopes.

Such dire infatuation seized the will                 [Str. 2]
25    of Koronis in her lovely robes:
    she bedded with a stranger

who came from Arkadia,
but not unnoticed by one watcher: Loxias,
    the lord of Pytho rich in sacred sheep, heard news
        within his temple,
persuaded into judgment by the surest confidant,
his all-knowing mind.
    He lays no hand on lies, and neither god
30   nor mortal man can cheat his vigilance in act or thought.

So now, knowing that Ischys, Eilatos' son,        [Ant. 2]
lay as a stranger in her arms, an act of impious deceit,
    he sent his sister
raging with irresistible might
to Lakereia, since it was there beside the shores of Boibias
    that the girl had her home. A hostile power,
35   swerving to evil, laid her low, and neighbors too
reaped woe, and with her many died.
    So, on a mountain, from one seed of flame,
fire leaps upon wide woods and pulls them down to dust.

But when on towering logs her kinsmen had        [Ep. 2]
laid the dead girl, and around her licked and roared
40   Hephaistos' hungry brightness, then Apollo said: "No
        longer
shall I endure at heart to make my son's destruction
a piteous incidental to his mother's heavy doom."
Thus he spoke, and within one stride was there, and from
    the corpse
ripped out the infant, standing in parted flame.
45   He took the child to the Centaur in Magnesia, to be taught
the art of healing mankind's many ills.

Some came afflicted by spontaneous sores,        [Str. 3]
some with limbs gashed by hoary
    bronze, or bruised
by stones slung from a distance;
50   others, their frames despoiled by summer's fire
    or wintry cold. Releasing each from his own ailment,
he drew them into ease, attending some with smooth
incantatory words, or gentle potions;

others he bound with poultices
or with the knife set upright on their feet.

But greed holds even the rarest skill in bondage.    [Ant. 3]
55   Turned by a lordly wage,
    the gleam of gold in hand,
he dared to fetch from death
a man already captive. Zeus then struck down both,
    snatched from the breast of each his very breath
with instant speed: the thunderbolt flashed forth and
    brought down havoc.
We must, with mortal minds,
    seek from the gods such things as are befitting,
60   knowing what lies before our feet, what destiny is ours.

Do not, my soul, pursue the life of gods     [Ep. 3]
with longing, but exhaust all practicable means.
Yes, if wise Chiron dwelt still in his cave, and if
the honeyed discourse of my songs had power
65   to charm his will, long since I would have won from him a
    healer
for worthy men who now live prey to feverish ills—
some son of Leto's son or of his father—
and would have sailed, cutting the Ionian sea,
to Arethousa's spring and Aitna's lord, my host and friend,

70   who in his rule at Syracuse is mild to townsfolk,     [Str. 4]
bears the nobility no grudge, and is revered
    by strangers as a father.
If to him I had brought the twofold joy
of golden health and a revel song
    to cast a brightness on the Pythian wreaths
which the triumphant Pherenikos garnered once at Kirrha,
75   I would, I say, have dawned
    upon him as a light outblazing any star
in heaven, passing over that deep sea.

But as it is, my wish is first to offer prayer     [Ant. 4]
to the great Mother, whom by night before my door
    girls often celebrate, with Pan,

in dance and song, that reverend goddess.
80      Next, Hieron, since you know how from old tales to glean
            essential truth, you have learned this lesson well:
        the gods apportion mortal kind two griefs for every good.
        Children and fools cannot
            endure such odds with grace or steadfastness;
        the noble do so, turning the fair side ever outward.


        Yours is a happy lot: upon a king,                      [Ep. 4]
85      leader of hosts, great Destiny casts smiles
        as on no other man. Yet life without sharp change
        was granted neither Peleus, Aiakos' son,
        nor godlike Kadmos, though they say these two
        prospered beyond all mortals, having heard the hymns
90      with which, upon the mountain and in seven-gated
            Thebes,
        the Muses blessed them when the one wed lovely-eyed
            Harmonia,
        the other, glorious Thetis, daughter of the deep-sea sage.


        The gods joined both in feasting;                       [Str. 5]
        they saw the royal sons of Kronos
            throned in gold, and won
95      from each a bridal gift. So Zeus, through grace
        releasing them from former anguish, set
            their hearts upright in cheer. In time, however,
        the bitter sufferings of three daughters wrenched from
            Kadmos
        a share of happiness; and yet
            the fourth, Thyone of white arms,
        drew by her loveliness great Zeus, the king and father, to
            her bed.


100     And Peleus' child, the only one to whom immortal   [Ant. 5]
        Thetis gave birth in Phthia, yielding up
            his life in war to bow shot,
        roused lamentation from the Greeks
        about his blazing pyre. If a man holds in his mind
            the truth's straight course, he will, when kindly handled
                by

the Blessed, be content. The winds at different times veer
from above
105 now this way and now that.
For men, prosperity does not long remain
secure, when it attends them weighted with abundance.

Small amid small things, great among things great     [Ep. 5]
my state shall be. Whatever momentary shifts
fortune may bring me I shall honor to the limits of my
means.
110 If heaven should hand me wealth and its delight,
I hope to earn through aftertime high fame.
Of Nestor and Lykian Sarpedon, names still on all
tongues,
only resounding verses shaped by skillful craftsmen give
us knowledge. Excellence confirmed in song
115 endures; to few is such achievement easy.

On Hieron, tyrant of Syracuse, see Glossary. Although this ode alludes in
passing to one or more victories won by Hieron's racehorse Pherenikos in the
Pythian games (73–74), it is not properly speaking an epinician but rather a
poem of consolation; in it Pindar seeks to balance Hieron's inescapable mor-
tality against the exceptional advantages of his rank, power, and wealth,
drawing particular attention to the opportunity which they afford him of
winning a measure of immortality through posthumous fame. Scholars have
generally assumed that Hieron was suffering from some serious illness at the
time the ode was composed, and such an assumption is in accordance with
the great emphasis that is laid on both the power and the limitations of medi-
cine through the figure of Asklepios. The lesson that both Asklepios and his
mother Koronis embody is that human beings must be content with what-
ever good fortune falls to their lot and not indulge themselves in unattain-
able hopes.

1 **Chiron** See Glossary. The poet's wish that Chiron were still alive is
the first element in an elaborate pattern of concentric "rings" through
which fully two thirds of the ode is structured: (A) "If only Chiron were
still alive . . ." (1–5); (B) Chiron rears Asklepios to be a physician (5–7); (C)
Asklepios' birth (8–9); (D) Koronis is punished by Artemis and Apollo (9–
12); (E) Koronis' sin (12–20); (F) the central "moral" of the story (21–23);
(E') Koronis' sin (24–26); (D') Koronis is punished by Apollo and Artemis
(27–37); (C') Asklepios' birth (38–44); (B') Asklepios is reared as a physician
by Chiron (45–53), then goes too far and is punished by Zeus (54–58),

leading to a restatement of the "moral" (59–62); (A') "If only Chiron were
still alive, then . . ." (63–76). Other (less elaborate) examples of "concentric
ring-form" can be found in Bacchylides, Odes 11 and 13, and in Alcaeus 3.

6 **Asklepios** the greatest physician of Greek legend, son of Apollo by a
mortal woman named Koronis (cf. Theognis 13. 4).

8 **the daughter of knightly Phlegyas** i.e., Koronis. Phlegyas was a
legendary king of the Lapiths in Thessaly.

9 **Eleithyia** goddess of childbirth.

11 **the wrath of Zeus's children** Koronis provoked this anger by having
a secret affair with an Arkadian named **Ischys** (31) while she was pregnant
with Apollo's child, thus showing contempt both for the god (13–15) and
for the due forms of marriage (16–19).

27 **Loxias** another name for Apollo (see Glossary).

28 **the surest confidant** Pindar may be implicitly correcting an earlier
version of the story (told by Hesiod) whereby Apollo received the news of
Koronis' affair from a raven.

34 **Lakereia, Boibias** a town and a lake in eastern Thessaly.

40 **Hephaistos' hungry brightness** i.e., fire (see Glossary).

45 **the Centaur** i.e., Chiron. He lived on Mt. Pelion, in the region of
eastern Thessaly known as **Magnesia**.

67 **some son of Leto's son or of his father** i.e., either another Asklepios
(as the son of Leto's son Apollo) or another Apollo (himself the son of
Zeus). Among his many other functions, Apollo was a god of medicine.

68 **the Ionian sea** the body of water that separates Greece from southern
Italy and Sicily.

69 **Arethousa** a spring in Syracuse. **Aitna's lord** i.e., Hieron, who
founded the city of Aitna and named it after the nearby volcano (cf.
*Pythian* 1. 30ff with note). On Pindar's description of Hieron as **my host
and friend**, see note on *Olympian* 1. 103.

74 **Pherenikos** Hieron's famous race-horse (cf. *Olympian* 1. 18–22 and
Bacchylides, Ode 5. 37–49), who had evidently won one or more victories
at the Pythian games (see **Kirrha** in Glossary) some years before the
composition of this ode.

78 **the great Mother** a fertility goddess of Phrygian origin, often
identified with Rhea or Kybele and associated with the god Pan.

81 This line apparently alludes to *Iliad* 24. 527–33. Although the Homeric
passage is usually interpreted to mean that in allotting individual human
fortunes Zeus draws upon two large jars, one full of bad things and the
other of good things, the phrasing of the original Greek also permits one to
understand that there are *two* jars of bad things, and it is this more
pessimistic ratio that Pindar adopts here.

86–103 On **Peleus** and **Kadmos** as paradigms of the greatest good
fortune attainable by human beings, see Glossary and cf. *Olympian* 2. 78.

90 **the mountain** Pelion, where Peleus and Thetis were married.

92 **the deep-sea sage** Nereus (see Glossary).

97–99 **three daughters** See under "Kadmos" in Glossary, and cf. *Olympian* 2. 22–30. **Thyone** was another name for Semele, who became the mother of Dionysos by Zeus (see Glossary).

101 **yielding up his life in war** Achilles' death was brought about by the combined efforts of Paris and Apollo.

110 **If heaven should hand me wealth** Pindar is probably to be understood here as speaking not so much about himself personally as about wealthy men like Hieron, whose willingness to spend money on the commissioning of poetry he is commending. Greek poets not infrequently use the first person ("I") to articulate and endorse general truths.

112 **Nestor and Lykian Sarpedon** What they seem to have in common (aside from both playing roles in the *Iliad*) is preternatural longevity; see Glossary.

# Pythian 8:

## for Aristomenes son of Xenarkes, from Aigina, victim in wrestling

You, Tranquillity of kindly mind, who as          [Str. 1]
daughter of Righteousness make cities great,
who hold the highest keys
of counsel and of war,

5       accept from Aristomenes the honor of his Pythian triumph.
For you are skilled in gentle acts, performing and
                experiencing them alike
with an unerring sense of time and circumstance.

Then too, whenever anyone drives home          [Ant. 1]
implacable resentment in his heart,

10      you sternly go forth to oppose
the might of enemies and plunge
their arrogance beneath the flood. Of this Porphyrion had
                no understanding
when his transgressions roused your anger. Gain gives
                greatest joy
if it is carried off from the home of one who is willing;

15   ·   but violence, in time, brings even the loudest          [Ep. 1]
                boaster down.

Kilikian Typhos with his hundred heads did not escape
    her power,
nor yet the king of Giants; they were mastered by the
    thunderbolt
and by the arrows of Apollo, who with kindly spirit
received Xenarkes' son from Kirrha, with a crown
20    of laurel from Parnassos and a Dorian revel-band.

Not distant from the Graces has                           [Str. 2]
this righteous city's portion fallen,
island of the Aiakidai renowned
for deeds of prowess. Glory without blemish
25    is hers from earliest times, extolled in song for many
successes at the games, and as a nurse of heroes
supreme in the quick shifts of battle;

but also for her men she is distinguished.              [Ant. 2]
And yet I have no leisure to rehearse
30    the whole of the long story
with lyre and gentle voice,
lest chafing tedium follow. My most urgent duty
is owed to you, son: let this newest glory
go forth on wings furnished by my great art.

35    For as a wrestler following in the footsteps of your   [Ep. 2]
    mother's brothers,
you do not shame Theognetos at Olympia
nor yet the bold-limbed Isthmian triumph of
    Kleitomachos.
And adding honor to the Meidylid clan, you earn the very
    praise
which Oïkles' offspring once pronounced in riddling
    form,
40    seeing the sons steadfast in war beside Thebes' seven
    gates,

that time when the Descendants came                     [Str. 3]
from Argos on a second expedition.
Thus he spoke as they struggled:
"By nature does the noble spirit passed

45     from fathers to their sons stand forth to view. I clearly see
the spotted serpent on Alkmaion's blazing shield,
there where he fights as first at Kadmos' gates.

But he who suffered earlier pain,          [Ant. 3]
Adrastos, now is gripped by news
50     of better omens to console
his hero's heart; yet touching his own household
he shall fare otherwise. For he alone of the Danaan army
shall gather up the bones of his dead son, and come
by the gods' grace with host unharmed

55     to Abas' spacious streets." Such were the things    [Ep. 3]
that Amphiaraos uttered. I myself am also glad
to pelt Alkmaion with wreaths, and sprinkle him with
         song as well,
because as neighbor and as guardian of my goods
he met me on my way to the storied navel of the earth
60     and laid his hands on prophecy by means of inborn arts.

But you, Far-Shooter, governing          [Str. 4]
your famous shrine that welcomes all
in Pytho's hollow valley,
the greatest of enjoyments you bestowed
65     in that place, but at home you had before dealt out,
amid your festival, a longed-for prize in the pentathlon.
O lord, I pray that with a willing mind

I may observe the claims of fittingness      [Ant. 4]
in each thing as I come to it.
70     Beside the revel-band with its sweet singing
stands Righteousness; I ask, then, that the gods
give unbegrudged regard, Xenarkes, to your family's
         fortunes.
If anyone acquires good things without long toil,
he seems to most a wise man among fools,

75     well armed in life by shrewdness of contrivance.    [Ep. 4]
But such a state is not within men's grasp; divinity
         provides it,

placing at different times one man aloft, another in
      subjection.
Let measure guide you, entering games. At Megara a prize
      is yours,
and on the plain of Marathon, and in Hera's contest on
      your native soil
80    three times you triumphed, Aristomenes, by mastery in
      action.

And from above you fell upon                    [Str. 5]
four bodies with inimical intent.
To them no glad return like yours
was meted out in Pytho's festival,
85    nor, as they came home to their mothers, did sweet
      laughter on all sides
arouse delight; but down back alleys, out of enemies' reach,
they skulk along, deep-bitten by calamity.

He who has newly won some noble object          [Ant. 5]
and feels himself buoyed up in luxury
90    soars in his kindled hopes
on winged deeds of manhood, his ambitions
outstripping mere concern for wealth. With suddenness,
      for mortals,
pleasure springs up and grows, but so it also falls to earth,
shaken by purposes of adverse power.

95    Beings defined by each new day! What is a man?   [Ep. 5]
      What is he not?
      A shadow's dream
is humankind. But when the gleam that Zeus dispenses
      comes,
then brilliant light rests over men, and life is kindly.
Aigina, our dear mother, on a course of freedom
conduct this city with the aid of Zeus and kingly Aiakos,
100   Peleus and brave Telamon, and with Achilles.

Aristomenes' wrestling victory in the Pythian games was won in 446, which
means that this is the latest of Pindar's odes that can be reliably dated.
Uniquely among Pindar's odes for Aiginetans, the central myth does not

concern Aigina's own lineage of heroes, the Aiakidai (23), but is drawn instead from the cycle of Theban legends. Introduced to illustrate the principle of inherited excellence that is manifest in Aristomenes as heir to his maternal uncles' wrestling prowess (35ff), the speech of Amphiaraos soon turns to the unpredictable alternation of joy and sorrow that governs human life, thus anticipating the general reflections on vicissitude so memorably expressed in the ode's final triad. Some scholars have posited a connection between the somber tone of those lines and Aigina's political situation in 446, which was one of forced subservience to the expanding Athenian empire.

1 **Tranquillity** The Greek word is *hesychia*, used elsewhere by Pindar (e.g., *Pythian* 1.70) to denote civic peace (i.e. the absence of factional conflict within a city-state). Here Hesychia is personified as the daughter of Dike ("righteousness" or "justice"), one of the three Horai (cf. *Olympian* 13. 6–8).

12 **Porphyrion** one of the Giants (on whom see Glossary); Pindar makes him their king (cf. 17).

16 **Typhos** See Glossary, and cf. *Pythian* 1. 15–28. **her power** i.e., that of Tranquillity.

19–20 **Kirrha, Parnassos** See Glossary.

21 **Not distant from the Graces** i.e., not uncelebrated in song.

23 **the Aiakidai** See Glossary; they were one of the most illustrious families of Greek legend and one of Aigina's chief claims to fame.

33 **this newest glory** i.e., Aristomenes' current victory.

38 **the Meidylid clan** the Aiginetan clan to which Aristomenes and his family belonged.

39 **Oïkles' offspring** the prophet Amphiaraos (see Glossary).

40–41 **the sons, the Descendants** For the story of the Epigonoi ("Descendants") and their expedition against Thebes, see Glossary under "Adrastos."

46 **Alkmaion** The son of Amphiaraos.

47 **Kadmos' gates** i.e., the gates of Thebes, of which Kadmos (see Glossary) was the legendary founder.

48 **earlier pain** i.e., the defeat of the so-called Seven against Thebes, of whom Adrastos (see Glossary) was the commander in chief.

53 **his dead son** Aigialeus, the only one of the Epigonoi to die in the attack on Thebes.

55 **to Abas' spacious streets** i.e., to Argos, of which Abas was an early king.

59 **navel of the earth** Delphi, believed to be the center of the world.

61 **Far-Shooter** Apollo, as god of archery.

64 **the greatest of enjoyments** i.e., Aristomenes' victory in the Pythian games.

65–66 **at home . . . amid your festival** Evidently on some earlier occasion
Aristomenes had been victorious at the Delphinia, an Aiginetan festival
dedicated to Apollo and his sister Artemis ("your" is plural in the Greek).
On the **pentathlon** see note on Xenophanes 2. 2.

78–79 **Megara, Marathon** See Glossary.

79 **Hera's contest** According to an ancient commentator, the Aiginetans
had modelled this athletic festival on the Argive Heraia; cf. *Nemean* 10. 23ff
with note.

81–82 **you fell upon four bodies** Apparently Aristomenes had to defeat
four competitors in successive bouts in order to win his victory.

95 **Beings defined by each new day!** Cf. Archilochus 28 and Stesichorus
6. 207–8 for the idea that the circumstances and attitudes of human beings
vary day by day according to the vicissitudes of fortune.

98 **on a course of freedom** a possible allusion to hopes that Aigina might
regain her independence from Athenian domination.

## *Pythian* 10:

for Hippokleas son of Phrikias, from Thessaly,
victor in the boys' double stade race

Happy is Lakedaimon,                                                            [Str. 1]
blessed is Thessaly; from a single father, Herakles
the best of warriors, derives the race that rules
    them both.
Why do I utter vaunts inopportunely? Rather, it
    is Pytho
and Pelinnaion that summon me,
5    as do Aleuas' sons, who wish to bring to Hippokleas
a victory-song rung out by men's clear voices.

For he has tasted contests,                                                    [Ant. 1]
and to the crowd of those who live nearby, the glen
    beneath Parnassos
has heralded his name, supreme in the boys' double
    stade race.
10    Apollo, for mankind the end, like the beginning,
    grows
to sweetness when divinity impels.
Doubtless your counsels aided him in this achievement;
then too, by inborn nature he has trodden in the footsteps
    of his father,

who triumphed twice at Olympia, running in the   [Ep. 1]
    arms
that bear the brunt of Ares' wars;
15    likewise the games held under Kirrha's cliffs, deep in the
    meadow,
gave mastery to Phrikias' swift feet.
May destiny in later days as well
attend them so that wealth blooms forth in lordliness.

Of the delights in Hellas    [Str. 2]
20    having won no small portion, may they meet, from
    heaven,
no grudging shifts of fortune: may the gods be
untroubled at heart. Prosperity and praise in song
    fall, by the judgment of the wise, to such a man,
whose mastery in hand or speed of foot
awards the greatest prizes to his strength and daring,

25    and who, still living, sees    [Ant. 2]
his young son fittingly attain to Pythian crowns.
Never to brazen heaven can he climb;
but all such splendors as our mortal kind
    lays hands upon are his, gained at the utmost end
of voyaging. By ship nor yet on foot can you discover
30    that wondrous road that leads to where the Hyperboreans
    gather.

With them prince Perseus feasted once,    [Ep. 2]
when, coming to their halls,
he found them offering hecatombs of asses to the god,
a splendid sacrifice. Their festivals and hymns of
    praise
35    always give special pleasure to Apollo,
who laughs to see the rampant uproar of the beasts.

The Muse is not absent from the country,    [Str. 3]
given their ways of life; for everywhere girls' choruses
whirl to the ringing cry of lyres and pipes,
40    and banqueters, their hair bound up
    with golden laurel, revel joyfully.

Neither diseases nor the wretchedness of old age taints
that holy race; apart from toils and battles

they dwell, beyond the reach                                    [Ant. 3]
of Retribution's stern exactions. Drawing breath with
    daring heart,
45    the son of Danaë came there once, led by Athena,
to join the throng of blessed men. He slew
    the Gorgon, and that head whose locks
were writhing snakes he brought back to the islanders
to be their stony death. To me no marvel

that gods bring to fulfillment ever seems                       [Ep. 3]
50    unworthy of belief.
Let go the oar, drop anchor quickly from the prow
to grip the bottom and stave off the rocky reef:
the choicest kind of victory song
darts like a bee from one theme to another.

55    It is my hope, as Ephyraians                            [Str. 4]
pour forth my sweet voice by Peneios' banks,
to make Hippokleas, by means of song, still more
an object of admiration for his crowns
    among age-mates and elders,
a favorite of unmarried girls as well. Indeed,
60    different desires excite the hearts of different people.

Whatever each man strives for,                                  [Ant. 4]
should he attain it, his immediate thought affords
    delight;
but things a year from now no token can foretell.
I place trust in the kindly hospitality of Thorax,
    who, toiling in his zeal on my behalf,
65    has yoked this four-horse chariot of the Pierian Muses,
with each of us the other's willing friend and guide.

To one who tests it on the touchstone, gold shows            [Ep. 4]
    forth,
as does an upright mind.
His worthy brothers also we shall praise, because

70     they raise on high the Thessalian polity
       and make it greater. In the hands of nobles lies,
       father to son, the careful piloting of cities.

This is the earliest of Pindar's extant odes, composed in 498 when the poet
was twenty years old. It was apparently commissioned not by the young
victor's father but by a certain Thorax (64–66), who belonged to one of
Thessaly's most important and powerful dynastic families, the Aleuadai or
"sons of Aleuas" (5). The central portion of the ode (31–46) concerns a visit by
the hero Perseus to the land of the Hyperboreans, a mythical people, beloved
by Apollo, who lived "beyond the north wind" (the literal meaning of their
name). The picture of these "blessed men" (46) engaged in continual merri-
ment and celebration may be intended to form an idealized background for
and parallel to the festivities occasioned in "blessed Thessaly" (2) by
Hippokleas' victory at the games of Apollo.

1–3 The ruling dynasties of both **Lakedaimon** (Sparta) and **Thessaly**
claimed to be descended from **Herakles**.

4 **Pytho and Pelinnaion** respectively, the place where Hippokleas won
his victory (also known as Delphi) and the town in west-central Thessaly
that was his home (also known as Pelinna).

5 **Aleuas' sons** See introductory note.

8 **the glen beneath Parnassos** i.e., Delphi (see Glossary).

9 **double stade race** approximately four hundred meters in length; it
was known as the *diaulos* in Greek.

12 **his father** Phrikias (16), whose two victories at Olympia were won in
the race in armor, in which contestants wore helmets and greaves and
carried heavy shields.

15 **under Kirrha's cliffs** i.e., in the Pythian Games (see Glossary).

19 **the delights in Hellas** i.e., victories in the various athletic festivals of
the Greek world.

30 **the Hyperboreans** See introductory note.

45–48 The **son of Danaë** is Perseus, the **Gorgon** is Medousa, and **the
islanders** are the people of Seriphos; see Glossary under "Perseus" and
"Medousa" for the story.

55 **Ephyraians** Ephyra (also known as Krannon) was a town in the same
general area of Thessaly as Pelinna. The **Peneios** was the chief river of
Thessaly.

64 **the kindly hospitality of Thorax** On Thorax, see introductory note; on
the reference to hospitality, see note on *Olympian* 1. 103.

65 **this four-horse chariot of the Pierian Muses** i.e., the present ode,
which Thorax appears to have commissioned from the poet on behalf of
Hippokleas.

## *Nemean* 5:

for Pytheas son of Lampon, from Aigina,
victor in the pankration

I am no statue-maker, fashioning images                    [Str. 1]
    that stand in idleness and do not budge
beyond their bases. No!
    On every cargo boat and skiff, sweet song,
go forth from Aigina, spreading wide the news
that Lampon's son, broad-sinewed Pytheas,
5   has won at Nemea the pankratiasts' crown,
not yet revealing on his cheeks
    the darkening bloom that summer's prime begets;

and that to spearman heroes sprung from Zeus               [Ant. 1]
    and Kronos and the golden Nereids,
the stock of Aiakos, he has brought glory's gift,
    as well as to their mother city, land endeared to
        strangers,
which once they prayed would flourish in renown
10  of men and ships, when, standing by the altar of Hellenian
        Zeus,
they stretched their hands to heaven all together,
Endeïs' true-born sons
    and Phokos, mighty prince

whom divine Psamatheia bore where breakers                 [Ep. 1]
    strike the sand.
I shrink from speaking of a deed
    portentous and not justly hazarded,
15  how they forsook the fair-famed island,
    and what divinity it was that drove
such valiant warriors from Oinone.
    I shall stand still: not every truth is better
for showing the strict lineaments of its face,
and often silence is the skill
    that men do best to observe.

But if prosperity or strength of hand or iron war          [Str. 2]
    is set as theme for praise, prepare the ground,

20       and from this spot I'll leap
                great lengths: impulsive nimbleness is in my knees,
         and eagles wing their way beyond the sea.
         Even for such as those the Muses sang on Pelion
         with ready will, fairest of choirs, and in their midst
         Apollo ranged with golden plectrum
                over the seven-tongued lyre,

25       leading the way in varied melodies. At first,          [Ant. 2]
                starting with Zeus, they sang of august Thetis
         and Peleus, telling how Hippolyta,
                Kretheus' delicate daughter, sought to entangle him in
                     guile,
         and brought her husband, guardian of Magnesians,
         into her plot, persuading him with intricate
                blandishments:
         she fashioned, fitting piece to piece, a lying tale,
30       alleging that the man,
                in Akastos' very bed, made trial of

         her bridal sleep. The opposite was true: time after      [Ep. 2]
                time, with all her heart,
         she begged and pleaded for his love.
                Aroused to passion by her precipitate words,
         at once he spurned her, married as she was,
                in fear of Zeus's wrath, who has a father's care
         for host and guest. And he, king of immortals
                and lord of clouds, took note in heaven,
35       and with a nod he pledged that soon the hero
         would gain a wife from among the Nereids
                who ply their golden distaffs in the sea,

         after their brother-in-law Poseidon was persuaded,    [Str. 3]
                he who often goes
         from Aigai to the illustrious Dorian Isthmus.
         There joyfully the crowds
                with cry of flutes receive him in his godhead,
         and meet in contests, bold and strong of limb.
40       Inborn destiny is what brings all actions to
         decision. You from Aigina twice, Euthymenes,

sank into Victory's embrace
and felt the touch of hymns of intricate art.

Now too indeed your uncle, rushing after you,          [Ant. 3]
does honor, Pytheas, to that hero's kindred stock.
Nemea holds him in firm favor,
as does the native month held dear by Apollo:
45    he bested youths who came against him both at home
and under Nisos' hollow ridge. I am delighted
that the whole city strives for noble ends.
It is, you may be certain, by Menandros' luck
and grace that sweet requital for hard toil

is yours to enjoy: one who builds athletes ought to    [Ep. 3]
hail from Athens.
50    But if you have come to sing, Themistios,
hang back no longer; lift
your voice, raise high the sail
to reach the very masthead,
proclaiming that as boxer and pankratiast
at Epidauros he displayed
prowess twofold; and to the doors of Aiakos' shrine
bring wreaths of flowers and greenery with
the fair-haired Graces' aid.

This is one of three odes (*Isthmian* 6 and *Isthmian* 5 are the others) which
Pindar composed for the family of an Aiginetan named Lampon. The poem
was written to celebrate a victory in the pankration which was won (prob-
ably in 483 or 481) by Lampon's elder son Pytheas; it is perhaps a measure of
Lampon's ambitions for Pytheas that he commissioned Bacchylides to pro-
duce a second epinician for the same occasion (Ode 13). As it happens, how-
ever, less attention is given here to Pytheas than to his maternal uncle
Euthymenes (41–46), a fact which is perhaps not surprising in view of
Pytheas' youth (see note on line 6). Fully half the ode, moreover, is devoted
to Aigina's great family of heroes, the Aiakidai or "stock of Aiakos" (8). Hav-
ing alluded to one dark episode from Aiakid history (14–16), the poet
promptly rejects it as inappropriate to the circumstances and launches en-
thusiastically upon a far more auspicious story: how Peleus rebuffed the
improper advances of his host's wife and was rewarded for his righteousness
with a divine bride (25–37).

5 **the pankratiasts' crown** On the pankration, a combination of boxing and wrestling, see Xenophanes 2. 5 with note.

6 This physical detail probably indicates that Pytheas won his victory competing in the age class known as the *ageneioi* ("beardless").

7 **spearman heroes** the Aiakidai generally, and in particular the three sons of Aiakos: Peleus, Telamon, and Phokos. Aiakos himself was a son of **Zeus**; his wife **Endeïs** (12), the mother of Peleus and Telamon, was a granddaughter of **Kronos** through her father Chiron; and **Psamatheia** (13), the mother of Phokos, was one of the **Nereids** (on which see Glossary).

10 **Hellenian Zeus** "Zeus of the Greeks," a cult title particularly associated with Aigina.

14 **a deed portentous and not justly hazarded** Phokos was killed by his half brothers Peleus and Telamon, who as a consequence were banished from Aigina by their father Aiakos. Peleus went to Phthia in Thessaly, while Telamon settled on the island of Salamis.

16 **Oinone** another name for Aigina.

19 **prepare the ground** To cushion a jumper's landing the soil was loosened by spading beforehand.

22 **such as those** i.e., such as the Aiakidai, and specifically Peleus, whose marriage to Thetis on Mt. Pelion was attended by the Olympians (cf. Alcaeus 4. 6, *Pythian* 3. 87–95).

24 **plectrum** a small device used to pluck the strings of a lyre or other stringed instrument.

26–34 **Hippolyta** was the wife of **Akastos** (30), king of Iolkos in **Magnesia**. She fell in love with Peleus and tried to seduce him; when he spurned her advances, she took revenge by persuading her husband that Peleus had attempted to rape her. A subsequent effort by Akastos to contrive the death of Peleus was unsuccessful.

36 **a wife** i.e., Thetis, one of the fifty daughters of Nereus (see Glossary).

37 **their brother-in-law** Amphitrite, Poseidon's wife, was also one of the daughters of Nereus. **Aigai** where Poseidon had an undersea palace, according to Homer (*Iliad* 13. 21–22).

39 **contests** the Isthmian games, held near Corinth in Poseidon's honor.

41 **Euthymenes** Pytheas' maternal uncle; cf. *Isthmian* 6. 58ff. The two victories here alluded to may have been won at the Isthmian games (cf. 39), but this is not certain.

43 **that hero** presumably Peleus, whose **kindred stock** is the Aiginetan people.

44–46 I.e., Euthymenes has won victories at Nemea, at home on Aigina, and at Megara. According to the ancient commentators, the **native month held dear by Apollo** was called Delphinios, during which both the Nemean games and the Aiginetan Delphinia (see note on *Pythian* 8. 65–66) took place. **Nisos** was a legendary king of Megara, on which see Glossary.

48 **Menandros** Pytheas' trainer, an Athenian (cf. Bacchylides, Ode 13. 191–98).

50 **Themistios** one of Pytheas' forebears, possibly his maternal grandfather (cf. *Isthmian* 6. 65).

52 **Epidauros** situated on the northeastern coast of the Peloponnesos, not far from Aigina. It was the site of an athletic festival held in honor of Asklepios.

## *Nemean* 10:

### for Theaios son of Oulias, from Argos, victor in wrestling at the Argive Heraia

The city of Danaos and his fifty                          [Str. 1]
    daughters enthroned in splendor, O you Graces,
Argos, the fitting home of Hera—take this as your theme
    of song. It is ablaze with greatness
in countless forms because of its bold deeds.
Long is the tale of Perseus with the Gorgon Medousa,
5  and many the towns in Egypt founded by
    the hands of Epaphos;
nor did Hypermestra go astray when, casting her sole
    vote
for life, she kept her sword within its sheath.

Diomedes the fair-haired gray-eyed Maiden once      [Ant. 1]
    transformed into a deathless god;
the earth in Thebes, blasted by Zeus's thunderbolts,
    gaped to receive
Oïkles' visionary son, stormcloud of war.
10 In women's loveliness it has excelled from old—
Zeus coming to Alkmene and to Danaë brought
    the truth of this claim to the light—
while in Adrastos' father and in Lynkeus it united
    the fruits of wisdom with straight-dealing justice;

it fostered, too, Amphitryon's warlike spirit. He,      [Ep. 1]
    supreme in blessedness,
attained to that god's kinship when, in arms of bronze,
15 he slew the Teleboans. In his likeness
the king of immortals came into his halls,

bearing the fearless seed of Herakles, whose wife is on
    Olympos,
walking beside her mother, queen of marriages—
    Hebe the loveliest of gods.

My mouth cannot encompass, in their telling,        [Str. 2]
    all of the glories which the hallowed soil of Argos
20    has as its portion; then too, tedium in men
    weighs heavy when one meets it face to face.
Nevertheless, awake the well-strung lyre
and turn your thought to wrestling bouts. The brazen
    contest
urges the people on to the sacrifice of cattle
    and to the judging of the games of Hera,
where Oulias' son Theaios, twice victorious, won
    forgetfulness of labors bravely borne.

25    He also mastered once the host        [Ant. 2]
    of Greeks at Pytho, and, arriving graced by luck,
he gained crowns at the Isthmus and at Nemea alike,
    and thereby gave the Muses fields for plowing,
three times at the sea's gates triumphant,
three times on ground made sacred by Adrastos' institution.
Father Zeus, what he covets in his heart, his mouth
    keeps locked in silence, but the consummation
30    of every enterprise lies in you. Not with a heart unused to
    toil
    does he beseech this favor, bringing courage to bear as
    well.

The things I sing of are known both to the god and    [Ep. 2]
    to whoever strives
for eminence at the utmost games: the highest festival is
    Pisa's,
established there by Herakles. Meanwhile, as prelude,
    sweet
voices have twice amid the Athenians' rites
35    reveled on his behalf, and oil, the olive's fruit, has come
to Hera's valiant populace in vessels
    of burnt clay intricately painted.

Theaios, your maternal ancestors'        [Str. 3]
    illustrious stock has often met
with honor in the games by favor of the Graces
    and of Tyndareos' sons.
I would demand it as my right, were I a kinsman
40   of Thrasyklos and Antias, not to keep my shining eyes
downcast in Argos. With how many victories has the town
    of Proitos, breeding ground of horses,
blossomed! Both in Corinth's hollows,
    and four times at the hands of Kleonai's men;

from Sikyon they went away          [Ant. 3]
    laden with silver drinking cups,
and from Pellene with their backs well clad
    in cloaks of soft-napped wool.
45   But it is impossible to ascertain
the mass of bronzes—counting them would take too much
       time—
set as prizes in Kleitor, Tegea, and the towns
    along Achaia's hilltops
and beside Zeus's race course on Lykaion,
    for one victorious by strength of foot or hand.

Given that Kastor and his brother Polydeukes    [Ep. 3]
    came
50   as guests to Pamphaës' house, it is no cause for wonder
    that
the family begets fine athletes. After all, those two
stewards of Sparta's wide lands oversee the thriving
contests which they, with Herakles and Hermes, have in
    charge,
showing great care for righteous men. In truth,
    the race of gods is to be trusted.

55   Changing their state in alternation,       [Str. 4]
    they spend one day beside their father Zeus,
the next within the hollows of the earth
    beneath Therapne's slopes.
The fates that they fulfill are identical, because
Polydeukes chose this mode of life, instead of being

altogether a god and dwelling in heaven,
  when Kastor met with death in war.
60   For Idas, angered, it would seem, about some cattle,
  had wounded him with his spear's brazen point.

Gazing from Mt. Taÿgetos,                                        [Ant. 4]
  Lynkeus spied him sitting in
an oak tree's hollow trunk,
  for of all mortals that man's eye
was sharpest. Swift of foot, at once
they reached the spot, and contrived a great deed with all
    haste,
65   and suffered fearfully at Zeus's hands,
  those sons of Aphareus. For straightway
the son of Leda came in close pursuit. They took
  their stand against him by their father's tomb.

Seizing the polished stone that was death's              [Ep. 4]
    monument,
they hurled it at Polydeukes' breast, but neither crushed
    him
nor forced him back. And so, attacking with quick javelin
    poised,
70   he drove the bronze point into Lynkeus' side,
while Zeus struck Idas down, in flame and smoke and
    thunder's roar:
they burned together in abandonment. Discord with
    stronger powers
  is for mankind a harsh companion.

Quickly Tyndareos' son came back                          [Str. 5]
  to where his mighty brother lay,
and found him not yet dead, but shuddering
  with labored breaths.
75   Shedding hot tears, he groaned
and cried aloud: "O son of Kronos, father, what release
from sorrows will there be? Death for me too decree
  along with him who lies here, lord!
Honor is gone forever when a man is stripped
  of friends, and in adversity few mortals can be trusted

to take a share of pain and trouble." Thus                [Ant. 5]
   he spoke; and Zeus approached him, face to face,
80     and uttered forth these words: "You are my son;
   but this man was conceived thereafter, when
your mother's husband came to her and sowed
a hero's mortal seed. But come, I lay before you
   nonetheless
this choice: if on the one hand you desire, eluding
   death and detestable old age,
to dwell yourself upon Olympos in my company
and with Athena and the black-speared Ares,

85     that lot is yours to claim. But if it is for your       [Ep. 5]
   brother's sake
that you contend, and your thought is to share all things
   alike,
half of the time you may draw breath beneath the earth,
half of the time in heaven, in my halls of gold."
Hearing this, in his mind he formed no double purpose:
90     he set free first the eye, and then the voice
of Kastor in his brazen belt.

Despite its traditional placement among the Nemean odes, *Nemean* 10 celebrates a victory won not at Nemea but in the Argive Heraia, a biennial festival in Hera's honor which was held near her temple a few miles north of Argos. To judge from what is said of him in the ode, Theaios was a highly talented wrestler, with multiple victories to his credit not only at the Heraia (24) and the Panathenaia (33–36), two of the most important "local" games, but also at three of the four Panhellenic festivals, the Pythian, Isthmian, and Nemean (25–28). Thus he needed only an Olympian victory in order to gain the title of *periodonikes* or "circuit victor," which was regarded as the crowning achievement of a Greek athlete's career; and this ambition is in fact alluded to, with appropriate circumspection, in lines 29–33. Theaios' maternal ancestors were themselves distinguished athletes (37–48), a fact which Pindar attributes to the lasting favor of Kastor and Polydeukes (49–54). The last two triads of the ode are devoted to one of Pindar's finest mythical narratives, which tells how Polydeukes, son of Zeus though he was, chose to give up a share of his immortality in order to rescue his mortal brother Kastor from death.

1–18 Consult Glossary for information on the figures in this lengthy catalogue of Argive heroes and heroines. The rhetorical purpose of the catalogue is to create an illustrious background against which Theaios' latest addition to the tale of Argive glory can show off to the greatest advantage; it is, in other words, part of a priamel (see introductory note to Tyrtaeus 7).

2 **the fitting home of Hera** Hera was the patron deity of Argos.

7 **gray-eyed Maiden** Athena.

9 **Oïkles' visionary son** Amphiaraos (see Glossary).

10, 12, 13 **it has excelled, it united, it fostered** The subject in each case is Argos.

12 **Adrastos' father** Talaos.

14 **that god** Zeus, with whom Amphitryon became linked in a relation of co-paternity through the begetting of Herakles. For the story, see under "Amphitryon" in Glossary and cf. *Isthmian* 7. 5–7.

18 **queen of marriages** Hera, as the goddess of marriage. Her daughter by Zeus, **Hebe** (Youth), became the wife of Herakles after he was transformed into a god at his death.

22 **The brazen contest** the Heraia (see introductory note), so called because bronze shields were given as prizes.

27 **at the sea's gates** i.e., at the Isthmian games, which were held near the narrow neck of land between the Saronic Gulf and the Gulf of Corinth.

28 **Adrastos' institution** i.e., at the Nemean games, reputedly founded by Adrastos (see Glossary) while leading the army of the Seven against Thebes.

29 **what he covets in his heart** an allusion to Theaios' unspoken longing for a victory at the Olympic games.

32 **Pisa** i.e., Olympia (see Glossary). On **Herakles** as founder of the Olympian festival, cf. *Olympian* 2. 3–4.

34 **the Athenians' rites** the Great Panathenaia, a festival held every four years in Athens in honor of Athena, the city's divine patron. Among the prizes awarded in the Panathenaic games were large decorated jars (*amphorae*) filled with olive oil.

36 **to Hera's valiant populace** i.e., to Argos (cf. note on 2).

38 **Tyndareos' sons** Polydeukes and Kastor, here in their function as patrons of athletes; see under "Tyndaridai" in Glossary.

40 **Thrasyklos and Antias** evidently relatives of Theaios on his mother's side and, like him, successful athletes.

41 **the town of Proitos** apparently a reference to Argos, although in fact Proitos was forced to abandon Argos, the city of his father Abas, and settle in Tiryns instead (see under "Akrisios" in Glossary and cf. Bacchylides, Ode 11. 59–81).

42 **Corinth's hollows** another reference to the Isthmian games. **Kleonai** a city not far from Nemea which administered the Nemean games.

43–44 **Sikyon, Pellene** See Glossary.

48 **Lykaion** On the festival of Zeus Lykaios in Arkadia, cf. *Olympian* 13. 107–8.

50 **Pamphaës** evidently one of Theaios' (maternal) ancestors. Pindar attributes the family's numerous athletic successes to a hereditary relationship of guest-friendship (*xenia*) between its members and the Tyndaridai.

56 **Therapne** a town not far from Sparta, site of an important shrine to Kastor and Polydeukes.

60–61 **Idas, Lynkeus** the two **sons of Aphareus** (65), whose quarrel with the Tyndaridai over some stolen cattle led to Kastor's death. Note that this Lynkeus is to be distinguished from the Lynkeus mentioned in line 12, who was one of the sons of Aigyptos and the husband of Hypermestra (6).

61 **spied him** i.e., Kastor. According to some editors "him" should be "them," i.e., Kastor and Polydeukes together. **Taÿgetos** is a steep mountain ridge to the west of Sparta.

64 **contrived a great deed** i.e., the fatal wounding of Kastor.

66 **the son of Leda** i.e., Polydeukes.

73 **Tyndareos' son** i.e., Polydeukes, although in fact he was the son of Zeus, not of Tyndareos (cf. lines 80ff, and see Glossary under "Tyndaridai").

81 **your mother's husband** Tyndareos, the husband of Leda (see Glossary).

90 **he set free** i.e., through the choice he made, Polydeukes brought Kastor back to life.


## *Isthmian* 5:

### for Phylakidas son of Lampon, from Aigina, victor in the pankration

O mother of the Sun, Theia of many names,                    [Str. 1]
it is because of you that men give currency
to gold as great in power above all other things.
Indeed, when rivalry is waged
5    by ships upon the sea and horses yoked to chariots,
it is, O lady, through the honor *you* bestow that they become
    objects of wonder in their whirling courses;

so too does he who in the games achieves                     [Ant. 1]
the glory he has longed for, his hair thick
with wreaths of victory won by hand

10   or speed of foot.
Men's prowess comes to judgment through the gods.
Two things alone hold life's most pleasing bloom secure
   within their fold: to flourish in the joys

of prosperous fortune, and to hear oneself be          [Ep. 1]
   praised.
Do not seek to become Zeus; all is yours,
15   if of these goods some share should come your way.
To mortals, mortal things are fitting.
In your case, excellence twice over at the Isthmus,
Phylakidas, lies ever-fresh in store; at Nemea also, for you
   both—
yes, Pytheas too—in the pankration. As for me,
20   the Aiakidai are not absent from the hymns that my heart
   tastes:
together with the Graces I have come on behalf of
   Lampon's sons

to this well-ordered city. If a turning has been made   [Str. 2]
onto the clear bright road of god-given deeds,
do not begrudge to offer fitting praise with song
25   mingled in recompense for toils.
So too among the men of old brave warriors
found profit in acclaim, and they have been made famous
   on lyres and through the urgent cry of pipes

age upon age, a theme of thought and song for          [Ant. 2]
   men of skill,
held high in reverence by grace of Zeus.
30   Amid the Aitolians' splendid sacrifices
Oineus' sons are mighty;
in Thebes horse-driving Iolaos
has honor; Perseus in Argos; and the fighting spirit of
   Kastor
   and Polydeukes by Eurotas' streams.

But on Oinone Aiakos and his sons,                     [Ep. 2]
35   the great in heart, take pride of place, who through fierce
   battles

twice sacked the Trojans' city, being led
at first by Herakles,
then with the sons of Atreus. Now drive on, and soar!
Tell me, who were the ones that slaughtered Kyknos,
       Hektor too,
40     and the undaunted leader of the Ethiopian host,
Memnon the brazen-armed? Who was it, then, whose
       spear
wounded the noble Telephos beside the banks of Kaïkos?

Those for whom mouths proclaim Aigina as            [Str. 3]
       fatherland,
that conspicuous island, long ago built high
45     to be a tower that deeds of lofty courage might climb.
My tongue is ready
with many an arrow of praise to launch at them
resoundingly: most recently in war the city of Ajax can
       bear witness
       whose sailors set her upright,

Salamis, there amid the rain of havoc loosed          [Ant. 3]
50     when on unnumbered men Zeus sent a storm of slaughter.
Nonetheless, drench this vaunt in silence!
Zeus gives out this and that,
Zeus, master of all things; then too, the honeyed sound
of victory hymns is welcomed on occasions such as this
       with no less gladness. Let a man fight hard

55     for prizes once he has studied Kleonikos' stock      [Ep. 3]
with thoroughness. No darkness dims the long
toil of their men, nor have thoughts of expense
yet marred their zealous hopes.
I praise too Pytheas among pankratiasts,
60     Phylakidas' skilled guide along the path of blows,
nimble of hand and with a mind to match.
Take up a crown for him, a headband of fine wool,
and send with it this winged new-made song.

This is chronologically the third and last of Pindar's odes for the family of
Lampon, on which see the introductory notes to *Nemean* 5 and *Isthmian* 6. It

was probably composed and performed in 478, or at any rate not too long after the battle of Salamis (480), in which the Greek alliance decisively defeated the Persian fleet—and in which a particularly distinguished role was played by the contingent of Aiginetan ships. Pindar introduces a reference to Aigina's role at Salamis as the climax of an extended celebration of Aiakid, and more generally of Aiginetan, valor (34–50). The ode begins with a hymnal invocation to the goddess Theia, who according to Hesiod (*Theogony* 371–74) was one of the Titans (see Glossary) and by Hyperion became the mother of Helios (the Sun), Selene (the Moon), and Eos (the Dawn). Here Pindar seems to represent her as the source of the radiance or splendor that casts a spell over human hearts when it shines forth from gold or from glorious achievements.

12–13 For the sentiment, cf. *Pythian* 1. 99–100.

17 **excellence twice over at the Isthmus** i.e., his current victory together with that celebrated in *Isthmian* 6.

19 **Pytheas** the older brother of Phylakidas; the Nemean victory here attributed to him is presumably that celebrated in *Nemean* 5. On the pankration see Xenophanes 2. 5 with note.

20 **the Aiakidai** the "descendants of Aiakos" (see Glossary), who were held in special reverence on Aigina (**this well-ordered city**, 22).

30–33 For information on the figures in this brief catalogue of regional heroes, consult Glossary. Rhetorically, the catalogue forms part of a priamel (see introductory note to Tyrtaeus 7) whose purpose is to highlight the special importance of the Aiakidai to the island of Aigina.

33 **by Eurotas' streams** i.e., in Sparta; see Glossary.

34 **Oinone** another name for Aigina.

35–42 Descendants of **Aiakos** were involved in two attacks on Troy in successive generations. The first of these was **Herakles'** punitive expedition against Laomedon (see Glossary), in which Aiakos' son Telamon took part (cf. *Isthmian* 6. 27ff); the second was the ten-year conflict waged by **the sons of Atreus** (Agamemnon and Menelaos) to recover Helen from Paris (the Trojan War). Although the correct answer to the questions posed in lines 39–42 is in each case Aiakos' grandson Achilles, he was not in fact the only member of the Aiakidai to participate in the Trojan War; others who did so were Ajax, Teukros, and Neoptolemos.

39–42 **Kyknos, Hektor, Memnon** The same three figures are cited as victims of Achilles' valor in *Olympian* 2. 81–83; see Glossary for particulars.

42 **Telephos** king of Mysia in northwestern Asia Minor. The Greeks mistakenly landed in his country on their way to Troy, and in the battle that followed Telephos was wounded by Achilles. Some time later Achilles healed the wound with rust taken from the same spear that had inflicted it. The **Kaïkos** was a river in southern Mysia.

48 **the city of Ajax** i.e., Salamis, the legendary home of Ajax and his father
Telamon; see Glossary. **whose sailors** i.e., Aigina's.
54 **occasions such as this** i.e., celebrations of victory won *in the athletic
competitions of peacetime* (as distinguished from victory gained through
war).
55 **Kleonikos** father of Lampon (cf. *Isthmian* 6. 16) and hence grandfather
of Phylakidas and Pytheas.
60 It would seem that Pytheas served as Phylakidas' trainer in the
pankration as well as being a pankratiast himself.

## *Isthmian 6:*

for Phylakidas son of Lampon, from Aigina,
victor in the boys' pankration

As when a drinking-party thrives and blooms,          [Str. 1]
we mix a second bowl of the Muses' melodies
for Lampon's family of fine athletes,
    having at Nemea first, O Zeus,
received from your hands the pick of crowns,
5       and now again from the master of the Isthmus
and Nereus' fifty daughters, since the youngest of
    his sons,
Phylakidas, is victorious. May there be a third
libation, one prepared for Olympian Zeus
    the Savior, to pour out upon
Aigina with the honeyed sounds of song.

10      For if a man who finds joy in expense          [Ant. 1]
and toil does deeds of prowess founded in divinity,
and if for him some power plants lovely fame,
    then at the utmost bounds of bliss
he has already cast his anchor, honored by the gods.
With feelings such as these
15      to meet and welcome death and white-haired age—this is
    the prayer
of Kleonikos' son, and I invoke
Klotho and her two sisters throned aloft,
    the Fates, to heed and grant
the noble wishes of a man who is my friend.

As for you, offspring of Aiakos in your golden                [Ep. 1]
    chariots,
20    I hold it as a clear-cut rule, when I set foot
upon this island, to besprinkle you with praise.
Numberless are the highways of fair deeds
    that you have cut, a hundred feet in breadth,
stretching beyond the springs of Nile and the
       Hyperboreans.
There is no city so uncouth,
    so backward and perverse of tongue,
25    that it has not heard word of Peleus the hero
    and his good fortune, son-in-law of gods,

nor heard of Ajax, Telamon's son,                             [Str. 2]
and of his father, who set off for brazen war,
an eager ally of Tirynthian men,
    over the sea to Troy, where heroes labored,
when vengeance for Laomedon's crimes
30    was taken by Alkmene's son.
He captured Pergamos, and with his friend he slew
the Meropian nation and that herdsman, mountain-huge,
Alkyoneus, whom he found in Phlegra's fields:
    there was no slackening of
the bow's deep music in the hands

35    of Herakles. But when he came to summon          [Ant. 2]
       Aiakos' son
to sail with him, he found the company at a feast.
And as he stood there in his lion's skin,
    Amphitryon's warlike son, the noble Telamon
urged him to pour the first libations
of fragrant wine, and gave him, held aloft
40    and amply filled, a cup embossed with bristling gold.
And he, lifting to heaven his unconquerable hands,
gave utterance to words like these:
    "If ever, father Zeus,
you heard my prayers before with willing heart,

now, now with fervent importunity                             [Ep. 2]
45    I beg that to this man a fearless son

be born from Eriboia, to be my destined guest friend.
In body let him be unbreakable,
    just like this hide in which I now am wrapped,
stripped from the beast I killed at Nemea once, the first of
        all my labors;
and let his spirit match." When he
    said this, the god sent down
50   a mighty eagle, king of birds. He felt
    joy's piercing sweetness deep within,

and spoke out like a man of prophecy:                    [Str. 3]
"You shall have the son you ask for, Telamon.
Name him after the bird that just now loomed above us:
    call him Ajax, wide in power, of all the host
most terrible amid the War God's toils."
55   Speaking thus, he at once
    sat down. But I lack time to go through all such deeds of
        prowess,
since it is for Phylakidas, O Muse, that I have come
as revel-master, and for Pytheas and Euthymenes.
    According to the Argive manner,
    it shall be stated in the briefest terms:

60   together they have won in the pankration          [Ant. 3]
    ˙three victories at the Isthmus, others too at leafy Nemea,
youths and uncle alike in splendor. What a trove
    of triumph songs have they brought forth to light!
The clan of the Psalychiadai they refresh
and nourish with the Graces' fairest dew,
65   and they raise high the house of Themistios, living
within this city loved by gods. Bestowing due
attention on all actions, Lampon shows
    special regard for Hesiod's familiar maxim;
expounding it, he urges his sons on,

bringing the city glory in which all can share.          [Ep. 3]
70   For good deeds done to strangers he is warmly loved;
his will is moderate in pursuit and moderate in possession;
his tongue does not outstrip his mind.
    For athletes, you would say he is

a Naxian whetstone, master of bronze, among all other rocks.
I shall give them Dirke's hallowed water
    to drink, water which the deep-girded daughters
75  of golden-mantled Memory made spring up
    beside the well-built gates of Kadmos.

Chronologically the second of Pindar's three odes for the family of the Aiginetan Lampon (the others being *Nemean* 5 and *Isthmian* 5), this poem takes as its ostensible occasion a victory won (probably in 480) by Lampon's younger son Phylakidas. Yet no more than a line or two is in fact devoted directly to Phylakidas, and it is Lampon himself that remains the main focus of attention throughout the ode. Although evidently not a successful athlete himself (there is, at any rate, no mention of any victories to his credit), he seems to have been deeply interested in furthering the athletic careers of his two sons and willing to spend money freely to that end, as his commissions to Pindar and Bacchylides testify. Even the ode's mythical centerpiece (drawn, as is usual in odes for Aiginetans, from the corpus of Aiakid legend) is oriented toward Lampon, for in it Pindar seems to suggest a parallel between Telamon in his role as father of Ajax, that longed-for son destined to be a superlative warrior, and Lampon in his role as father of Phylakidas and Pytheas, who have won glory as pankratiasts. It is noteworthy that the qualities in Ajax singled out for attention in Herakles' prayer (42–49), namely an unbreakable body and an equally unbreakable spirit, are precisely the qualities that were required to survive and triumph in the all-out combat of the pankration.

1–9 Pindar alludes to the Greek custom of pouring out three libations in the course of a banquet or drinking-party, the first to Olympian Zeus, the second to Earth and the heroes, the third to Zeus Soter (Savior). According to the metaphor, the first "libation of song" was *Nemean* 5 (composed for Phylakidas' brother Pytheas), which paid honor to Zeus as patron of the Nemean games, while the second is the present ode for Phylakidas himself, which honors Poseidon as patron of the Isthmian games. In hoping that there may be yet a third "libation of song," one poured out for **Olympian Zeus the Savior** (8), the poet is in effect praying that Phylakidas may go on to win at Olympia.

5 **the master of the Isthmus** Poseidon. On his association with the Nereids, cf. *Nemean* 5. 37.

16 **Kleonikos' son** Lampon; cf. *Isthmian* 5. 55.

18 **a man who is my friend** Cf. note on *Olympian* 1. 103.

19 **offspring of Aiakos** the Aiakidai (see Glossary), who were held in special reverence on Aigina (**this island**, 21).

23 **the springs of Nile and the Hyperboreans** representing, respectively, the southern and northern limits of the habitable world. Not only has the fame of the Aiakidai spread everywhere, but the range of themes open to one who wishes to praise them is equally wide.

25 **Peleus . . . son-in-law of gods** as husband of the Nereid Thetis; cf. *Nemean* 5. 34–36.

27–30 On **Telamon's** journey to Troy as part of **Herakles'** expedition against Laomedon, see Glossary under "Laomedon" and cf. *Isthmian* 5. 37 with note. Herakles' forces were **Tirynthian** because he was a resident of Tiryns at the time.

30 **Alkmene's son** Herakles (see Glossary).

31 **with his friend** i.e., with Telamon. **Pergamos** was another name for Troy; the Meropes (or **Meropian nation**) were the legendary inhabitants of Kos, an island off the southwestern coast of Asia Minor; **Alkyoneus** was a cattle-stealing giant whom Herakles killed at **Phlegra** in Thrace.

37 **Amphitryon's warlike son** Herakles again.

46 **Eriboia** Telamon's wife.

48 **the beast I killed at Nemea** On Herakles' killing of the Nemean lion, see Glossary under "Nemea" and cf. Bacchylides, Ode 13. 46–54.

53 **Name him after the bird** a play on the name *Aias* (the Greek form of Ajax) and *aietos* "eagle."

58 **Pytheas and Euthymenes** Phylakidas' older brother (cf. *Nemean* 5. 4–6 and *Isthmian* 5. 59–63) and maternal uncle (cf. *Nemean* 5. 41–46).

58–59 The **Argives**, like the Spartans and other Lakonians, were known for their brevity of speech.

63–66 **the Psalychiadai** the clan to which Phylakidas' family belonged. On **Themistios**, one of the family's ancestors, cf. *Nemean* 5. 50–53.

67 **Hesiod's familiar maxim** an allusion to Hesiod, *Works and Days* 412 ("attention furthers one's work").

73 **a Naxian whetstone** Naxos, an island in the Cyclades, was well known as a source of hard, fine-grained rock suitable for use in sharpening metal tools and weapons. The implication is that Lampon served an analogous role in "whetting" or "honing" his sons' athletic abilities.

74–75 **Dirke** a spring in Thebes, Pindar's native city, of which **Kadmos** was the legendary founder. **daughters of golden-mantled Memory** the Muses; hence the **water** referred to is a metaphor for poetry.

## *Isthmian* 7:

for Strepsiades of Thebes, victor in the pankration

In which, O blessed Thebe, of your land's                                    [Str. 1]
earlier glories has your heart most taken

delight? Was it the time you raised up Dionysos
to sit with flowing hair beside
5   Demeter of the clashing bronze? Or having once received,
     at midnight in a shower of golden snow, the mightiest
        of gods,

when, standing in the doorway of Amphitryon's        [Ant. 1]
        house,
he came to bring to that man's wife the seed of Herakles?
Or owing to Teiresias' shrewd counsels?
Or for the sake of Iolaos, skilled in horsemanship?
10  Or for the Sown Men with their tireless lances? Or when
        from the midst
     of ardent battle shouts you sent Adrastos back, bereft

of countless friends, to Argos famed for horses?        [Ep. 1]
Or because you set upright on its feet
the Dorian outpost of
the Spartans, when the Aigeidai, your descendants,
15  captured Amyklai by command of Pythian oracles?
But ancient grace
slumbers, and mortals are forgetful

of that which fails to reach the summit of poetic        [Str. 2]
        skill,
yoked to loud-sounding streams of verse.
20  Celebrate, therefore, with melodious song
Strepsiades as well, for he brings from the Isthmus
a triumph in the pankration, fearsome in his strength and
        beautiful
     to look upon, his valor in no way disgracing his
        physique.

He is made radiant by the dark-haired Muses,        [Ant. 2]
and shares a garland with the uncle he is named for,
25  whom Ares of the brazen shield embroiled in doom;
yet honor lies in store to recompense the brave.
Let him know well, whoever in that stormcloud drives
     the hail of blood away from his dear fatherland,

heaping havoc upon the opposing host,                            [Ep. 2]
that he greatly augments the glory of his townsmen,
30      both in his life and after death.
Son of Diodotos, in emulation
of warlike Meleagros, in emulation too of Hektor
and Amphiaraos,
you breathed out the full flower of your youth

35      amidst the press of forefighters, where the bravest      [Str. 3]
checked the fierce clash of war with final hopes.
I suffered grief unspeakable, but now
the Earthholder has granted me fair weather
after the storm. I shall sing out, fitting my hair
        with garlands. May the envy of immortals stir no
        trouble.

40      Pursuing day by day what is delightful,                   [Ant. 3]
I shall move calmly toward old age and my allotted
span of life. For all of us die alike,
although our fortunes are unequal; and however far
        a man
may gaze, he is too small to reach the gods' bronze-floored
        dwelling place. Winged Pegasos, of course, threw off

45      his master when Bellerophon was seeking                   [Ep. 3]
to make his home in heaven amid the company
of Zeus. For sweetness contrary to right
the bitterest of outcomes lies in wait.
To us, however, Loxias, whose thick hair gleams with gold,
50      grant from your contests
a garland in full flower at Pytho also.

This ode, which cannot be reliably dated, was written for one of Pindar's fellow Thebans, a certain Strepsiades (his father's name, very unusually, appears nowhere in the ode). Although it would seem that the family was not athletically distinguished (at any rate no victories by relatives are mentioned), it did have a cause for pride in Strepsiades' maternal uncle, also named Strepsiades, who died in battle while fighting for his fatherland. In fact the central section of the ode, which in the typical epinician is likely to be occupied by a mythical narrative, instead contains an extended tribute to the patriotic heroism of the elder Strepsiades (25–36). Although it is quite likely that such a commemorative passage was requested when the poem was commissioned, it also heightens the importance of the younger Strepsiades' victory in the pankration (which was in any case the most "warlike" of all Greek sporting events) by partially assimilating it to an ideal of martial valor as old as Homer's *Iliad* and prominent as well in the poems of Tyrtaeus.

1–22 Like *Nemean* 10, this ode begins with a priamel (see introductory note to Tyrtaeus 7) in which Thebes' "earlier glories" are reviewed (1–15) and then set aside (16–19) in favor of the city's most recent claim to fame, Strepsiades' victory at the Isthmus (20–22). For information on most of the figures mentioned in 1–15, consult Glossary.

1 **Thebe** the eponymous nymph of Thebes, here representing the city as a whole.

3, 5 **Dionysos, Demeter** naturally associated with one another as divinities of, respectively, wine and grain (and hence bread). Bronze cymbals seem to have been used occasionally in the worship of Demeter.

5 **the mightiest of gods** Zeus; on his begetting of **Herakles** see under "Amphitryon" in Glossary. The shower of gold was more usually associated with Zeus's impregnation of Danaë, the mother of Perseus.

10 **the Sown Men** Known in Greek as the Spartoi, they sprang up out of the earth when Kadmos (see Glossary) sowed it with the teeth of a dragon he had killed on his first arrival at the future site of Thebes. The chief aristocratic families of Thebes traced their descent from the Spartoi.

14 **the Aigeidai** a Theban clan which, according to legend, assisted the Dorians (see Glossary) in their invasion of the Peloponnesos, having been prompted to do so by the Delphic oracle.

25 **whom Ares . . . embroiled in doom** The specific circumstances of the elder Strepsiades' death in battle are not known.

31 **Son of Diodotos** the elder Strepsiades.

32–33 Both **Meleagros** and **Hektor** (though not **Amphiaraos**) died while defending their homelands; see Glossary.

38 **the Earthholder** Poseidon, patron deity of the Isthmian games; the **fair weather** that he has granted is Strepsiades' current victory.

40–42 The first person here probably has general reference (see note on *Pythian* 3. 110): Pindar is recommending a particular attitude toward life.

44–48 On **Pegasos** and **Bellerophon**, see *Olympian* 13. 63–92. Here the point of the mythical exemplum is explicitly to illustrate the dangers that arise when human beings lose sight of the limitations imposed upon them by their mortal status.

49 **Loxias** Apollo in his role as the oracular god of Delphi; evidently Strepsiades was hoping to win a further victory in the Pythian games.

# Paean 4 (Fr. 52d)

... Karthaia                                                   [Ant.]
is only a short-backed ridge of land,
but I shall not exchange it for Babylon ...
     [5 lines missing]

Truly, I too, though dwelling on a rocky crag, am far    [Ep.]
    and wide
5      known for my deeds of prowess in the games
of Hellas, known as well for the songs
    that I furnish in abundance.
Although my soil yields in some measure the life-giving
cure that Dionysos grants to helpless troubles,
10   I have no horses and am largely ignorant about the
     pasturing of cattle.
But Melampous, at any rate, was not willing
to leave his native land and become sole ruler in Argos,
putting aside his augur's gift and office.
Ië, ië, o ië Paian!

15   The city of one's home, one's friends          [Str.]
and kinsmen—a man with these
can be content. Foolish are they who long
    for what lies far away. The speech of king Euxantios
has my approval, made when he refused the Cretans'
    eager offer
20   that he become their absolute ruler, and out of a hundred
    cities
take a seventh share along with Pasiphaë's sons.
    A marvel of his own witnessing
he proclaimed to them: "I am afraid of war
with Zeus, and of Poseidon's thunderous roar.

25   Once, you know, land and people all together       [Ant.]
they hurled with lightning bolt and trident
into the depths of Tartaros, sparing
    my mother and all her well-fenced house.
After that, am I to try for wealth? Am I to thrust aside
    what the blessed gods

30      ordained for this land, forsaking it utterly,
        to claim broad acres elsewhere as my own? Too constant
            would be the fear I felt.
        Let the cypress be, my heart!
        Let be the pasture-lands of Ida!

35      To me little has been given . . .                              [Ep.]
        but no sorrows have fallen to my lot, no civil conflicts. . . ."
            [8 lines missing]
        Ië, ië, o ië Paian!

A fragmentary paean (*paian*), composed for the people of Keos. Paeans were
traditionally associated with the worship of Apollo, who in his aspect as the
god of healing was frequently addressed as Paian (cf. note on Solon 7. 57).
Characteristic features of the form, at least as it was handled by Pindar, in-
clude a ritual refrain invoking Paian and praise of the state or community
which commissioned the poem. In this case, however, the Kean chorus's loyal
praise of their native island is tempered by an equal readiness to acknowl-
edge its shortcomings; indeed, the basic gist of the piece (what we have of it,
at any rate) could be paraphrased as "Be it ever so humble, there's no place
like home." In confirmation of that thought the chorus cites the example of
Euxantios, a legendary king of Keos whose strong attachment to his home-
land led him to decline an opportunity to gain power and wealth on the large
and fertile island of Crete.

1 **Karthaia** a town on Keos.
3 **Babylon** a great city on the Euphrates River in Mesopotamia, prover-
bial for its size and magnificence.
4 **I too** The members of the chorus speak collectively in the person of
their native island.
5 **my deeds of prowess in the games** On the athletic prowess of the
Keans in Panhellenic competition cf. Bacchylides, Odes 2. 6–10 and 6. 4–9.
6–7 **the songs that I furnish** chiefly, no doubt, an allusion to Simonides
and Bacchylides, who were natives of Keos.
8–10 Like most of the islands in the Cyclades, Keos was not suitable for
much in the way of agriculture or animal husbandry, being rocky and
without ample sources of water, but it did produce wine (cf. Bacchylides,
Ode 6. 5).
11–13 **Melampous** a famous prophet and augur of Greek legend. A rather
different story from that presupposed by this allusion can be found in
Herodotus (9. 34).

15–18 For the idea that one should be content with what one already has and not yearn for things beyond one's sphere, cf. *Pythian* 3. 20–23 and 59–62, *Isthmian* 7. 40–48.

18 **Euxantios** See introductory note and cf. Bacchylides, Ode 2. 8. Euxantios was borne by Dexithea of Keos to Minos, the king of Crete (on whom see Bacchylides' Dithyramb 17).

20 **a hundred cities** Homer refers to "Crete of the hundred cities" (*Iliad* 2. 649).

21 **Pasiphaë's sons** Pasiphaë was the wife of Minos, and hence her sons were Euxantios' half brothers.

27 **Tartaros** See Glossary.

34 **Ida** a mountain in central Crete.

## Dithyramb 2 (Fr. 70b)

In former times, dithyrambic song moved                    [Str.]
    in long-drawn fashion, like a rope,
and the letter *san* rang falsely on men's lips.
But new gates now are flung wide for
5      the circling dance . . .    . . . knowing
what kind of rites for Bromios
the descendants of Ouranos, beside the scepter of Zeus
    himself,
hold in their halls. Beside the august Great Mother
the whirl and clash of tambourines begin;
10   there the castanets ring out, and torches
    blaze beneath the tawny pines;
there the Naiads' wailing cries resound
as clamorous frenzy stirs amid the throng
and heads are tossed from side to side.
15   There the all-mastering thunderbolt, breathing fire,
is set into motion, and the spear
of Enyalios, while the stalwart aegis borne by Pallas
gives voice with the strident hiss of countless snakes.

And Artemis, with light step, approaches                   [Ant.]
    unaccompanied,
20   once she has yoked a pride
of savage lions, their tempers bent to Bacchos . . .
while he himself is spellbound by the herds

of wild beasts dancing. I as chosen
herald of skillful words
25    have been raised up by the Muse for Hellas . . .
offering prayers for Thebes, that city of weighty chariots
where once, the story tells, Harmonia was won in
         marriage
by Kadmos with his lofty thoughts:
         she heard the voice of Zeus,
30    and brought forth progeny of fair fame among mankind.
Dionysos, you . . .
your mother . . .

As a type of poetic composition, the dithyramb was originally associated
with Dionysos (cf. Archilochus 22, Pindar, *Olympian* 13. 18–19), and that as-
sociation is retained in the form of dithyramb represented by this fragment,
which was composed for performance in Thebes (cf. 26ff). Other poems tra-
ditionally identified as dithyrambs, for example Dithyrambs 17 and 18 of
Bacchylides, are predominantly narrative in character and lack any connec-
tion in subject matter with Dionysos or the Dionysiac cult. In its depiction of
Dionysiac revelry among the Olympians, this fragment exhibits interesting
similarities to and contrasts with the opening of *Pythian* 1.

1–5 It is not clear what precisely Pindar has in mind when he draws this
contrast between earlier and contemporary forms of the dithyramb. *San*
was an alternative form of *sigma*, the Greek *s*. Lasos of Hermione, a
generation before Pindar, is reported to have composed "asigmatic" poems
in which the *s* sound was avoided as aurally displeasing.
    6 **Bromios** "the roaring one," an epithet of Dionysos.
    7 **the descendants of Ouranos** i.e., the Olympian gods, who were
ultimately descended from the primal union between Ouranos (Sky) and
Gaia (Earth).
    8 **Great Mother** See note on *Pythian* 3. 78. Her worship resembled that of
Dionysos in involving loud, percussive music and ecstatic dancing, and
the two deities were frequently associated with one another.
    12 **Naiads** nymphs closely associated with springs and streams.
    17 **Enyalios** Ares. **Pallas** Athena; for her association with the aegis, see
Glossary.
    27 **Harmonia** daughter of Ares and Aphrodite and wife of Kadmos (on
whom see Glossary); cf. Pindar, *Pythian* 3. 91.
    30 **progeny** Among the four daughters of Kadmos and Harmonia was
Semele, who became mother of Dionysos by Zeus (cf. *Olympian* 2. 26–27,
*Pythian* 3. 98–99).

## *Partheneion* 2 (Fr. 94b)

... for Loxias has come                                                  [Str.]
   with ready mind to confer on Thebes
immortal glory.


But quickly girding up my robe                                           [Ant.]
5    and carrying in my gentle hands a splendid bough
of laurel, I shall make
   Aioladas' illustrious house
and his son Pagondas


matter for song, my head entwined with garlands                         [Ep.]
10   in virginal profusion,
   and to the sound of lotus pipes
I shall imitate in song
   that resonant siren call


which stills the West Wind's sudden gusts                                [Str.]
15   to silence, and whenever with the strength
of winter shuddering Boreas
   rages onward, and quickly....
   ... the blast, and turmoil ...


[either 10 or 25 lines missing]


Many deeds of earlier times I have as themes                            [Str.]
20   for artful embellishment in verse, while of others
      only
Zeus has knowledge. But in my case it is fitting
   to think a maiden's thoughts
and utter them in speech;


nor, for a man and woman to whose blooming                              [Ant.]
25   offspring I am devoted, ought I to forget appropriate
      song.
As a sure witness I have come
   to join the dancing, for Agasikles
and for his noble parents,

because of their acts of friendliness to strangers. For     [Ep.]
30     both of old and recently they have won honor
among their neighbors
for famous victories gained
with horses swift of foot:

on the shores of glorious Onchestos                          [Str.]
35     and by Itonia's temple of fair fame
they decked their hair with garlands,
and at Pisa. . . .

      [either 10 or 25 lines missing]

. . . at seven-gated Thebes.

Thereafter too, ill-natured anger                            [Str.]
40     at these men's moderate ambitions
gave rise to odious conflict, which the tongue did not
    retract; yet still the paths of righteousness
they loved and trusted as their own.

Son of Damaina, step forth now on feet blessed by           [Ant.]
    good omens
45     and lead the procession; after you, in joyful mood,
    will follow
your daughter, first upon the path,
her sandals treading close upon
the laurel bough with lovely leaves,

she whom Andaisistrota                                        [Ep.]
50     has trained in arts. . . .

A fragmentary "maiden song" or *partheneion*, like Alcman 1 and 2; see the
introduction to that poet for a brief characterization of the genre. The refer-
ences to Apollo **Loxias** (1) and to the carrying of a laurel bough (5–6, 48)
indicate that the poem was composed for performance at a Theban festival of
Apollo known as the Daphnephoria ("Bearing of the Laurel"). Its purpose is
apparently to celebrate a particular Theban family, that of **Aioladas** and his
son **Pagondas** (7–8). Also named are **Agasikles** (27), who is probably the son
of Pagondas, **Damaina** (44), who is presumably the mother either of
Pagondas or of Agasikles, and **Andaisistrota** (49), who may be the mother
and/or the trainer of the young woman who led the chorus.

34–36 I.e., members of Aioladas' family won chariot victories at the
festival of Poseidon at **Onchestos** (a town on the shores of Lake Kopais in
central Boiotia) and at the Pamboiotia, an "all-Boiotian" festival held at the
sanctuary of Athena **Itonia** near Koroneia.

## *Enkomion* for Theoxenos (Fr. 123)

One ought, my heart, to cull desires                                    [Str.]
    in season, in youth's prime.
And yet whoever, catching sight of the flashing
      radiance
of Theoxenos' eyes,
does not surge with longing, that man's murky heart
5     must have been forged from adamant or iron

by a cold flame: held in dishonor                                      [Ant.]
    by quick-glancing Aphrodite,
he either toils compulsively for money
or by women's impudence
is carried along a path of utter coldness, doing
      service.
10    But I, stung through that goddess's power, melt like the
      wax

of holy bees in the sun's heat whenever I look                         [Ep.]
on the youth and freshness of boys' limbs.
On Tenedos too, it seems,
Attraction dwells, and Charm,
15    in the person of Hagesilas' son.

This poem, which may be complete, honors a youth named Theoxenos, son
of Hagesilas, from Tenedos, a small island off the northwest coast of Asia
Minor. The Alexandrian critics labeled it an *enkomion*, a poem of praise and
celebration of a type often intended for performance within the context of a
*symposion* or drinking-party.
6–9 The point seems to be that any man who remains unaffected by the
beauty of Theoxenos must be either (a) single-mindedly devoted to
money-making at the expense of all erotic feeling or (b) enslaved in an
unworthy and unsatisfactory fashion to heterosexual desire. The text and
interpretation of lines 8–9 are, however, disputed.

### *Enkomion* for Thrasyboulos (Frs. 124a + b)

I send you, Thrasyboulos, this chariot of lovely          [Str. 1]
    songs
to follow your feasting. Amid the gathering, it may well be
a sweet spur to your fellow revelers, to the fruit

of Dionysos, and to the drinking cups from Athens,    [Str. 2]
5   at the time when men's fatiguing anxieties have vanished
out of their hearts and minds, and on a sea of golden
    wealth

we all alike go voyaging toward illusory shores.         [Str. 3]
The man without possessions is rich then, and in turn the
    wealthy . . .
          [1 line missing]

          [1 line missing]
11  . . . their thoughts grow great, subdued by the        [Str. 4]
arrows of the vine. . . .

Thrasyboulos was the nephew of Theron, tyrant of Akragas, whose Olympian chariot victory is celebrated in *Olympian* 2. This poem, clearly intended for performance at a drinking-party (*symposion*), exhibits close parallels in theme and treatment with Bacchylides' "*Enkomion* for Alexandros," which was composed for similar circumstances.

### *Enkomion* for Xenophon (Fr. 122)

Young women hospitable to many guests,                 [Str. 1]
    attendants
of Attraction in wealthy Corinth,
you who burn the amber tears of blooming
frankincense and often in your thoughts
    soar toward Aphrodite,
5   the heavenly mother of desires,

to you it has been granted, girls,                         [Str. 2]
without reproach on beds of love
to pluck the fruit of your youth's delicate prime.
Under compulsion, everything is honorable. . . .

[1 line missing]

[2 lines missing]                                        [Str. 3]
But I wonder what the masters of the Isthmus
will say of me, having hit on such a starting point
15      for a banquet song sweet as honey to the mind,
linked as it is with women shared by all.

We make gold known by means of the pure         [Str. 4]
         touchstone. . . .
              [at least 5 lines missing]

[2 lines missing]                                        [Str. 5]
O mistress of Cyprus, into your sacred precinct here
a herd of a hundred ranging maidens has
20      been brought by Xenophon,
rejoicing in the fulfillment of his prayers. . . .

A notable feature of the cult of Aphrodite at Corinth was an institution
known as "sacred prostitution," whereby women (usually slaves) worked as
courtesans in the service of the goddess. This fragmentary poem was written
to celebrate the dedication to Aphrodite of one hundred such "sacred prosti-
tutes" by the same Xenophon of Corinth who commissioned Pindar's *Olym-
pian* 13. According to the ancient source that quotes the lines (Athenaeus 13.
573–74), Xenophon had vowed to make such a dedication as a thank offering
if he should achieve an Olympian victory; in fact, as we know from *Olympian*
13, he won not one but *two* victories in a single Olympiad. The poem was
classified as an *enkomion* by the Alexandrians; Pindar himself refers to it as a
"banquet song" or *skolion* (15).

13 **the masters of the Isthmus** the people of Corinth (see Glossary).
18 **mistress of Cyprus** Aphrodite (see Glossary).

## *Threnos* 7 (Fr. 129)

For them the sun's force shines below
while here it is night,
and in meadows filled with crimson roses their place of
         residence
is shady with boughs of frankincense
5       and trees hung thick with golden fruit.

> Some find delight in horses and bodily exercise,
>     others in playing checkers,
> still others in the lyre, while all about them
>     complete felicity is thrivingly in bloom.
> A fragrance spreads throughout the lovely spot
> continually as they cast mingled incense of all kinds
> 10    into flame burning brightly on the altars of the gods. . . .

Like Simonides 3, 4, and 5, these lines are from a dirge (*threnos*). As a depiction of the happy state enjoyed by at least some of the dead in the afterlife, the fragment bears comparison with *Olympian* 2. 61–83.

2 **here** i.e., on earth in the realm of the living.

# BACCHYLIDES

Bacchylides was the nephew of Simonides and, like him, was born on Keos, an island in the western Cyclades. His exact dates are not known, but he appears to have been a close contemporary of Pindar. Like Pindar, with whom on occasion he shared patrons, Bacchylides composed choral lyrics in a wide variety of types, including hymns, paeans, dithyrambs, epinicians, and *enkomia*. His works were collected by Alexandrian scholars into nine books. Substantial portions of two of these books, the epinicians (victory odes) and the dithyrambs, were discovered at the end of the nineteenth century on a fragmentary papyrus scroll in Egypt. For a brief account of the epinician as a poetic type, see the introduction to Pindar.

## Ode 2:

for Argeios son of Pantheidas, from Keos,
victor in boys' boxing at the Isthmian games

|   | | |
|---|---|---|
| | Hurry, O giver of glorious gifts, Report, | [Str.] |
| | to holy Keos, bringing | |
| | a message whose name is gracious, | |
| | that in the battle of bold hands | |
| 5 | Argeios has won victory, | |

|   | | |
|---|---|---|
| | and so has brought to mind all those fair deeds | [Ant.] |
| | which at the Isthmus' famous neck, | |
| | leaving Euxantios' holy island, | |
| | we brought to light along | |
| 10 | with seventy crowns. | |

|   | | |
|---|---|---|
| | The Muse, home-born, summons | [Ep.] |
| | the sweet shrill cry of pipes, | |
| | doing honor in victory song | |
| | to Pantheidas' beloved son. | |

This brief epinician was evidently composed and performed while Argeios and his party were still at Olympia following his victory; thereafter Bacchylides produced a second, and much more substantial, ode (not included in this volume) for performance on Keos.

7 **at the Isthmus' famous neck** i.e., at the Isthmian games (see Glossary).
8 **Euxantios' holy island** i.e., Keos. On Euxantios, a legendary ancestor of the Kean people, see Pindar, Paean 4.
9 **we** i.e., the citizens of Keos, of whom Bacchylides himself was one.
11 **The Muse, home-born** See previous note. According to an alternative interpretation of the epithet (which literally means something like "born on the spot"), Bacchylides is alluding to the extemporized character of the poem (see introductory note).

## Ode 3:

> for Hieron son of Deinomenes, from Syracuse,
> victor in the chariot race at the Olympic games

In praise of Demeter, queen of fruitful Sicily,                    [Str. 1]
    and of the Maiden, violet-crowned,
sing, Kleio, giver of sweet gifts; and sing as well
    of Hieron's horses that ran swiftly at Olympia.

5    For with the aid of Victory that excels, and Glory      [Ant. 1]
        too,
they rushed alongside the banks of Alpheos
with its wide eddies, where they made Deinomenes' son
    blessed with the crowns that they attained.

The people shouted . . .                                          [Ep. 1]
10    Oh, three times fortunate the man
who, having as his lot from Zeus
    the widest kingship of all Greeks,
knows not to hide his towering piles of wealth
    beneath a shrouding cloak of darkness.

15    The shrines abound with festal sacrifices,              [Str. 2]
    the streets abound with hospitality;
gold gleams and sparkles forth
    from tripods of high craftsmanship that stand

before the temple, there where the greatest          [Ant. 2]
    precinct
20    of Phoibos, near the waters of Kastalia,
lies in the Delphians' charge. The god, the god
    let each man glorify, since that is the best of blessings.

For once, when Zeus had brought                      [Ep. 2]
    his destined judgment to fulfillment
25    and Sardis was being captured by the Persian army,
    Apollo of the golden lyre
kept Croesus, king
    of horse-taming Lydia,

safely guarded. When the unexpected day              [Str. 3]
30    came, he had no intention of awaiting
slavery with its many tears. Instead,
    before the bronze walls of his palace

he had a pyre heaped up, and with his faithful       [Ant. 3]
    wife
and fair-haired daughters wailing piteously,
35    he climbed upon it, and with arms
    uplifted to steep heaven

he cried aloud: "Almighty Power,                     [Ep. 3]
    where is the gratitude of gods?
And where is Leto's lordly son?
40    Gone are the halls of Alyattes . . .
    . . . countless . . .
        [one line missing]

. . . the city. . . .                                 [Str. 4]
Red with blood are the golden eddies
45    of Paktolos, and with unseemly violence women
    are being dragged from well-built houses.

Things that before were hateful now are dear: to     [Ant. 4]
    die is sweetest."
So much he said, and ordered the soft-stepping servant
to set the tower of logs ablaze. The maidens
50    shrieked, and toward their mother they

kept reaching out their arms, for mortals find the                [Ep. 4]
    death
that is foreseen to be most hateful.
But when the fire's bright force
    was darting fearsomely about,
55    Zeus brought a black cloud over
    and quenched the tawny flames.

Nothing is unbelievable which the gods' concern               [Str. 5]
brings about. At that time Apollo, Delos-born,
carried the old man off to the Hyperboreans
60    and settled him there with his trim-ankled
        daughters

by reason of his piety, since of all mortals he                  [Ant. 5]
sent up the greatest gifts to holy Pytho.
And yet of those who dwell in Hellas, none,
    O Hieron worthy of great praise, will wish

65    to claim that he has sent to Loxias                         [Ep. 5]
    more gold than you.
There is ample cause to praise,
    for anyone who does not grow fat on envy,
that warlike man . . .
70    . . . holding Zeus's scepter

and a share of the dark-haired Muses' gifts.                   [Str. 6]
        [one line missing]
. . . what the day brings. . . .
. . . you look for. Life is short,

75    and winged hope undoes the understanding              [Ant. 6]
of beings whom the day defines. The lord Apollo,
far-shooter, said to Pheres' son:
    "Being mortal, you must cherish two

thoughts at once: that tomorrow you will see                   [Ep. 6]
80    the radiance of the sun for one last time,
and that for fifty years
    you will live out your life amid deep wealth.

> Delight your heart with pious actions, for that is
>     the highest form of profit."

85      To one of wit, the things I say are intelligible. The        [Str. 7]
            deep
        sky above cannot be stained; the water of the sea
        does not decay; gold is a thing of joy;
            but man is not allowed to shake off hoary

        old age and once again recover blooming                     [Ant. 7]
90      youth. However, the luster of accomplishment
            does not
        waste away along with the flesh of mortals; rather,
            the Muse sets it to growing. Hieron, you have

        shown forth to men prosperity's most splendid               [Ep. 7]
            flowers. To one who gains success,
95      silence furnishes no adornment.
            Together with the truth of noble deeds,
        many a man will sing the graceful gift of Keos'
            honey-tongued nightingale.

On Hieron, tyrant of Syracuse, see Glossary. The chariot victory that this ode
celebrates was won in 468, eight years after Pindar had articulated Hieron's
hopes for such a triumph at the end of *Olympian* 1. The main themes of the
ode are Hieron's great wealth and his recognition that such riches are not to
be hoarded in miserly fashion but rather expended freely in displays of piety,
generosity, and magnificence. In illustration of these themes Bacchylides re-
lates how Croesus, a Lydian king of proverbial wealth, was rescued by the
gods from imminent death because of his righteousness.

2  **the Maiden** Persephone (see Glossary under "Demeter").
3  **Kleio** one of the Muses (see Glossary).
17–21 Hieron had donated golden tripods to the sanctuary of Apollo
(**Phoibos**) at Delphi. **Kastalia** was a spring not far from the temple.
25–62 On **Croesus** and the conquest of **Lydia** by the **Persians**, see Glossary
under "Croesus." A quite different depiction of Croesus on the pyre is to
be found in Herodotus (1. 86–90).
37  **Almighty Power** Croesus is addressing Zeus.
40  **Alyattes** Croesus's father and predecessor on the Lydian throne.
45  **Paktolos** a river near Sardis, famous for the gold that it carried in its
waters.

59 **Hyperboreans** See Glossary and cf. Pindar, *Pythian* 10. 30ff.
62 **the greatest gifts** Herodotus (1. 50–51) lists the many objects of gold
and silver that Croesus dedicated to Delphian Apollo.
65 **Loxias** Apollo.
76 **beings whom the day defines** For this characterization of human
beings cf. Archilochus 28 and Pindar, *Pythian* 8. 95 with note.
77 **Pheres' son** Admetos, a legendary king of Pherai in Thessaly, who
enjoyed Apollo's special favor.
85–92 In this priamel (see introductory note to Tyrtaeus 7) three imperish-
able and unchanging substances (the sky, the sea, and gold) are first
*contrasted* with man's bodily nature, doomed as it is to irreversible decay,
and then (implicitly) *likened* to the lasting fame that poetry can bestow on
mortals even after their physical extinction.
97–98 **Keos' honey-tongued nightingale** a reference to Bacchylides
himself, who was a native of Keos (cf. Ode 2. 11 with note).

# Ode 5:

for Hieron son of Deinomenes, from Syracuse,
victor in the horse-race at the Olympic games

Fortunate leader of the Syracusans                              [Str. 1]
    renowned for their whirling chariots,
you will know how to judge the violet-crowned
    Muses' sweet gift and ornament, if any can
5    of those now living on the earth,
    correctly. Let your thought, intent on justice,
relax a while in peace, cares laid aside,
    and turn your mind's gaze hither:
this hymn, woven with the aid
10    of the deep-girded Graces,
is being sent from the holy isle
    to your illustrious city by a guest-friend,
the celebrated servant of
    gold-banded Ourania. He is ready
15    to pour forth from his breast loud song

in praise of Hieron. Quickly                                    [Ant. 1]
    cutting the depth of air
on high with tawny wings,
    the eagle, messenger of Zeus

20      who thunders in wide lordship,
            is bold, relying on his mighty
        strength, while other birds
            cower, shrill-voiced, in fear.
        The great earth's mountain peaks do not hold him
                back,
25          nor the tireless sea's
        rough-tossing waves, but in
            the limitless expanse
        he guides his fine sleek plumage
            along the west wind's breezes,
30          manifest to men's sight.


        So now for me too countless paths extend in all        [Ep. 1]
                directions
            by which to praise your prowess
        in song, by the grace of dark-haired Victory
            and Ares of the brazen breastplate,
35      O lordly sons of Deinomenes!
            May god not tire in his beneficence.
        When Pherenikos with his auburn mane
            ran like the wind
        beside the eddies of broad Alpheos,
40          Dawn, with her arms all golden, saw his victory;


        and so too at most holy Pytho.                         [Str. 2]
            Calling the earth to witness, I declare
        that never yet has any horse outstripped him
            in competition, sprinkling him with dust
45      as he rushed forward to the goal.
            For like the north wind's blast,
        keeping the man who steers him safe,
            he hurtles onward, bringing to Hieron,
        that generous host, victory with its fresh applause.
50          Blessed is he on whom the gods
        bestow a share of noble things
            and, along with enviable success,
        a life passed amid wealth. For no
            mortal on earth is born
55          to be in all ways fortunate.

Once, they say, that ruiner of gates, [Ant. 2]
    the unconquerable son of Zeus
whose thunderbolt is bright, went down
    into the halls of slender-ankled Persephone,
60    seeking to fetch the saw-toothed hound
    from Hades up into the light,
the offspring of the terrible Echidna.
    There he observed the souls
of wretched mortals by Kokytos' streams,
65    like leaves tossed by the wind
up and down the clear-edged heights
    of Ida where sheep graze.
Conspicuous among them was the shade
    of Porthaon's grandson,
70    bold-hearted shaker of the spear.

Seeing him in his shining armor, [Ep. 2]
    Alkmene's son, the wondrous hero,
stretched a clear-sounding sinew on his bow;
    then, lifting up the lid
75    of his quiver, he took out
    a brazen-headed arrow. But right there before him
the soul of Meleagros loomed
    and with full knowledge spoke to him:
"Great Zeus's son,
80    stand where you are, and, making your heart calm,

do not launch from your hands [Str. 3]
    a rough-edged arrow to no purpose
against the souls of those who have perished.
    You have no cause to fear." He spoke thus, and
    amazement seized
85    Amphitryon's lordly son.
    He said, "Who is it of immortals
or mortals that has nurtured such
    a sapling, and in what great land?
Who killed him? Truly, Hera of the lovely belt
90    will soon send such a one
against me, to my hurt—but then perhaps
    the fair-haired Pallas has the matter already in mind."

Then Meleagros said to him
   in tears: "To turn aside
95     the gods' intent is difficult

for men who live upon the earth.          [Ant. 3]
   For otherwise my father, horse-driving Oineus,
       would
have put an end to the wrath of Artemis,
   august, white-armed, with rosebuds in her hair,
100   by means by prayers and
     the sacrifice of many goats
and cattle, ruddy-backed.
   But not to be conquered was the wrath
which the goddess had conceived. And so the Maiden
     sent a boar,
105   wide-ranging in violence, a ruthless fighter,
into the lovely fields of Kalydon,
   and there, strength overflowing,
it ravaged vineyards with its tusks
   and slaughtered flocks, and any man
110   who met it face to face.

Against it we waged hateful battle—we, the best    [Ep. 3]
   among the Greeks—with force and fury,
six days on end; but when some power
   had handed victory to the Aitolians,
115   we buried those who had been killed
     by the boar's impetuous, bellowing charge:
Ankaios and Agelaos, bravest
   of my dear brothers,
whom in Oineus' celebrated halls
120   . . . Althaia bore.

   . . . destroyed by baleful destiny . . .      [Str. 4]
   . . . for not yet had Leto's wild
and fiery-hearted daughter brought
   her wrath to an end. Contesting for the gleaming hide,
125   we fought with force and fury
     against the Kouretes staunch in war.
And then I killed, along

with many others, Iphiklos
and noble Aphares, my mother's quick-limbed brothers;
    for in truth
130      strong-hearted Ares
does not distinguish friends in war:
    blindly do weapons leave the hand,
aimed against the lives
    of enemies but bringing death
135      to those that heaven chooses.


Of these things Thestios' fiery-hearted        [Ant. 4]
    daughter took no thought,
although she was my mother—and my evil fate.
    Plotting my death, that woman whom no fear could
      shake
140      took from a chest of intricate workmanship
    the log that spelled my speedy doom
and set it burning: destiny
    had so spun out its thread that then
and thus would be the limit of my life. It happened
145      that I was stripping Klymenos
of armor, Deïpylos' valiant son
    whose body was without flaw;
before the ramparts I had overtaken him,
    as they fled toward the stout
150      walls of that ancient city,


Pleuron. But the sweet breath of life began to fail    [Ep. 4]
    me,
and I felt my strength grow less.
Alas! With one last gasp, I burst out weeping, grieved
    to leave behind the radiance of youth."
155      They say that Amphitryon's son,
    whom cries of battle did not daunt, at that time and
      no other
shed tears, in pity for
    the man's calamitous fate;
and answering him
160      he said, "For mortals, not to be born is best,

nor to gaze upon the sun's                                        [Str. 5]
   bright light. And yet no good
can come of such lamentation:
   a man should speak of what he really means to
      accomplish.
165   Tell me, is there within the halls
   of Oineus, dear to Ares,
one of his daughters still unwedded,
   bearing your likeness in her form?
Her I would gladly make my lustrous wife."
170   To him the shade
of Meleagros staunch in war
   replied: "I left one with youth's bloom about her neck
there in the house, Deïaneira,
   as yet without experience of golden
175   Kypris who casts her spells on mortal men."

White-armed Kalliope,                                             [Ant. 5]
   halt the well-wrought chariot
right here! Make Zeus the son of Kronos
   your theme of song, the Olympian ruler of the gods,
180   and the untiring current
   of Alpheos, and Pelops' might,
and Pisa, where famed Pherenikos
   won victory on the race course
by speed of feet, and came then to the towers of
      Syracuse,
185   bearing for Hieron
the leaves of happiness.
   One must for the sake of truth
give praise, with both hands thrusting
   envy aside,
190   if anyone among mortals is successful.

A man from Boiotia said this,                                     [Ep. 5]
   Hesiod, servant of the sweet
Muses: he whom immortals honor
   has men's report attending him as well.
195   I readily am persuaded
   to see that glorious speech, not straying from the path of
      justice,

be sent to Hieron, for from that source
the roots of all nobility draw strength and flourish.
May Zeus, the greatest of all fathers,
200          preserve them in unshaken peace.

On Hieron, tyrant of Syracuse, see Glossary. Like Pindar's *Olympian* 1, this ode celebrates the Olympic victory won in 476 by Hieron's racehorse Pherenikos, whose speed and grace are vividly evoked in lines 37–49. The extended mythical narrative that occupies the central portion of the ode (56–175) brings together two great figures of Greek legend: Herakles, who has descended into the realm of the dead while performing one of his famous labors, and the Aitolian warrior Meleagros, whose ghost or shade Herakles encounters there. At Herakles' prompting Meleagros tells the story of his own untimely death, which was brought upon him by fate and the burning anger of his mother Althaia. The narrative as a whole ends with an allusion to Meleagros' sister Deïaneira (172–175), whom Herakles will later marry and at whose hands he in turn is destined to die. In this way Bacchylides contrives to suggest a parallel between the two heroes that underscores the truth of the maxim which the myth is introduced to illustrate: "no mortal on earth is born in all ways fortunate" (53–55).

11–14  The **holy isle** is Keos, Bacchylides' homeland, and Bacchylides himself, in his role as poet, is both a **guest-friend** (see note on *Olympian* 1. 103) and a **servant of gold-banded Ourania** (Ourania being one of the Muses; see Glossary).

16–30  The extended description of the eagle obviously has symbolic force, but scholars are undecided whether it should be referred to Hieron as victor, to Bacchylides as poet, or to both at once.

31–35  On the military exploits of Hieron and his brother Gelon (the **sons of Deinomenes**) see Glossary under "Hieron" and cf. *Pythian* 1. 47–52 and 71–80.

39  **beside the eddies of broad Alpheos** i.e., at Olympia.

57  **the unconquerable son of Zeus** Herakles; likewise **Alkmene's son** in 72.

60  **the saw-toothed hound** Kerberos (see Glossary).

64  **Kokytos** a river in the underworld; its name means "Wailing."

69  **Porthaon's grandson** i.e., Meleagros, Porthaon being the father of **Oineus** (97)

89–92  Zeus's wife **Hera** persecuted Herakles throughout his life; it was through her machinations, for example, that he was compelled to perform his famous twelve labors. **Pallas** Athena, on the other hand, was his patron and protector throughout his various trials.

97  **Oineus** the king of the city of **Kalydon** (106) in Aitolia. According to the account given at *Iliad* 9. 529ff, **Artemis** became angry at Oineus when

he inadvertently neglected to include her among the gods whom he honored with sacrifice at a harvest festival; as a punishment she sent a monstrous boar to ravage Oineus' land.

111–35 Heroes from all over Greece joined forces in the famous "Kalydonian boar hunt," which ended in the boar's death. Thereafter, however, a quarrel over its hide led to armed conflict and bloodshed between the Aitolians of Kalydon and the **Kouretes** (126) of **Pleuron** (151). In this battle Meleagros accidentally killed two uncles, the brothers of his mother **Althaia** (120). Althaia was the daughter of **Thestios** (136), king of Pleuron.

136–44 Shortly after Meleagros was born, the Fates predicted that he would die if and when the log that was then burning on Oineus' hearth was consumed to ashes; in order to protect her son, therefore, Althaia removed the log from the fire and put it into a chest for safekeeping. Years later, seeking revenge for the killing of her brothers (see previous note), she burned the log and so brought about the death of Meleagros.

160–62 For the sentiment, cf. Theognis 12.

173 **Deïaneira** Herakles' future wife; her name means "man-destroyer." As the story is presented in Sophocles' *Trachiniae*, Deïaneira unintention- ally caused Herakles' death when she attempted to regain his affections by means of what she thought was a love potion but what was in reality a deadly poison. It is possible, however, that Bacchylides was thinking of an earlier version of the story according to which Deïaneira killed Herakles deliberately in revenge for his infidelity. In either case, the allusion has ominous undertones that are only intensified by the abruptness with which the poet calls a halt to the story in lines 176–78.

175 **Kypris** Aphrodite (see Glossary).

176 **Kalliope** one of the Muses (see Glossary).

181 **Pelops** is mentioned here in his role as mythical founder of eques- trian competition at Olympia (cf. Pindar's *Olympian* 1).

193–94 This sentiment is not in fact found in any of the extant works of Hesiod.


# Ode 6:

### for Lachon son of Aristomenes, from Keos, victor in the stade race at the Olympian games

Lachon from mightiest Zeus                                    [Str. 1]
has with his feet obtained the best
of glories, winning beside the streams of Alpheos.
How often in the past
5     has Keos, nurse of vines,

been celebrated at Olympia
for mastery gained in boxing and the stade race,
through songs sung by young men

whose hair is thick with wreaths.                        [Str. 2]
10  But you are now the one to whom Ourania,
queen of music, directs a hymn by Victory's grace,
O wind-foot son
of Aristomenes,
doing you honor with songs sung before
15      your house, because by gaining mastery in the stade
race
you brought fair fame to Keos.

In this ode, as in Ode 2, one sees the epinician reduced to little more than its
factual essentials: the victor's name (1), his father's name (13), his homeland
(5, 16), the victory itself as defined by venue (3) and event (15), and previous
victories, in this case won not by the victor but by his community at large
(4–9).

1–2 In the original Greek there is a play on words between Lachon's
name and the verb *lache* ("obtained").
7 **the stade race** see note on Pindar, *Olympian* 13. 30.
10 **Ourania** one of the Muses (see Glossary).

# Ode 11:

for Alexidamos son of Phaïskos, from Metapontion,
victor in boys' wrestling at the Pythian games

Victory, giver of sweet gifts. . . .                        [Str. 1]
to you the father . . .
enthroned on high . . .
and on Olympos rich in gold
5   you stand at Zeus's side
and bring to decision, for immortals
and mortals too, the outcome of achievement.
Be gracious, daughter of long-tressed
Styx who keeps justice upright. Thanks to you,
10  now it is Metapontion that is filled
with young men, strong of limb, intent

on revelry and good cheer throughout a city honored by
       the gods,
for they are singing of the Pythian victor,
Phaïskos' wondrous son.

15    With gracious glance the Delian-born                    [Ant. 1]
          son of deep-girdled Leto
      made him welcome, and many were
          the wreaths of flowers that fell
      about Alexidamos on the plain
20        of Kirrha, thanks to the strength
          that conquered all in wrestling.
      At no time on that day, at least,
      did the sun see him fall upon the earth.
      And I shall vow that so too on the sacred soil
25        of hallowed Pelops
      by Alpheos' lovely stream, if only someone had
      not turned aside the course of upright justice,
          the leaves of gray-green olive open to all comers

      would as a crown have decked his hair                  [Ep. 1]
30    when he returned to his Italian homeland, nurse of calves.
      In truth, he brought to earth
      in that land's lovely meadows
          many a boy with subtle stratagems.
      But either some god was to blame, or
35        men's judgments, wandering far astray,
      snatched from his hands the loftiest of prizes.
      But now Artemis, She of the Wilderness
      who wields a golden distaff and a far-famed bow,
      the Gentle One, has granted lustrous victory.
40    To honor her the son of Abas
          once built an altar used for prayer by many,
          he and his daughters in their pretty robes.

      They had been driven in stark terror                   [Str. 2]
          from Proitos' lovely palace
45    by the almighty Hera, who had yoked
          their wits to maddening compulsion.
      With hearts still blithely girlish

they came into the precinct of
the goddess of the crimson belt
50   and claimed that their own father
greatly surpassed in wealth the fair-haired one who shares
the throne of Zeus, revered for his wide power.
    Provoked to wrath against them,
she turned their thoughts around to delirium.
55   They fled into the wooded hills,
    uttering dreadful cries,

leaving behind the town of Tiryns            [Ant. 2]
    with its god-built streets.
Already it had been ten years
60     since the people left god-cherished Argos
and dwelt instead in Tiryns, demigods
    fearless in warfare with bronze shields,
    along with their much-envied king.
For irresolvable conflict,
65   beginning from some trifle, had sprung up between the
        brothers
Proitos and Akrisios.
    When discord, overstepping justice,
and battle's woes loomed close to crush the people,
they begged that since the sons of Abas
70     shared the inheritance of a crop-rich land,

the younger should make Tiryns           [Ep. 2]
his place of settlement before they fell into disaster's grip.
Then too, it was the will of Zeus, the son of Kronos,
who honored the race of Danaos
75     and Lynkeus, driver of horses,
that there should be an end to hateful sorrows.
    The monstrous Cyclopes came
and built a rampart of surpassing beauty
about the famous city, where the godlike
80   heroes of great renown thereafter dwelt,
having left glorious Argos grazed by horses.
    From there in panic haste
    Proitos' unwedded daughters
    fled, their dark hair streaming.

85    But he himself was seized at heart by sorrow,          [Str. 3]
          and strange perplexity struck him like a blow:
      he had in mind to thrust his two-
          edged sword into his breast.
      His bodyguards, however,
90        with soothing words
          and force of hands restrained him.
      Thirteen full months
      they wandered in the shadowy woods,
      fleeing throughout Arkadia,
95        that nurse of flocks. But when at last
      their father reached the lovely streams of Lousos,
      he bathed his body in them and then called
          upon the ox-eyed daughter

      of Leto in her crimson veil.                            [Ant. 3]
100       Lifting his arms toward the sun's
      splendor, whose speed is that of horses,
          he begged her to release his children from
      the wretchedness of their mad frenzy:
          "And I shall offer you in sacrifice twenty oxen
105       whose ruddy necks have not yet felt the yoke."
      She heard his prayer, that stalker of wild beasts
      whose father is supreme, and, swaying Hera,
      she brought the girls, heads wreathed with flowers,
          at long last to an end of impious madness.
110   They built for her, at once, a precinct and an altar,
      and stained it with the blood of sheep,
          and instituted women's choruses.

      From there, accompanying                                [Ep. 3]
      Achaians, men whom Ares loves, you journeyed to a city
115   that is a nurse of horses, and with happy effect
      you dwell in Metapontion,
          the people's golden mistress.
      For you a charming grove
          beside the waters of the Kasas
120   was founded by the men who in due time,
      by the counsels of the blessed gods,
          sacked Priam's well-built city

along with Atreus' sons in brazen armor. Any man
whose thoughts are set on justice
125       will find a theme in the countless deeds of prowess
that have through all of time been done by Achaians.

Metapontion was a Greek city in southern Italy, founded by colonists from
the region of Greece known as Achaia. The cult of Artemis Hemera ("The
Gentle One") was of special importance in Metapontion, having been
brought there by its Achaian founders (cf. 113–117). Bacchylides avails him-
self of this circumstance in choosing a subject for the ode's central narrative,
which is structured through an elaborate (and potentially confusing) series
of temporal regressions and returns: (A) Proitos and his daughters built an
altar to Artemis Hemera (40–42) because (B) the girls had been driven in
madness from Tiryns (43–58), where (C) Proitos had been living for ten years
(59–63) because (D) he had quarreled with his brother Akrisios (64–76), which
resulted (C') in his settling in Tiryns (77–81), from whence (B') his daughters
fled and wandered in madness until Artemis cured them (82–109) and (A')
they and Proitos built her an altar as an expression of gratitude (110–12). For
other examples of such "concentric ring-form" cf. Alcaeus 3, Pindar, *Pythian*
3, and Bacchylides, Ode 13.

1–9  According to Hesiod (*Theogony* 383–85), **Victory** (Nike) is one of
four children borne by **Styx**, the others being Emulation (Zelos), Power
(Kratos), and Force (Bia). Styx herself was the eponymous nymph of a
river in the Underworld which had the power of binding any god that
swore an oath by its waters. It is this capacity that Bacchylides alludes to
when he says that Styx **keeps justice upright** (9).
16  **son of deep-girdled Leto**  Apollo, here acting in his role as patron
deity of the Pythian games.
19–20  **the plain of Kirrha**  below Delphi (Pytho); see Glossary.
24–25  **the sacred soil of hallowed Pelops**  On Pelops' tomb and hero
shrine at Olympia cf. Pindar, *Olympian* 1. 90–93.
24–36  Bacchylides claims that the only reason why Alexidamos had
failed to win a wrestling victory at Olympia was that he was defrauded of
what was rightfully his either by supernatural power or by human error.
40  **the son of Abas**  Proitos; for his story see Glossary under "Proitos"
and "Akrisios."
51  **the fair-haired one**  i.e., Hera.
74  **the race of Danaos**  the people of Argos; see Glossary under
"Danaos."
75  **Lynkeus**  father of Abas; see Glossary.
77  **Cyclopes**  See Glossary.

110 **a precinct and an altar** The sanctuary of Artemis here alluded to was
at Lousoi (cf. 96) in northern Arkadia, where the goddess was worshipped
as "The Gentle One" (Hemera) in commemoration of her curing of the
daughters of Proitos.
113–20 The **you** in these lines is Artemis Hemera, whose worship was
transferred to Metapontion by its Achaian founders.
119 **Kasas** the river on which Metapontion was situated.

## Ode 13:

### for Pytheas son of Lampon,
### from Aigina, victor in the pankration

[lines 1–43 missing]
". . . shall put an end to arrogance with its high
thoughts,
45           meting out punishments to mortal men.

So crushing is the hand that Perseus'                      [Ant. 2]
descendant wields
against the savage lion's neck
with stratagems of every kind!
50      For flashing bronze, which masters
mortals, refuses to pass through
that unapproachable bulk,
which bends a sword
back on itself. The time shall come, I say,
55      when on this spot, for wreaths
offered in the pankration, Greeks
will sweat and toil."

Since then, beside the altar of Zeus who rules             [Ep. 2]
supreme,
the flowers of glory-laden Victory have
60           caused golden fame
to flourish in the sight of many
for a few men throughout
their lifetimes; and when death's
dark cloud conceals them, there remains
65      renown undying for a thing well done
as their unfailing portion.

Such honors you too have attained at Nemea,         [Str. 3]
     O son of Lampon;
your hair decked out with wreaths
70   of flowers all in bloom,
you have come home to the city's high-built streets . . .
     . . . so that the gentle sounds
     of revelry that gives delight
     hold sway on your ancestral
75   island, as you show forth the strength that gained
the upper hand in combat with pankratiasts.
O daughter of the river's
     eddying flow, Aigina of the kindly mind,

truly to you the son of Kronos                      [Ant. 3]
80       has given great honor,
showing forth this victory
in view of all the Greeks
like a bright torch. Your might is hymned
by many a high-vaunting girl,
85       who . . .
         . . . with skipping feet,
like an untroubled fawn
upon the flowering hills,
lightly leaping in company
90       with worthy friends and neighbors.

Wreathed in the local fashion                       [Ep. 3]
with crimson flowers and reeds
     woven as ornaments,
the maidens celebrate your son,
95       O mistress of a land that welcomes guests,
and Endeïs too, the rosy-armed,
     who bore the godlike Peleus
and Telamon the warrior,
     when she had lain with Aiakos in love.

100  Their battle-rousing offspring,                 [Str. 4]
         the swift Achilles
and lovely Eriboia's
high-spirited son, I shall proclaim—

Ajax the hero with his mighty shield,
105    who standing on the stern
      brought the bold-hearted
      bronze-helmed Hektor to a halt
as he was rushing at the ships
to set them awesomely ablaze,
110    that time when Peleus' son
      let the harsh anger in his breast

rise up, thus setting the Dardanians        [Ant. 4]
    free from their woes.
Previously, they never left
115    the many towers of Ilion's
prodigious citadel, but in a bewilderment of fear
they cowered out of battle's stinging reach
      whenever on the plain Achilles raged,
      driving his foes before him in confusion,
120    shaking the spear that slaughtered multitudes.
But when the violet-crowned
Nereid's son, who never trembled,
    ceased to take part in warfare,

then just as on the sea that blooms in darkness    [Ep. 4]
125    the north wind rends the hearts of men
      amid the waves,
coming upon them with the fall of night,
      but ceases when the light of dawn
shines forth for mortals, and a fair breeze stills
130      the sea; the south wind billows in
the sails, and joyfully they make their way
      beyond all hope to land—

in this way, when the Trojans heard        [Str. 5]
    that the spearman Achilles
135    was staying in his quarters
for the fair-haired woman's sake,
Briseïs of the longed-for limbs,
they stretched their hands up to the gods,
      glimpsing a patch of brightness
140      agleam beneath the storm-clouds.

And with all speed they left
Laomedon's walls
and raced out on the plain,
   bringing fierce battle with them

145     and rousing fear in the Danaans.        [Ant. 5]
      Urged on by Ares
of the strong spear and by Apollo
Loxias, lord of Lykia,
they reached the shore of the sea,
150    and there beside the ships' fair sterns
      they fought; and with the blood
      of slaughtered men
the dark earth reddened
under Hektor's hand.
155     . . . to the demigods . . .
      . . . through the god-like heroes' onslaught.

     . . . truly, with great hopes        [Ep. 5]
did they draw breath and utter
      their overweening cries,
160    those Trojan horsemen, when they stormed
      the dark-eyed ships . . .
      . . . banquets . . .
      . . . would hold sway throughout the god-built city.
But they were destined before then to make
165     Skamandros' eddying waters crimson,

dying beneath the tower-razing hands      [Str. 6]
      of Aiakos' descendants.
Of them, however much . . .
169    either on deep-piled logs . . .
         [five lines missing]
175    For under night's dark veil
Excellence, visible to all,
      does not grow dim in hiding,

but, burgeoning always with        [Ant. 6]
      untiring fame,
180    she wanders over land

and widely shifting sea.
Moreover, she does honor to the glory-laden
island of Aiakos, and with Good Fame
    who holds wreaths dear
185    she steers the city on its course,
together with Good Order, sound of mind,
who claims festivities as her portion
and keeps the towns of reverent men
    under safe guard in peace.

190    Celebrate, O young men, the glorious victory          [Ep. 6]
of Pytheas, and also the attentive care
    shown by Menandros in assisting athletes.
The training that he gives has often,
    by Alpheos' stream, found honor at the hands
195    of the august Athena, great in heart, whose chariot is golden,
    and before now it has set crowns
upon the hair of countless men
    at games attended by all Greeks.

Unless a person is overmastered                              [Str. 7]
200    by envy and its reckless speech,
he must give praise to such a man of skill
as justice bids. Men's censure, to be sure,
lies heavy on all actions,
but truth is likely to win out,
205    and time that conquers everything
    always brings into public view
the thing which has been nobly done.
The ill-disposed, intemperate
209    of tongue, dwindle and fade away from sight . . .
            [one line missing]

            [nine lines missing]                            [Ant. 7]
220    . . . he warms his heart with hope.
Trusting to that myself, and to
    the Muses with their crimson veils,

this newly plaited crown of song                             [Ep. 7]
I show forth, doing honor

225          to the resplendent hospitality
             which, Lampon, you have offered me. May you look
                with favor on my gift—no slight one—to your son.
             If Kleio, giver of all bloom, has truly
                instilled this in my mind,
230          songs of delightful utterance
             will herald forth his name to all the people.

When Pytheas, an Aiginetan youth, won a victory in the pankration at the Nemean games, his father Lampon took the unusual (and presumably quite costly) step of commissioning epinicians from *two* eminent poets simultaneously; this poem and Pindar's *Nemean 5* were the result. As in *Nemean 5* and in Pindar's two other odes for Lampon's family, *Isthmian 6* and *Isthmian 5*, the central section of this ode (91–167) celebrates the exploits of Aigina's own lineage of heroes, the descendants of Aiakos. Two are singled out for special attention: Achilles, whose temporary withdrawal from the Trojan War emboldened Hektor and his fellow Trojans to mount an energetic counterattack on the Greek forces, and "Ajax the hero with his mighty shield" (104), whose courage and tenacity in defending the Greek ships put a halt to the Trojan onslaught. Such martial exemplars seem particularly appropriate in an ode for a pankratiast in view of the fiercely violent character of that sport.

44–57 The identity of the speaker of these lines is concealed by the preceding lacuna; it may be Nemea herself, the eponymous nymph of the game site. The subject of line 44 must be Herakles, who was **Perseus' descendant** through his mother Alkmene (see Glossary). On Herakles' killing of the invulnerable Nemean lion, see Glossary under "Nemea" and cf. Pindar, *Isthmian* 6. 47–48. Lines 54–57 make it clear that Herakles' fierce struggle against the lion is to be understood as a mythical prototype of the pankration.

77 **Aigina** eponymous nymph of the island Aigina, whose father was the river god Asopos.

94 **your son** i.e., Aiakos, whom Aigina bore to Zeus.

96 **Endeïs** Aiakos' wife, who was one of the daughters of Chiron the Centaur; cf. Pindar, *Nemean* 5. 12.

102 **Eriboia** Telamon's wife; cf. Pindar, *Isthmian* 6. 46.

104–67 The central narrative of the ode shows "concentric ring-form" (see note on Alcaeus 3 and cf. Bacchylides, Ode 11, and Pindar, *Pythian* 3): (A) Ajax stood defending the Greek ships against Hektor (104–9) after (B) Achilles in anger had withdrawn from battle and thus heartened the Trojans (110–13), who (C) previously had kept themselves safe within the walls of Troy (114–20); but when (B') Achilles became angry at

Agamemnon and stopped fighting, the Trojans took heart and went on the offensive (121–45), until (A') they began attacking the Greek ships (146–67).

110 **Peleus' son** Achilles, whose **harsh anger** against Agamemnon (see note to line 137) prompted him to withdraw temporarily from the Trojan War and thus opened the way for a Trojan attack on the Greek camp.

112 **the Dardanians** the Trojans (see Glossary).

122 **Nereid's son** Achilles, as son of Thetis (see Glossary).

137 **Briseïs** a young woman awarded to Achilles as a war prize and then taken away from him by Agamemnon, the commander in chief of the Greek forces at Troy. The anger provoked in Achilles by that action and the various consequences that flowed from it make up the main theme of Homer's *Iliad*.

142 **Laomedon** king of Troy (and father of Priam), at whose behest the city's walls were built by Poseidon and Apollo.

145 **the Danaans** the Greeks.

165 **Skamandros** the chief river of Troy.

167 **Aiakos' descendants** Bacchylides is alluding in particular to Achilles, who slaughtered many Trojans on the banks of the Skamandros once the death of his friend Patroklos had spurred him to begin fighting again.

192 **Menandros** Pytheas' trainer (cf. *Nemean* 5. 48).

194 **by Alpheos' stream** i.e., at Olympia (see Glossary).

225 **the resplendent hospitality** Cf. note on *Olympian* 1. 103.

227 **my gift** i.e., the present ode.

228 **Kleio** one of the Muses (see Glossary).

## Dithyramb 17: "The Youths, or Theseus"

|  | With darkly gleaming prow the ship | [Str. 1] |
|---|---|---|

      With darkly gleaming prow the ship          [Str. 1]
          was cutting through the Cretan sea,
          carrying Theseus, staunch in the battle din,
      and twice seven splendid young Ionian folk;
5     for into the far-shining sail
          a breeze from the north was falling,
          thanks to glorious Athena, shaker of the aegis.
      And Minos' heart was pricked
          by lust, the holy gift
10    of Aphrodite, goddess diademed with desire.
          No longer did he keep his hand
          away from the girl, but touched
          her white cheeks.
          And Eriboia shouted to
15    Pandion's grandson in his bronze

breastplate. When Theseus saw it,
   his dark eyes rolled
under his brows, and cruel pain
   tore at his heart,
20    and he said, "Son of mightiest Zeus,
no longer are your passions steered
   in righteousness within the compass of
your wits. Hero that you are, restrain your vaunting
    violence.

Whatever thing all-mastering destiny          [Ant. 1]
25    has stipulated for us from the gods, and Justice swings
    her scales
   in confirmation, that apportionment
we shall fulfill as fated when
it comes. But as for you, hold back
   from the grave wrong that you are planning. Even if it is
    true
30    that Phoinix's cherished daughter, famed
for beauty, lay with Zeus beneath the crest of Ida
   and bore you to be foremost
of mortals, still I too
   am son of a god,
35    born to Poseidon of the sea
from his union with opulent
Pittheus' daughter, who received
a golden veil from the dark-haired Nereids.
Therefore I urge you, warlord of the Knossians,
40    to curb your arrogance, which will otherwise
be cause of many groans. I would not wish
   to see the immortal loveliness
of Dawn's light after you had forced
any of these young people to your will;
45    before that comes to pass, the power of our hands
will be shown forth, and what ensues will be as heaven
    determines."

So much the hero said, that valiant spearman.     [Ep. 1]
Amazement gripped the sailors
at the man's inordinate

50   boldness, but it enraged the Sun-god's son-in-law.
     Beginning to weave a new and cunning
     plan, he said: "O you whose strength is mighty,
     Zeus, father, listen: if indeed your white-armed
     bride from Phoinikia bore me as your son,
55   now send forth from the sky a swift
     lightning flash with fiery tresses
     as a sign easy to recognize. And if
         in turn Troizenian Aithra
         engendered *you* by earth-shaking
60      Poseidon, fetch this ring of gold,
     my hand's splendid
         ornament, out of the sea's depths,
     hurling yourself with boldness into your father's home.
     You will learn whether my prayer
65      is heeded by the son of Kronos,
     the lord of thunder who rules all things."

     Then Zeus, whose strength is mighty, heeded          [Str. 2]
         the unimpeachable prayer. Engendering honor
             unsurpassed
         for Minos his beloved son, and wishing
70   to make it visible to all,
     he sent a flash of lightning. At the sight
         of a portent that so fitted his desires, the hero staunch in
             war
         stretched up his hands toward the glorious sky
     and said, "Theseus, here you see
75      the clear gifts given to me
     by Zeus. Now you in turn must leap into
         the sea's loud turbulence, and Kronos' son,
         your father, lord Poseidon, will
         bring your fame to unequaled heights
80      throughout the earth with its fair trees."
         Thus he spoke, and the other's spirit
     did not give way. Upon
         the well-built sterndeck
     he took his stand and leapt, and the precinct of the sea
85      welcomed him willingly.
     Amazement filled the heart

of Zeus's son, and he commanded that
    the ship, so intricately crafted, should keep on
      before
the wind; but Destiny was readying a different course.

90     The vessel under swift escort rushed along, being   [Ant. 2]
      driven
    by a gale that blew behind it from the north.
    The crowd of young
Athenians had trembled when
the hero leapt into the sea, and from
95      their lily-lustrous eyes they shed
    tears, expecting compulsion's heavy grip.
Dolphins, meanwhile, those salt-sea dwellers,
    quickly carried the great
Theseus to the home of his
100     father, the god of horses; and he came
    to the sea gods' hall. There, at the sight
    of blessed Nereus' glorious daughters,
    fear seized on him, for from their radiant limbs
    brightness shone forth
105    like that of fire, and about their hair
    bands plaited out of gold
were twisting, as they took delight
    in dancing on supple feet.
He also saw the dear wife of his father
110    there in the lovely house, august
    ox-eyed Amphitrite,
who clothed him in a mantle of sea-purple

and set upon his thick-curled locks           [Ep. 2]
a plaited garland without flaws,
115    which earlier, at her marriage,
deceitful Aphrodite had given her, dark with roses.
Nothing willed to be so by higher powers
is unbelievable to mortals of sound mind.
By the ship's slender stern he rose to view, and ah!
120    amid what thoughts did he cut short
the Knossian commander, when
he came unwetted from the sea,

a wonder to all, and round his limbs
        the gods' gifts shimmered, and the bright-
125        throned maidens, settled
        anew in joyousness,
    cried aloud, and the sea
        resounded, and nearby the youths
    sang a paean with lovely voice.
130    O god of Delos, warmed at heart
        by the dances of the Keans,
    grant that heaven may send good fortune.

Although in the Alexandrian edition of Bacchylides' works this poem was classified as a dithyramb, it shows no trace of the Dionysiac associations that seem to have marked the dithyramb in its original form (see the introductory note to Pindar, Dithyramb 2). Apart from the last three lines, which point to a festival of Apollo on the island of Delos as a likely occasion for its performance, the ode is purely narrative in character, plunging *in medias res* without preliminaries of any sort. The story it tells concerns Theseus, the greatest figure of Athenian legend, and his confrontation with King Minos of Crete, who had decreed that a yearly tribute of youths and maidens be sent from Athens to Crete in order that they might be fed to the Minotaur, a monster half human and half bull in form.

4 **young Ionian folk** i.e., Athenian; Athens considered itself to be the mother city of the Ionian Greeks (cf. Solon 3).

7 **shaker of the aegis** See Glossary under "Athena."

14 **Eriboia** one of the fourteen young Athenians.

15 **Pandion's grandson** Theseus; see Glossary for the complexities of his lineage.

20 Minos was the son of Zeus by Europa (**Phoinix's cherished daughter**, 30), on whom see Glossary.

31 **Ida** a mountain massif in central Crete.

37 **Pittheus' daughter** Aithra (cf. 58).

50 **the Sun-god's son-in-law** i.e., Minos, whose wife Pasiphaë was the daughter of Helios the Sun-god.

58 **Troizenian Aithra** Aithra's father Pittheus was king of Troizen in the northeastern Peloponnesos.

59 **engendered** *you* Minos is obviously addressing Theseus now, not Zeus.

102 **Nereus' glorious daughters** the fifty Nereids, of whom Poseidon's wife Amphitrite (111) was one.

## Dithyramb 18: "Theseus"

"King of holy Athens, [Str. 1]
    lord of Ionians living in luxury,
why, just now, did the trumpet, brazen-mouthed,
    sound forth a warlike song?
5    Is some enemy pressing close
    on the boundaries of our land,
    some leader of armies?
Or are pirates, contrivers of evil,
driving away the flocks by force,
10    in defiance of their shepherds?
If not, what is it then that tears your heart?
    Speak out; for I think that if any mortal
has brave young men at hand
    to call on for assistance, it is you,
15    O son of Pandion and Kreousa."

"Just now a herald came from the Isthmus, [Str. 2]
    having made the whole long journey on foot;
and deeds beyond telling he reports, done by a mighty
    man: he slaughtered the overbold
20    Sinis, who in strength was greatest
    of mortals, being the child of Kronos' son,
    the Earthshaker and Loosener;
the man-killing sow that haunted
Kremmyon's glens he also killed,
25    and reckless Skiron;
he put a halt to the wrestling school
    of Kerkyon; and Polypemon's mighty
hammer has fallen from the hand
    of Prokoptes now that he has met a better
30    man. I fear the way these things may end."

"Who does he say that this man is, [Str. 3]
    and from where? How is he equipped?
Is he bringing a great host with him
    under hostile arms,
35    or does he walk alone with his attendants,
    the way a traveler does who roams

         through foreign lands,
    so strong and brave
    and bold that he has brought the might
40       and power of so many men
    to naught? Surely a god is urging him along,
         that he may visit justice on the unjust;
    for it is not easy, doing deed on deed,
         not to meet at last with calamity.
45  All things, in time's long course, come to an end."


    "Two men only are at his side,                [Str. 4]
         he says; about his shining shoulders
    an ivory-hilted sword is strapped;
         two polished spears are in his hands,
50  and a Lakonian cap, well-made,
         sits on his head of fiery hair;
    a crimson tunic
    covers his chest, and a woolen cloak
    from Thessaly; and from his eyes
55       there gleams a red
    Lemnian flame. He is a boy
         on manhood's very verge; the sports of Ares
    are what his mind is fixed on, war
         and battle with its brazen din;
60  and what he seeks is splendor-loving Athens."


This poem, like the preceding one, was classified as a dithyramb by
Bacchylides' ancient editors. Unlike the preceding poem, it is dramatic rather
than narrative in form, being a dialogue between King Aigeus of Athens and
an anonymous interlocutor. The formidable young man whom they are dis-
cussing is none other than Aigeus' own son Theseus, although at this point
the king is still ignorant of his identity. Years before, while visiting King
Pittheus of Troizen, Aigeus had slept with Pittheus' daughter Aithra. Before
leaving Troizen, Aigeus hid a sword and a pair of sandals under a large rock
and told Aithra that when their son was able to lift the rock and retrieve the
tokens, he should travel north across the Isthmus of Corinth to Athens.


   2 **lord of Ionians** Athens regarded itself as the mother city of Ionian
Greeks; cf. Bacchylides 17. 4 and Solon 3.
   15 According to Apollodorus (3. 15. 5), the mother of Aigeus was named
Pylia, not Kreousa.

20–29 **Sinis, Skiron, Kerkyon, Prokoptes** notorious malefactors of legend
who preyed on people traveling across the Isthmus. **Sinis** would draw
several pine trees down toward the ground, tie men to their branches, and
then release the trees; **Skiron** would force passersby to wash his feet and
then, as they did so, kick them over a cliff into the sea; **Kerkyon** would
force them to wrestle with him and kill them during the bout; **Prokoptes**
(better known as Procrustes) would offer them accommodation for the
night and then adjust their bodies to fit the bed, pounding out (or stretch-
ing) those who were too short and sawing off portions of those who were
too long. Theseus dispatched each one of these criminals by his own
particular method.
21–22 **Kronos' son, the Earthshaker** i.e., Poseidon.
27 **Polypemon** perhaps Prokoptes' father; his name, appropriately
enough, means "he who causes much pain."
30 **I fear the way these things may end** The anonymous young man is
evidently so formidable as a fighter that Aigeus feels his own security to
be threatened.
56 **Lemnian flame** Lemnos was a volcanic island in the northeastern
Aegean, and as such was closely associated with Hephaistos, the god of fire.

## *Enkomion* for Alexandros (Fr. 20b)

O lyre, no longer hang on the peg, [Str. 1]
nor check the clear sound of your seven-toned voice,
but come here to my hands! I long to send
a golden wing of the Muses to Alexandros,

5    as an adornment of his banquet on festal days, [Str. 2]
when young men's tender spirits are warmed
by the sweet compulsion of the circling cups,
and hopes of Aphrodite are kindled in their hearts.

That power, mingled with Dionysos' gifts, [Str. 3]
10   sends a man's thoughts soaring highest.
Straightway he sacks cities crowned with towers;
he thinks that he will be sole ruler of all mankind;

his houses gleam with gold and ivory; [Str. 4]
over the shining sea wheat-laden ships
15   sail from Egypt bringing him limitless
wealth—such are the heart's desires of one who drinks. . . .

See Pindar's "*Enkomion* for Thrasyboulos" for another treatment of the joys of drunkenness.

4 **a golden wing of the Muses** i.e., a song. **Alexandros** king of
Makedonia during the first half of the fifth century B.C. He was an ancestor of Alexander the Great.
8 **hopes of Aphrodite** i.e., hopes that amorous activity is imminent.
9 **Dionysos' gifts** i.e., wine.

# GLOSSARY OF NAMES

The names listed here are primarily mythological or geographical; a limited number are historical. Any name in **boldface** has an entry of its own which can be consulted for additional information.

**Abas** An early king of **Argos**, father of **Proitos** and **Akrisios**.

**Achaia** A region in the northern **Peloponnesos**.

**Achaians** (1) The inhabitants of **Achaia**. (2) More generally, a poetic term for the Greeks of the heroic age collectively, like **Danaans**.

**Acheron** A river in the Underworld which the souls of the dead had to cross in order to reach the house of **Hades**.

**Achilles** Son of **Peleus** and hence one of the **Aiakidai**; his mother was the sea goddess **Thetis**. The greatest of the Greek warriors to fight at **Troy**, he died there while still young, in the tenth and final year of the war.

**Adrastos** Son of Talaos, grandson of **Proitos**, and brother-in-law of **Amphiaraos**. As king of **Argos**, he was commander in chief of the ill-starred and ultimately unsuccessful campaign against the city of **Thebes** called the Seven against Thebes, the purpose of which was to make **Polyneikes** king of the city. Adrastos was the only one of the seven leaders to survive the battle and return home safely. In the next generation he led the Epigonoi ("Descendants"), the sons of the original Seven, on a second—and this time successful—attempt to take Thebes.

**Aegean (Sea)** The body of water between the Greek mainland and Asia Minor.

**Agamemnon** Son of **Atreus**, grandson of **Pelops**, and brother of **Menelaos**. As king of **Argos**, he was commander in chief of the combined Greek forces that fought at **Troy** to regain possession of **Helen**.

**Aiakidai** The descendants of **Aiakos**. In addition to Aiakos' three sons **Peleus**, **Telamon**, and **Phokos**, the Aiakidai included Peleus' son **Achilles**, Telamon's sons **Ajax** and Teukros, and Achilles' son

Neoptolemos. One of the most illustrious families of Greek legend, the Aiakidai were held in special honor on the island of **Aigina**.

**Aiakos** Son of **Zeus** by **Aigina**. By his wife **Endeïs** Aiakos had two sons, **Peleus** and **Telamon**; by the sea nymph Psamatheia he had a third, **Phokos**. There was a hero cult of Aiakos on Aigina in historical times.

**Aigina** An island (and city-state) in the Saronic Gulf, not far from **Athens**; also, a nymph of the same name, daughter of the river **Asopos** and mother of **Aiakos**.

**Aiolians** One of several ethnic and linguistic subdivisions within the larger category of Hellenes (speakers of Greek). The northwestern coast of Asia Minor was settled by Aiolians, including the island of **Lesbos**. One of the so-called modes or styles of Greek music was known as Aiolian.

**Aiolos** Father of **Sisyphos** and great-grandfather of **Bellerophon**.

**Aitna (Etna)** A volcano in eastern **Sicily**, subject to periodic eruptions both in antiquity and in modern times; also, a city founded not far from the mountain by **Hieron** of **Syracuse**.

**Aitolia** A region of west-central Greece in which the city of **Kalydon** was located.

**Ajax (Aias)** (1) Son of **Telamon** and **Eriboia**, born and raised on the island of **Salamis**. Among the Greek warriors who fought at **Troy**, Ajax was generally recognized to be second only to **Achilles** in courage and effectiveness. (2) Son of Oileus of Lokros; sometimes referred to as "Ajax the Lesser" to distinguish him from Ajax son of Telamon. He also fought at Troy, but he was chiefly notorious for his brutal and sacrilegious treatment of **Kassandra** during the sack of the city.

**Akragas** A large and wealthy city in southwestern **Sicily**, situated on a river of the same name.

**Akrisios** One of the twin sons of Abas, king of **Argos**. Upon the death of Abas, Akrisios contended with his brother **Proitos** for the kingship, a dispute that was eventually resolved when the two agreed to divide their father's realm between them. Akrisios was the grandfather of **Perseus** through his daughter **Danaë**.

**Alkmaion** Son of **Amphiaraos** and one of the so-called Descendants or Epigonoi (see under **Adrastos**).

**Alkmene** Granddaughter of **Perseus**, wife of **Amphitryon**, and mother of **Herakles** by **Zeus**.

**Alpheos** A river in the western **Peloponnesos**. **Olympia**, the site of the Olympian Games, was situated on its northern bank.

**Althaia** Wife of **Oineus** of **Kalydon**, and mother of **Meleagros**.

**Amphiaraos** Son of Oïkles, cousin and brother-in-law of **Adrastos**. He was an Argive warrior and prophet who reluctantly took part in the expedition of the Seven against **Thebes**; while fleeing from the battle, he was swallowed up by the earth and became an oracular power.

**Amphitrite** One of the fifty **Nereids** and wife of **Poseidon**.

**Amphitryon** Grandson of **Perseus**, cousin and husband of **Alkmene**. He and Alkmene, both Argives, were living in exile in **Thebes** when **Zeus** begot **Herakles** on Alkmene; he did so by visiting her in Amphitryon's shape while Amphitryon himself was away taking vengeance on a people called the Teleboans, who had murdered Alkmene's brothers. Amphitryon's own son by Alkmene, Iphikles, was born at the same time as Herakles. Despite Zeus's undoubted paternity, Herakles is frequently referred to as the son of Amphitryon.

**Amyklai** A town near **Sparta**, captured by the **Dorians** when they invaded the **Peloponnesos**.

**Aphrodite** Goddess of physical beauty and sexual love. According to one tradition she was born from the sea foam (*aphros*); according to another she was the daughter of **Zeus** by the goddess Dione. She is frequently called Kypris ("the Cyprian") because she first came ashore on the island of **Cyprus**.

**Apollo** Son of **Zeus** by Leto, who gave birth to him on the island of **Delos**. As a god Apollo took a special interest in (among other things) archery, music, prophecy, and medicine. He was also known as Phoibos (Phoebus) and Loxias, the latter name being particularly associated with his role as the oracular god of **Delphi**. The **Pythian Games** were held in his honor.

**Ares** The god of war, son of **Zeus** and **Hera**; also known as Enyalios. His name is frequently used simply as a synonym for war.

**Argos** A city in the northeastern **Peloponnesos**; both mythologically and historically, one of the most important cities in Greece. It was the site of a famous temple to the goddess **Hera** and of a festival held in her honor known as the Heraia.

**Arkadia** The ruggedly mountainous central portion of the **Peloponnesos**.

**Artemis** Daughter of **Zeus** by Leto and sister of **Apollo**; a virgin goddess devoted to the hunting of wild animals.

**Asklepios** Son of **Apollo** by **Koronis**. Reared and educated by **Chiron**, he became the greatest physician of Greek legend and a patron of doctors. His skill was such that he was even able to bring a dead man temporarily back to life, as is told by Pindar in *Pythian* 3.

**Asopos** A river in **Boiotia**; also, a river god, father of various nymphs, including **Thebe** and **Aigina**.

**Athena** Daughter of **Zeus**; having been born from his head, she remained particularly close to her father and frequently carried the aegis, a magical shield that inspired terror in enemies. A virgin goddess, Athena took special interest in warfare and handicrafts. She was the patron and protector of various heroes in Greek legend, among them **Perseus, Herakles**, and **Bellerophon**. As its name suggests, her association with the city of **Athens** was particularly strong. She was also known as Pallas.

**Athens** The chief city of **Attika**. One of its legendary kings was **Theseus**. A picture of the city's troubled economic, political, and social state c. 600 B.C. emerges from the extant fragments of the poet Solon. In the fifth century B.C. Athens was one of the two most powerful city-states in Greece (the other being **Sparta**), and its fleet contributed largely to the Greek victory over the Persians at the battle of **Salamis**. Athenian ceramics were of high quality and constituted (along with olive oil) one of the city's chief exports. Athens was the site of the Great Panathenaia, a festival (including athletic contests) that was held every four years in Athena's honor.

**Atreidai** See **Atreus**.

**Atreus** Son of **Pelops** and father of **Agamemnon** and **Menelaos**, who are often referred to as the Atreidai ("sons of Atreus").

**Attika** The territory of **Athens**, northeast of the **Peloponnesos**. Its inhabitants spoke an Ionic dialect known as Attic.

**Bellerophon** Grandson of **Sisyphos** and great-grandson of **Aiolos**. He tamed the winged horse **Pegasos** and with his aid performed various exploits at the command of Iobates, king of **Lykia**, who was seeking to bring about his death. Later, when Bellerophon tried to fly up to **Olympos** and join the gods, he was thrown off by Pegasos and direly crippled in his fall to earth.

**Boiotia** A fertile region of central Greece, immediately northwest of **Attika**. Among its cities were **Thebes** and Orchomenos. In addition to the Theban Pindar, Boiotia could boast of the poets **Hesiod** and Corinna.

**Boreas** The North Wind, which was particularly associated with **Thrace**. Both Boreas and his sons Kalaïs and Zetes were proverbial for their speed.

**Centaurs** Creatures that combined the body of a horse with the torso, upper limbs, and head of a man. With the exception of **Chiron**, Centaurs were notorious for their lawlessness and violence.

**Chiron** A Centaur, son of **Kronos** and Philyra. He was renowned for his wisdom and for his role as educator of heroes; among those reared in his cave on Mt. **Pelion** were Jason, **Asklepios**, and **Achilles**.

**Corinth** A wealthy and powerful commercial city at the southern end of the **Isthmus of Corinth**; its inhabitants were of **Dorian** extraction. Various legends were associated with it, and it was the site of a famous temple to **Aphrodite**. Corinth administered the **Isthmian Games**.

**Crete** A large island in the southern **Aegean**; one of its most important cities was **Knossos**.

**Croesus** The last king of **Lydia**, who became proverbial for his wealth, piety, and benevolent generosity. His empire, with its capital of **Sardis**, was conquered in 546 B.C. by **Kyros**.

**Cyclades** A group of islands in the middle of the **Aegean** Sea.

**Cyclopes** One-eyed giants of great size and strength. Various large-scale structures of great antiquity in Greece (e.g. the walls of **Tiryns**) were said to have been built by the Cyclopes.

**Cyprus** An island in the eastern Mediterranean, closely associated with **Aphrodite** and famous for the incense and perfumes that it produced.

**Danaans** A collective name for the Greeks of the heroic age.

**Danaë** Daughter of **Akrisios**, the king of **Argos**, and mother of **Perseus** by Zeus.

**Danaos** An Argive king, father of fifty daughters (the Danaids) who fled to **Argos** from their home in Egypt in an attempt to avoid marriage with their cousins, the sons of Danaos' brother Aigyptos. When the Danaids were forced to go through with the marriage, Danaos persuaded forty-nine of them to murder their husbands on the night of the wedding, but the fiftieth, Hypermestra, had fallen in love with her husband **Lynkeus** and so spared him.

**Dardanians** See **Dardanos**.

**Dardanos** An ancestor of the Trojan people, and of the Trojan royal family in particular. In his honor the region around **Troy** was sometimes called Dardania and the Trojans themselves Dardanians.

**Dawn (Eos)** Daughter of **Hyperion** and **Theia** and sister of the sun-god **Helios**. She was the mother of **Memnon**.

**Deiphobos** One of the sons of **Priam**.

**Delos** A small island in the middle of the **Cyclades**, birthplace of **Apollo**.

**Delphi** A place sacred to **Apollo**, on the southern slopes of Mt. **Parnassos**; also known as Pytho. Delphi was the site of the Delphic (or Pythian) oracle, a religious institution that claimed to transmit Apollo's prophecies to mankind. With **Kirrha**, Delphi was also the site of the **Pythian Games**, held every four years in Apollo's honor.

**Demeter** Sister of **Zeus** and mother by him of **Persephone**. Demeter was the goddess of agriculture (specifically of grain crops) and, together with her daughter, had particularly strong associations with **Sicily**.

**Descendants (Epigonoi)** See under **Adrastos**.

**Diomedes** Son of **Tydeus** and a great Argive warrior and hero.

**Dionysos** Son of **Zeus** by **Semele**; also known as Bakchos. Among other functions, he was the god of wine.

**Dorians** One of several ethnic and linguistic subdivisions within the larger category of Hellenes (speakers of Greek). The Dorians were the last to come down into Greece from the north; they settled mainly in the **Peloponnesos**, the southern islands of the Aegean, and the southwestern coast of Asia Minor. One of the so-called modes or styles of Greek music was called Dorian.

**Echidna** A snakelike monster, mother by **Typhos** of **Kerberos** and the **Hydra**.

**Elis** A region of the western **Peloponnesos** in which **Olympia** was located.

**Endeïs** Daughter of **Chiron**, wife of **Aiakos**, and mother of **Peleus** and **Telamon**.

**Enyalios** See **Ares**.

**Epaphos** Son of **Zeus** by an Argive princess named Io; he was born in Egypt because his mother had been driven there through the hostility of **Hera**.

**Eriboia** (1) Wife of **Telamon** and mother of **Ajax**; another form of her name is Periboia. (2) According to Bacchylides (in Dithyramb 17), one of the fourteen young Athenians transported to **Crete** by **Minos**.

**Eros** God of love in the sense of sexual desire (*eros* in Greek). He was sometimes represented as being the son of Aphrodite.

**Eteokles** One of the two sons of **Oedipus** and **Iokaste**, brother of **Polyneikes**.

**Ethiopians** A semimythical people who were believed to live on the eastern edge of the habitable world; see **Memnon**.

**Euboia** A long, narrow island lying off the northeast coast of **Boiotia** and **Attika**.

**Europa** Sister of **Kadmos** and mother by **Zeus** of **Minos**, **Rhadamanthys**, and **Sarpedon**. According to Bacchylides (in Dithyramb 17), she was the daughter of Phoinix, the eponymous founder of the Phoenician people; other authorities make her the daughter of Agenor and the sister of Phoinix.

**Eurotas** The chief river of **Lakonia**; **Sparta** was situated on its west bank.

**Fates (Moirai)** Three goddesses who were thought to assign human beings their destinies at birth by spinning and cutting different lengths of thread. Their names are Klotho ("Spinner"), Lachesis ("Allotment"), and Atropos ("Inflexible").

**Ganymede** A young Trojan prince whose beauty prompted **Zeus** to abduct him and bring him to **Olympos**, where he served as cupbearer to the gods.

**Geryon** A triple-bodied giant, living in Erytheia in the extreme west of the world. As one of his twelve labors **Herakles** had to steal Geryon's cattle and bring them back to Greece; in accomplishing this task he also killed Geryon. To reach Erytheia, Herakles traveled in the golden cup of **Helios**.

**Giants** Monstrous offspring of the goddess Earth (Gaia) who rebelled against the rule of the **Olympians** but were defeated by them in battle. Individual Giants include Alkyoneus, who was overcome by **Herakles**, and Porphyrion, who (at least according to Pindar) was killed by **Apollo**.

**Gorgons** See **Medousa**.

**Graces (Charites)** The three daughters of **Zeus** and Eurynome, named Aglaia ("Splendor"), Euphrosyne ("Cheerfulness"), and Thalia ("Abundance"). As embodiments of grace and charm (*charis* in Greek), they were particularly associated with poetry, festivity, physical attractiveness, and athletic victory.

**Hades** Son of **Kronos** and **Rhea** and hence brother of **Zeus** and **Poseidon**. With his wife **Persephone**, Hades ruled over the shades of the dead in the Underworld. By extension his name was frequently used to denote (a) his realm of the Underworld and (b) death itself.

**Harmonia** Daughter of **Ares** and **Aphrodite** and wife of **Kadmos**.

**Hebe** Daughter of **Zeus** and **Hera**, and wife of **Herakles** after his death and subsequent apotheosis. Her name means "youth."

**Hektor** The eldest son of **Priam**, and husband of Andromache. As the greatest of the Trojan warriors to fight in the **Trojan War**, Hektor represented Troy's only hope for victory, and with his death at the hands of **Achilles** the city's doom was sealed.

**Helen** Daughter of **Zeus** and **Leda** and wife of **Menelaos**, king of **Sparta**, by whom she had a daughter named Hermione. Her removal from **Sparta** to **Troy** in the company of **Paris** gave rise to the **Trojan War**. She is sometimes referred to as the daughter of **Tyndareos**, who was Leda's husband.

**Helikon** The highest mountain in **Boiotia**. On its eastern slope there was a sanctuary dedicated to the **Muses**.

**Helios** The Sun-god, son of **Hyperion** and **Theia** and father of Pasiphaë (see under **Minos**). He was said to travel each night from west to east in a golden cup or bed.

**Hellas** The Greek word for all the various lands that were inhabited by Greeks (Hellenes). These included not only the mainland and islands that make up modern Greece but also the western coast of Asia Minor and much of Sicily and southern Italy.

**Hephaistos** God of fire and patron of craftsmen, particularly blacksmiths; he himself served as smith to the **Olympians** and as such was responsible for the manufacture of many miraculous devices. His name is often used simply as a synonym for fire.

**Hera** Daughter of **Kronos** and **Rhea**, sister and wife of **Zeus**. The goddess of marriage, she was fiercely hostile toward the various objects of Zeus's extramarital affections and, often, toward the resulting offspring as well (e.g., **Herakles**). She was the patron deity of **Argos**

and was honored with athletic festivals there and on **Aigina**, among other places.

**Herakles**  Son of **Zeus** by **Alkmene**, although he is often referred to as the son of **Amphitryon**, who was his mother's husband. As a result of the enmity of **Hera**, Herakles found himself in servitude to Eurystheus, king of **Tiryns**, at whose behest he had to perform his famous Twelve Labors; among these were the killing of the Nemean lion (see **Nemea**) and of the **Hydra**, the theft of the cattle of **Geryon**, and the fetching of **Kerberos**. In addition, Herakles fought a war against **Laomedon** of **Troy** and founded the festival of **Zeus** at **Olympia** with the spoils of his campaign against Augeas, king of Elis. Upon his death, as a reward for his life of toil and suffering, Herakles became a god and lived thereafter on **Olympos**, with **Hebe** as his wife.

**Hermes**  Son of **Zeus** and Maia; born on Mt. **Kyllene** in Arkadia and hence occasionally called "Kyllenian." Among his various functions, he was associated with thieves, heralds, and athletes.

**Hesiod**  A poet from Askra in **Boiotia**, who lived c. 700 B.C.; his works include the *Theogony* and the *Works and Days*.

**Hieron**  Tyrant of **Syracuse** from 478 until his death in 467 B.C., having succeeded his elder brother Gelon in that office. In 480 he and Gelon joined forces with Theron, tyrant of **Akragas**, to defeat the Carthaginians in the battle of Himera; in 474 he defeated the Etruscans in a sea battle off the coast of Kyme (near present-day Naples). He was also a notable patron of poets: Simonides, Pindar, and Bacchylides all wrote poems on commission for him.

**Horai**  The three daughters of **Zeus** and Themis, named Eunomia ("Good Order"), Dike ("Justice"), and Eirene ("Peace"). Their collective name is sometimes translated as "Hours" or "Seasons."

**Hydra**  A many-headed monster, offspring of **Typhos** and **Echidna**. It was killed by **Herakles** as the second of his twelve labors.

**Hyperboreans**  A mythical people beloved by **Apollo** and living a paradisal existence somewhere "beyond the North Wind" (the literal meaning of their name). According to Pindar (in *Pythian* 10) **Perseus** visited the Hyperboreans under the guidance of Athena, and according to Bacchylides (in Ode 3) Apollo settled **Croesus** in their midst.

**Hyperion**  One of the **Titans**, father by **Theia** of **Helios**.

**Hypermestra**  See **Danaos**.

**Ida** The highest mountain on **Crete**; also, a mountain in the vicinity of Troy.

**Idas** Brother of **Lynkeus** (2).

**Ilion** Another name for the city of **Troy**.

**Ino** One of the four daughters of **Kadmos**. In a fit of madness Ino killed her son Melikertes and then threw herself into the sea, thereupon becoming a sea goddess.

**Iokaste (Jocasta)** Wife of Laios, mother (and wife) of **Oedipus**.

**Iolaos** Son of **Herakles'** half brother Iphikles; he served as Herakles' squire and helper in a number of his labors and other exploits.

**Ionia** The central part of the western coast of Asia Minor.

**Ionians** One of several ethnic and linguistic subdivisions within the larger category of Hellenes (speakers of Greek). In addition to **Ionia** itself, most of the **Cyclades** were inhabited by Ionians, and **Athens** claimed to be their mother city.

**Isthmian Games** An athletic festival dedicated to **Poseidon**, held every two years on the **Isthmus of Corinth** and administered by the city of **Corinth**. The prizes given at the Isthmian games were wreaths of wild parsley or pine.

**Isthmus of Corinth** The narrow neck of land that connects the **Peloponnesos** to the northern half of the Greek mainland; site of the **Isthmian Games**.

**Kadmos** Brother of **Europa** and legendary founder of **Thebes**, which therefore is frequently referred to as the "city of Kadmos." Though a mortal, Kadmos was privileged to marry the goddess **Harmonia**; the gods attended this wedding as they did that of **Peleus** and **Thetis**. By Harmonia Kadmos had four daughters, each of whom suffered tragic losses in life and/or met with a tragic end. Two of them were **Ino** and **Semele**; the others were Agauë, who murdered her son Pentheus in a state of bacchic frenzy, and Autonoë, whose son Aktaion was torn to pieces by his hunting dogs.

**Kalliope** One of the nine **Muses**; her name means "beautiful voice."

**Kalydon** A city in **Aitolia**, home of **Oineus** and **Meleagros**.

**Kassandra** Daughter of **Priam**. During the sack of **Troy** by the Greeks, Kassandra took refuge in the temple of **Athena** but was dragged from that sanctuary by **Ajax** son of Oileus and raped.

**Kastor** Son of **Tyndareos** and **Leda** and half brother of **Polydeukes**. His mortal wounding and subsequent resuscitation are narrated by Pindar in *Nemean* 10. See also **Tyndaridai**.

**Keos** One of the **Cyclades**, birthplace of the poets Simonides and Bacchylides.

**Kerberos** A monstrous three-headed hound, offspring of **Typhos** and **Echidna**, which guarded the realm of **Hades** and **Persephone**. As one of his twelve labors **Herakles** had to descend into the Underworld, subdue Kerberos, and bring him back to **Tiryns**.

**Kinyras** A legendary king of **Cyprus**, famous for his wealth.

**Kirrha** A town on the plain beneath **Delphi**. A number of events in the **Pythian Games** took place at Kirrha, including all equestrian contests.

**Kithairon** A mountain on the southwestern border of **Boiotia**, near which the battle of **Plataia** was fought.

**Kleio** One of the nine **Muses**; her name means "she who brings fame."

**Kleonai** See under **Nemean Games**.

**Klotho** See under **Fates**.

**Knossos** A city on the north-central coast of **Crete**, home of **Minos**.

**Koronis** Daughter of Phlegyas, a Thessalian king, and mother by **Apollo** of **Asklepios**. Her story is told by Pindar in *Pythian* 3.

**Kouretes** (1) Semidivine beings who helped to protect the newborn **Zeus** from the hostility of his father **Kronos** by drowning out the infant's cries with noisy dancing. (2) A people who lived in the Aitolian city of Pleuron; their king was Thestios, father of **Althaia**. War broke out between the Kouretes and the people of **Kalydon** after the Kalydonian boar hunt, as is narrated by Bacchylides in Ode 5.

**Kronos** Son of Sky (Ouranos) and Earth (Gaia), husband of **Rhea**, and king of the **Titans**. After being deposed by his son **Zeus**, he was (according to one tradition) imprisoned in **Tartaros** with his fellow Titans; according to the tradition followed by Pindar in *Olympian* 2, however, he presided over the Islands of the Blessed, to which great heroes went after death. The phrase "son of Kronos" usually (though not always) refers to Zeus.

**Kyknos** A son of **Poseidon**, who fought on the side of the Trojans in the **Trojan War** until he was slain by **Achilles**.

**Kyllene** A mountain in northeastern **Arkadia**, birthplace of **Hermes**.

**Kypris** See **Aphrodite**.

**Kyros (Cyrus)** Founder of the Persian Empire (see under **Persia**).

**Laios** King of **Thebes** and father of **Oedipus**.

**Lakedaimon** Another name for **Sparta**.

**Lakonia** A region in the southeastern **Peloponnesos**; its most important city was **Sparta**.

**Laomedon** King of **Troy** in the generation before the **Trojan War**, and father of **Priam**. He contracted with **Herakles** to destroy a sea monster that was ravaging the region, but once the deed was done he refused to hand over the reward which he had promised, so Herakles organized a punitive expedition against him and captured Troy. On this campaign Herakles was accompanied by **Telamon**.

**Leda** Wife of **Tyndareos**. She was the mother of **Kastor** and Klytaimnestra by Tyndareos and of **Helen** and **Polydeukes** by **Zeus**.

**Lesbos** A large island off the western coast of Asia Minor. Its most important city, Mytilene, was the hometown of the poets Alcaeus and Sappho.

**Leto** Mother by **Zeus** of **Apollo** and **Artemis**.

**Loxias** See **Apollo**.

**Lydia** A region of western Asia Minor, well known in the archaic period for its natural wealth (especially its gold) and for the fine craftsmanship of its luxury goods. One of the so-called modes or styles of Greek music was known as Lydian.

**Lykia** A region of southwestern Asia Minor. During the **Trojan War** the Lykians fought as allies on the Trojan side under the command of Glaukos and **Sarpedon**. There was a famous temple of **Apollo** at Patara in Lykia, and perhaps as a result he was often called Lykian.

**Lynkeus** (1) One of the fifty sons of Aigyptos and husband of Hypermestra (see under **Danaos**). Lynkeus succeeded **Danaos** as king of **Argos**; he and Hypermestra had one son, **Abas**. (2) One of the two sons of Aphareus, Idas being the other; their fight with **Kastor**

and **Polydeukes** and subsequent deaths are narrated by Pindar in *Nemean* 10.

**Magnesia** (1) A region in eastern **Thessaly** in which Mt. **Pelion** was located. (2) A city in **Ionia**.

**Maia** Mother of **Hermes** by **Zeus**.

**Marathon** A town in eastern **Attika**, site of an athletic festival in honor of **Herakles**.

**Medes** An Iranian people whose empire passed into the control of **Kyros** and his fellow Persians. The Greeks tended to use the terms "Mede" and "Persian" interchangeably.

**Medousa** One of the three Gorgons, female monsters whose heads were entwined with snakes and whose gaze was so penetrating that anyone who met it directly was turned to stone. **Perseus** was able to decapitate Medousa with the assistance of **Athena**.

**Megara** A city on the Saronic Gulf halfway between **Athens** and **Corinth**; hometown of the poet Theognis and site of an athletic festival in honor of Alkathoos, a legendary king of the city.

**Meleagros** An Aitolian warrior and hero, son of Oineus of **Kalydon**. Having fought bravely in the war that broke out between the people of Kalydon and the Kouretes after the Kalydonian boar hunt (see under **Kalydon**), he died as a result of the anger of his mother **Althaia**. His story is told by Bacchylides in Ode 5.

**Memnon** Son of the goddess **Dawn** by **Tithonos**. Memnon was king of the **Ethiopians** at the time of the **Trojan War** and came to Troy's assistance as an ally; he was killed by **Achilles**.

**Memory (Mnemosyne)** One of the **Titans** and mother by **Zeus** of the nine **Muses**.

**Menelaos** Son of **Atreus**, brother of **Agamemnon**, and husband of **Helen**. He succeeded his father-in-law **Tyndareos** as king of **Sparta**.

**Messenia** A region in the southwestern **Peloponnesos**. The Spartans fought several wars with the Messenians in order to gain and maintain control of the region; the first of these took place in the eighth century B.C., the second in the seventh. The Spartan poet Tyrtaeus was active at the time of the Second Messenian War.

**Midas** A legendary king of Phrygia in Asia Minor, famous for his great wealth.

**Minos** Son of **Zeus** by **Europa**, brother of **Rhadamanthys** and **Sarpedon**. His wife Pasiphaë, daughter of **Helios** the Sun-god, gave birth to the Minotaur, half man and half bull in form, which was eventually killed by **Theseus**.

**Muses** The nine daughters of **Zeus** and **Memory** (Mnemosyne); goddesses of poetry and song. They were born in **Pieria**, lived on **Olympos**, and had a sanctuary on Mt. **Helikon**; hence they are often referred to as Pierian, Olympian, or Helikonian. Among the individual Muses are **Kalliope, Kleio, Ourania**, and **Terpsichore**.

**Nemea** A valley in the northeastern **Peloponnesos**, site of the **Nemean Games**. The first of the twelve labors of **Herakles** was to kill an invulnerable lion that was ravaging Nemea; this he achieved by strangling it with his bare hands. He habitually wore its hide thereafter.

**Nemean Games** An athletic festival dedicated to **Zeus**, held every two years at **Nemea**; it was administered by the neighboring city of Kleonai. The prizes given were wreaths of wild parsley.

**Nereids** The daughters of **Nereus**; like their father, they lived in the sea. There were fifty of them, including **Thetis**, Poseidon's wife **Amphitrite**, and Psamatheia, the mother of **Phokos**.

**Nereus** Son of Sea (Pontos) and Earth (Gaia) and father of the fifty **Nereids**. Renowned for his wisdom, he was sometimes referred to as the "Old Man of the Sea."

**Nestor** King of Pylos in the southwestern **Peloponnesos**. He led a contingent of Pylians to the **Trojan War** but did not actually take part in battle, being advanced in years (according to one tradition he ruled through three generations); his role was that of wise counselor and eloquent speaker.

**Nymphs** Minor female deities, usually attached to particular places, springs, streams, etc. Eponymous nymphs of cities and islands were common, e.g., **Thebe** and **Aigina**.

**Oedipus** Son of **Laios** and **Iokaste**. In fulfillment of a Delphic prophecy (see under **Delphi**), he unwittingly killed his father and married his mother, becoming king of **Thebes** in the process; when the nature of his crime was discovered, he was banished from the city. His sons by Iokaste were **Polyneikes** and **Eteokles**.

**Oïkles** Son of **Proitos**, brother of Talaos, and father of **Amphiaraos**.

**Oineus** King of **Kalydon**; father of **Meleagros** and **Tydeus**.

**Oinone** Another name for **Aigina**.

**Olympia** A sanctuary of **Zeus** in **Elis**, site of the **Olympic Games**.

**Olympians** The gods who succeeded the **Titans** as the ruling powers of the world, i.e., the generation of **Zeus** and his siblings (**Hera, Poseidon**, etc.) and that of Zeus's children (**Athena, Apollo**, etc.). They were called the Olympians because they were believed to live on the summit of Mt. **Olympos**, although they were also often spoken of as living in the sky or heaven.

**Olympic Games** An athletic festival dedicated to **Zeus**, held every four years at **Olympia**. It was the oldest and most important of the four "Panhellenic" contests, the others being the **Pythian**, **Isthmian**, and **Nemean** games. At the Olympic games wreaths of olive leaves were given as prizes.

**Olympos** The highest mountain in Greece, situated on the northern border of **Thessaly**. Its summit was commonly regarded as the residence of **Zeus** and the other **Olympians**.

**Ourania** One of the nine **Muses**; her name means "heavenly."

**Pallas** See **Athena**.

**Paris** A Trojan prince, son of **Priam** and brother of **Hektor**. While being entertained as a guest by **Menelaos**, he ran away with his host's wife, **Helen**, thus giving rise to the **Trojan War**.

**Parnassos** A mountain in central Greece just north of the Gulf of Corinth; the second highest in Greece after Mt. **Olympos**. **Delphi**, site of the **Pythian Games**, was situated on its southern side.

**Paros** One of the **Cyclades**, birthplace of the poet Archilochos.

**Pasiphaë** Daughter of **Helios** the Sun-god and wife of **Minos**.

**Pegasos** A winged horse that sprang from the blood that was spilled when **Perseus** decapitated the Gorgon **Medousa**. He joined the gods on **Olympos** soon after his birth and returned there permanently once his association with **Bellerophon** had ended.

**Peleus** Son of **Aiakos** and **Aigina**, brother of **Telamon**, and father by **Thetis** of **Achilles**, who was his only child. After his banishment from the island of Aigina (see under **Phokos**) he settled in Phthia, a town in southern **Thessaly**. His marriage to Thetis, which took place on Mt. **Pelion**, was attended by the **Olympians**. Like **Kadmos**, who also married a goddess, Peleus was conventionally taken to exemplify the greatest good fortune attainable by human beings.

**Pelion** A mountain in eastern **Thessaly**, home of **Chiron** and site of the wedding of **Peleus** and **Thetis**.

**Pellene** A city in eastern **Achaia**. It was the site of an athletic festival at which woolen cloaks were given as prizes.

**Peloponnesos** The southern half of the Greek mainland, connected to the northern half by the **Isthmus of Corinth**. The name means "island of **Pelops**."

**Pelops** Son of **Tantalos**. He was brought from **Lydia** to **Elis** by **Poseidon** in order to win and marry Hippodameia, as is told by Pindar in *Olympian* 1; among their children was **Atreus**. The tomb of Pelops at **Olympia** was the center of an active hero cult in historical times.

**Pergamos** Another name for the city of **Troy**; strictly speaking, the term refers to the citadel rather than to the city as a whole.

**Persephone** Daughter of **Zeus** and **Demeter** and wife of **Hades**, hence queen of the dead. In conjunction with her mother Persephone, she was worshipped as "The Maiden" (Kore).

**Perseus** Son of **Zeus** and **Danaë**. When he was born, he and Danaë were cast out to sea in a large wooden chest by Danaë's father **Akrisios**, who had been warned by an oracle that Danaë's daughter would produce a son who would kill him. The chest came ashore on the island of Seriphos, where Perseus grew to manhood. On the orders of Polydektes, king of Seriphos, Perseus undertook to kill **Medousa**; discovering on his return to the island that Polydektes had attempted to rape Danaë in his absence, he used the Gorgon's head to turn the king and other members of his court to stone.

**Persia** The region occupied by modern-day Iran; the heart of an empire founded by **Kyros** and extended by his successors. Under Xerxes the Persians tried to annex mainland Greece to their empire by mounting a full-scale invasion, but this attempt failed when their forces were defeated at **Salamis** and **Plataia**. The Persians were also known to the Greeks (inaccurately) as **Medes**.

**Pherenikos** A racehorse belonging to **Hieron**. His name means "Victory-Bringer"; his successes were celebrated by both Pindar (in *Olympian* 1 and *Pythian* 3) and Bacchylides (in Ode 5).

**Philyra** Mother of **Chiron** by **Kronos**.

**Phoibos** See **Apollo**.

**Phokos** Son of **Aiakos** by the Nereid Psamatheia. He was murdered by his half brothers **Peleus** and **Telamon**, who as a consequence were banished from **Aigina** by Aiakos.

**Pieria** A region immediately to the north of Mt. **Olympos**, birthplace of the **Muses**, who thus are often called Pierian.

**Pisa** The district around **Olympia**; the name is frequently used as a synonym for Olympia in references to the **Olympian Games**.

**Pittakos** Ruler of Mytilene on the island of **Lesbos** in the early sixth century B.C. and a target of vituperative attack in the extant fragments of the poet Alcaeus. Along with Solon, Pittakos was accounted one of the "Seven Wise Men" of archaic Greece.

**Plataia** A city in **Boiotia** under the northern slopes of Mt. **Kithairon**; site of the battle in 479 B.C. which put an end to Persian hopes of annexing Greece (see under **Persia** and **Sparta**).

**Polydeukes** Son of **Zeus** and **Leda** and half brother of **Kastor**. His decision to renounce part of his immortality on behalf of Kastor is narrated by Pindar in *Nemean* 10. See also **Tyndaridai**.

**Polyneikes** One of the sons of **Oedipus** and **Iokaste**, brother of **Eteokles**. Upon Oedipus' banishment from **Thebes**, conflict broke out between the two brothers over the succession to the kingship. The quarrel led eventually to the famous expedition of the Seven against Thebes (see under **Adrastos**), which was an attempt by Polyneikes to wrest the Theban throne from Eteokles; during the war the two brothers killed one another in single combat. Before that, however, Polyneikes had married Argeia, a daughter of Adrastos, and produced a son named Thersandros.

**Poseidon** Son of **Kronos** and **Rhea**, brother of **Zeus**; he was god of the sea, of horses, and of earthquakes (he was frequently called Earthholder and Earthshaker). He was closely associated with the **Nereids** through his wife **Amphitrite**. The **Isthmian Games** were held in his honor.

**Priam** Son of **Laomedon** and king of **Troy** at the time of the **Trojan War**. According to Homer, he had fifty sons and twelve daughters, only some of whom (among them **Hektor, Paris,** and **Kassandra**) were the children of his wife Hekabe.

**Proitos** Son of **Abas** and brother of **Akrisios**. As a result of a quarrel that broke out between the two brothers (see under **Akrisios**), Proitos became king of **Tiryns**, which he fortified with the help of the

**Cyclopes**. His daughters offended **Hera** and were punished by her with madness, as is narrated by Bacchylides in Ode 11.

**Pythian Games** An athletic festival dedicated to **Apollo**, held every four years at **Delphi**. The Pythian games were second only to the Olympian in antiquity and prestige. The prizes given were wreaths of bay or laurel, a tree sacred to Apollo.

**Pytho** Another name for **Delphi**.

**Rhadamanthys** Son of **Zeus** by **Europa** and brother of **Minos** and **Sarpedon**. He was so renowned for his wisdom and justice while he was alive that he became one of the judges of the dead in the afterlife.

**Rhea** Daughter of Sky (Ouranos) and Earth (Gaia), sister and wife of **Kronos**, mother of **Zeus** and his five siblings. When Zeus was born Rhea hid him away in order to prevent **Kronos** from swallowing him (see under **Kouretes**). Rhea was sometimes known as the "Great Mother" (Magna Mater).

**Salamis** An island off the southwest coast of **Attika**. **Telamon** was king of Salamis at the time of the **Trojan War**, but it was his son **Ajax** who led the Salaminian contingent to Troy. In the time of Solon the city of **Athens** wrested control of Salamis from **Megara** and settled the island with Athenians. In 480 B.C. Salamis was the site of a sea battle in which the fleet of the invading Persians was decisively defeated by the Greek alliance. The sailors of Athens and of **Aigina** particularly distinguished themselves in the battle.

**Sardis** Capital of **Lydia**.

**Sarpedon** One of **Zeus**'s sons by **Europa**, the others being **Minos** and **Rhadamanthys**. He lived in **Lykia** and fought and died as an ally of the Trojans during the **Trojan War**, by which point he had lived through three generations. (Another tradition makes the Sarpedon who fell at Troy the son of Zeus by Laodamia, a daughter of **Bellerophon**.)

**Seasons** See **Horai**.

**Semele** One of the four daughters of **Kadmos** and **Harmonia**, also known as Thyone. She became the mother of **Dionysos** by **Zeus**. Although **Hera**, in a fit of her usual jealousy, contrived to have her rival incinerated by Zeus's thunderbolt, Semele enjoyed a posthumous existence among the gods on **Olympos**.

**Sicily** A large triangular island off the toe of Italy. Due to the local vulcanism (see under **Aitna**), the soil of Sicily was exceptionally fertile. Among its most important cities were **Syracuse** and **Akragas**.

**Sikyon** A city not far to the west of **Corinth**. It was the site of an athletic festival in honor of **Apollo**, at which silver wine cups were given as prizes.

**Sisyphos** Son of **Aiolos** and the legendary founder of **Corinth**. Famous for his consummate cunning, he even managed to return from the dead by persuading **Hades** and **Persephone** that he needed to punish his wife for neglecting (on his own prior instructions) to carry out the proper funeral rites. Upon dying for the second time, he was condemned to spend eternity repeatedly rolling an enormous boulder up a hill (cf. *Odyssey* 11. 593–600).

**Sparta** The chief city of **Lakonia**. In legend it was the home of **Tyndareos**, the **Tyndaridai**, and **Menelaos** and **Helen**. In the fifth century B.C. it was one of the two most powerful city-states in Greece (the other being **Athens**); its commanders and forces contributed largely to Greek resistance against the Persian invasion, particularly at the battles of Thermopylai (480 B.C.) and **Plataia** (479 B.C.). The Spartans were of **Dorian** extraction.

**Sun-god** See **Helios**.

**Syracuse** The largest and most powerful city in **Sicily**, on its southeastern coast. It had originally been settled as a colony of **Corinth**.

**Tantalos** King of Sipylos in **Lydia** and father of **Pelops**. He was guilty of an offense against the gods and endured endless torment in Hades as a consequence, but the exact nature of both the crime and the punishment differs in different versions of his story; see Pindar's *Olympian* 1. 25–64 with notes.

**Tartaros** In its original conception, a subterranean region as far below **Hades** as Hades was below the upper world, where the **Titans** and **Typhos** were imprisoned. Later, however, Tartaros was occasionally identified with Hades as the realm of the dead.

**Taÿgetos** A steep mountain ridge immediately to the west of **Sparta**.

**Teiresias** A Theban prophet of great renown.

**Telamon** Son of **Aiakos** and **Aigina**, brother of **Peleus**, and father of **Ajax** by **Eriboia**. After his banishment from the island of Aigina (see under **Phokos**), Telamon settled on **Salamis**. He accompanied

**Herakles** and **Iolaos** on an expedition against the city of **Troy** and its king, **Laomedon**.

**Teleboans**  See under **Amphitryon**.

**Terpsichore**  One of the nine **Muses**; her name means "delighting in dancing."

.  **Thasos**  An island in the northern Aegean just off **Thrace**. It was colonized from **Paros**, a process in which the poet Archilochos seems to have taken part.

**Thebe**  (1) The eponymous nymph of **Thebes**. (2) A town in the vicinity of **Troy**, original home of **Hektor**'s wife, Andromache.

**Thebes**  The largest city in **Boiotia**, and mythologically and historically one of the most important cities in Greece. Founded by **Kadmos**, it was the birthplace of both **Dionysos** and **Herakles** and the locus of an extensive cycle of legends concerning the fortunes of **Oedipus** and his family.

**Theia**  One of the **Titans**, mother by **Hyperion** of **Helios** the Sun-god.

**Thersandros**  Son of **Polyneikes**.

**Theseus**  The most important hero of Athenian legend. He was traditionally credited with a double paternity, being accounted the son both of **Poseidon** and of Aigeus son of Pandion, king of Athens, whose throne he inherited on Aigeus' death. His mother was Aithra, daughter of Pittheus, the king of Troizen, in the northeastern **Peloponnesos**.

**Thessaly**  A region in northern Greece, of which **Magnesia** (1) was a part.

**Thetis**  One of the fifty daughters of **Nereus** and mother of **Achilles** by **Peleus**.

**Thrace**  The region immediately to the north of the Aegean Sea. Among other things, it was known for its horses, the uncouthness of its inhabitants, and the north wind that blew down from it into Greece.

**Thyone**  Another name for **Semele**.

**Tiryns**  A city not far from **Argos**. For a time it was ruled by **Proitos**, and several generations later it was the residence of **Herakles** during one period of his life. Eurystheus, in whose service Herakles was compelled to perform his twelve labors, was a king of Tiryns.

**Titans** The second generation of the gods, children of Earth (Gaia) and Sky (Ouranos); chief among them were **Kronos** and **Rhea**. The Titans were deposed from power when **Zeus** and his fellow **Olympians** defeated them in battle and imprisoned them in **Tartaros**.

**Tithonos** A Trojan prince famous for his beauty; father of **Memnon** by the goddess **Dawn**.

**Troilos** The youngest of the sons of **Priam** by his wife Hekabe; he was slain by **Achilles**.

**Trojan War** The war that was waged by the combined forces of many Greek cities and regions, united under the general command of **Agamemnon**, against the city of **Troy** and its various allies. The purpose of the war on the Greek side was to assist **Menelaos** in reclaiming **Helen** from **Paris**. The siege of Troy lasted ten years and ended with the complete destruction of the city.

**Troy** A city in the northwest corner of Asia Minor, also known as Ilion and Pergamos. Until its destruction at the end of the **Trojan War**, Troy and the surrounding territory (known as the Troad) were ruled by a royal dynasty descended from **Dardanos**.

**Tydeus** One of the sons of **Oineus**, and father of **Diomedes**.

**Tyndareos** King of **Sparta**, husband of **Leda**, and father by her of **Kastor** and Klytaimnestra.

**Tyndaridai (Tyndarids)** The "sons of Tyndareos," i.e., **Kastor** and **Polydeukes**; also known as the Dioskouroi or "sons of Zeus." Neither term is strictly accurate, however, since although Kastor and Polydeukes were the twin sons of **Leda**, each had a different father, Kastor being the son of **Tyndareos** and Polydeukes the son of **Zeus**; see Pindar's *Nemean* 10 for an account of their begetting. As objects of hero cult they were held in particular reverence in Sparta, their hometown. Among their other functions, they were regarded as patrons and protectors of sailors, horsemen, and athletes.

**Typhos** An unruly monster who attempted to overthrow **Zeus** but was vanquished by Zeus's thunderbolt and imprisoned in the nether realm of **Tartaros**, pinned there by the weight of Mt. **Aitna**. He was said to have been born in Kilikia, a region in southeastern Asia Minor. Among his offspring by **Echidna** were the **Hydra** and **Kerberos**.

**Zeus** Son of **Kronos** and **Rhea**, ruler of the **Olympians** and of the world at large, "father of gods and men." **Hera** was his wife and royal consort, but he had a large number of offspring by other goddesses (e.g., **Demeter**, **Leto**, Themis, **Maia**) and by mortal women (e.g., **Alkmene**, **Danaë**, **Semele**, **Leda**). As a sky god he was the master of all weather phenomena (e.g., clouds, storms, lightning, thunder), and the eagle, "king of birds," was sacred to him. The **Olympian** and **Nemean Games** were held in his honor.

# SELECT BIBLIOGRAPHY
# FOR FURTHER READING

## General

W. Barnstone, *Sappho and the Greek Lyric Poets* (New York 1988).

C. M. Bowra, *Greek Lyric Poetry from Alcman to Simonides* (Oxford 1961).

———, *Early Greek Elegists* (Cambridge, Mass., 1938, Cambridge 1960).

A. R. Burn, *The Lyric Age of Greece* (London 1961).

D. A. Campbell, *The Golden Lyre: The Themes of the Greek Lyric Poets* (London 1983).

———, *Greek Lyric*, Vols. 1–5 (Cambridge, Mass., and London 1982, 1988, 1991, 1992, 1993).

P. E. Easterling and B.M.W. Knox, *The Cambridge History of Classical Literature, Volume I, Part 1: Early Greek Poetry* (Cambridge 1985).

J. M. Edmonds, *Greek Elegy and Iambus*, 2 vols. (Cambridge, Mass., and London 1931).

B. Fowler, *Archaic Greek Poetry: An Anthology* (Madison 1992).

H. Fränkel, *Early Greek Poetry and Philosophy*, tr. M. Hadas and J. Willis (Oxford 1975).

B. Gentili, *Poetry and Its Public in Ancient Greece: From Homer to the Fifth Century*, tr. A. T. Cole (Baltimore and London 1981).

W. Jaeger, *Paideia: The Ideals of Greek Culture*, Vol. 1, tr. G. Highet (Oxford 1939).

G. M. Kirkwood, *Early Greek Monody: The History of a Poetic Type* (Ithaca 1974).

R. Lattimore, *Greek Lyrics* (Chicago 1960).

M. R. Lefkowitz, *The Lives of the Greek Poets* (Baltimore 1981).

G. Most, "Greek Lyric Poets," in T. J. Luce, ed., *Ancient Writers: Greece and Rome*, Vol. 1 (New York 1982): 75–98.

D. Mulroy, *Early Greek Lyric Poetry* (Ann Arbor 1992).

A. J. Podlecki, *The Early Greek Poets and Their Times* (Vancouver 1984).

D. J. Rayor, *Sappho's Lyre: Archaic Lyric and Women Poets of Greece* (Berkeley and Los Angeles 1991).

B. Snell, *The Discovery of the Mind: The Greek Origins of European Thought*, tr. T. G. Rosenmeyer (Cambridge, Mass., 1953).

M. L. West, *Studies in Greek Elegy and Iambus* (Berlin 1974).

————, *Greek Lyric Poetry: The Poems and Fragments of the Greek Iambic, Elegiac, and Melic Poets (Excluding Pindar and Bacchylides) Down to 450 B.C.* (Oxford 1993).

## Alcaeus

A. P. Burnett, *Three Archaic Poets: Archilochus, Alcaeus, Sappho* (London 1983).

H. Martin, *Alcaeus* (New York 1972).

D. L. Page, *Sappho and Alcaeus: An Introduction to the Study of Ancient Lesbian Lyric* (Oxford 1955).

## Alcman

C. Calame, *Choruses of Young Women in Ancient Greece*, tr. J. Orion and D. Collins (Lanham, Md., 1994).

G. Davenport, *Archilochos, Sappho, Alkman: Three Lyric Poets of the Seventh Century B.C.* (Berkeley and Los Angeles 1984).

D. L. Page, *Alcman: The Partheneion* (Oxford 1951, repr. Salem, N.H., 1985).

## Archilochus

A. P. Burnett, *Three Archaic Poets: Archilochus, Alcaeus, Sappho* (London 1983).

G. Davenport, *Archilochos, Sappho, Alkman: Three Lyric Poets of the Seventh Century B.C.* (Berkeley and Los Angeles 1984).

H. D. Rankin, *Archilochus of Paros* (Park Ridge, N.J., 1977).

F. Will, *Archilochus* (New York 1969).

# Bacchylides

A. P. Burnett, *The Art of Bacchylides* (Cambridge, Mass., and London 1985).

R. Fagles, *Bacchylides: The Complete Poems* (Westport, Conn., 1976).

# Corinna

D. L. Page, *Corinna* (London 1953).

# Pindar

C. M. Bowra, *Pindar* (Oxford 1964).

E. L. Bundy, *Studia Pindarica* (Berkeley and Los Angeles 1962, repr. 1986).

R.W.B. Burton, *Pindar's Pythian Odes* (Oxford 1962).

D. S. Carne-Ross, *Pindar* (New Haven and London 1985).

L. Kurke, *The Traffic in Praise: Pindar and the Poetics of Social Economy* (Ithaca and London 1991).

M. R. Lefkowitz, *First-Person Fictions: Pindar's Poetic 'I'* (Oxford 1991).

H. Lloyd-Jones, *Pindar* (London 1982).

F. Nisetich, *Pindar's Victory Songs* (Baltimore and London 1980).

G. Norwood, *Pindar* (Berkeley and Los Angeles 1945).

W. H. Race, *Pindar* (Boston 1986).

——— , *Style and Rhetoric in Pindar's Odes* (Atlanta 1990).

D. C. Young, "Pindar," in T. J. Luce, ed., *Ancient Writers: Greece and Rome*, Vol. 1 (New York 1982): 157–77.

# Sappho

M. Barnard, *Sappho: A New Translation* (Berkeley and Los Angeles 1958).

A. P. Burnett, *Three Archaic Poets: Archilochus, Alcaeus, Sappho* (London 1983).

G. Davenport, *Archilochos, Sappho, Alkman: Three Lyric Poets of the Seventh Century B.C.* (Berkeley and Los Angeles 1984).

R. Jenkyns, *Three Classical Poets: Sappho, Catullus and Juvenal* (Cambridge, Mass., 1982).

D. L. Page, *Sappho and Alcaeus: An Introduction to the Study of Ancient Lesbian Lyric* (Oxford 1955).

## Semonides

H. Lloyd-Jones, *Females of the Species: Semonides on Women* (Park Ridge, N.J., 1975).

## Simonides

J. H. Molyneux, *Simonides: A Historical Study* (Wauconda, Ill., 1992).

## Solon

E. K. Anhalt, *Solon the Singer: Politics and Poetry* (Lanham, Md. 1993).

## Theognis

T. J. Figueira and G. Nagy (eds.), *Theognis of Megara: Poetry and the Polis* (Baltimore and London 1985).

## Xenophanes

J. H. Lesher, *Xenophanes of Colophon: Fragments* (Toronto 1992).